Kansas City, America's Crossroads

Century of Missouri History Scholarship Series

A series edited by Lynn Wolf Gentzler and Gary R. Kremer

Kansas City, America's Crossroads: Essays from the Missouri Historical Review, 1906-2006

Edited with an introduction by Diane Mutti Burke and John Herron

The State Historical Society of Missouri
Columbia

Volume Editors: Diane Mutti Burke and John Herron are assistant professors of history at the University of Missouri-Kansas City.

Series Editors: Lynn Wolf Gentzler is associate director of The State Historical Society of Missouri. Gary R. Kremer is executive director of The State Historical Society of Missouri.

The State Historical Society of Missouri
Columbia, Missouri 65201
© 2007 by The State Historical Society of Missouri

ISBN: 978-0-9622891-6-3

Contents

Preface   vii

Introduction   1
  Diane Mutti Burke and John Herron

Historical Sketch of Kansas City from the Beginning   12
to 1909
  H. C. McDougal

Confluence of People and Place: The Chouteau Posts on the   27
Missouri and Kansas Rivers
  David Boutros

The Expulsion of the Mormons from Jackson County,   47
Missouri
  Warren A. Jennings

From Virginia to Missouri in 1846: The Journal of Elizabeth   71
Ann Cooley
  Edited by Edward D. Jervey and James E. Moss

General Orders No. 11 and Border Warfare During the Civil   96
War
  Ann Davis Niepman

Beginning of the Park and Boulevard Movement in Frontier   122
Kansas City, 1872-1882
  William H. Wilson

The Kansas City Meat Packing Industry Before 1900   141
  G. K. Renner

Kansas City Free Speech Fight of 1911   153
  Tom N. McInnis

The 1918 Kansas City Influenza Epidemic   170
  Kevin C. McShane

"Nearest by Air to Everywhere": Aviation Promotion   185
in Kansas City, 1925-1931
  James P. Leyerzapf

Criminal Aspects of the Pendergast Machine   206
  Lawrence H. Larsen and Nancy J. Hulston

Chester A. Franklin and Harry S. Truman: An African   220
American Conservative and the "Conversion" of the Future
President
  Thomas D. Wilson

"Just Like the Garden of Eden": African American   252
Community Life in Kansas City's Leeds
  Gary R. Kremer

It Finally Happened Here: The 1968 Riot in Kansas City,   277
Missouri
  Joel P. Rhodes

Contributors   300

Index   302

Preface

Kansas City, America's Crossroads: Essays from the Missouri Historical Review, 1906-2006 is the second volume in the State Historical Society of Missouri's *Century of Missouri History Scholarship Series*. Since the first issue of the *Review* appeared in October 1906, more than seventy articles on the history of the Kansas City region have graced its pages.

Professors John Herron and Diane Mutti Burke, both faculty members in the Department of History at the University of Missouri-Kansas City, surveyed each of these articles and selected fourteen to be reproduced in this commemorative anthology. Their introduction to this volume explains how and why they chose the essays to be included here.

Professor Herron arrived in Kansas City in 2003 after completing a doctorate at the University of New Mexico and doing postdoctoral work at the University of San Diego. His areas of specialty include environmental history, the American West, and modern America. Diane Mutti Burke joined the University of Missouri-Kansas City history department in 2004 after completing doctoral work under a distinguished scholar of the South, Elizabeth Fox-Genovese, at Emory University in Atlanta the same year. Her specialties include the American South and African American and women's history.

The *Century of Missouri History Scholarship Series*, projected to be twelve volumes over the next five years, celebrates the first century of publication of the *Missouri Historical Review*. It also brings together some of the best Missouri history writing over the past one hundred years.

In 2008 the Society plans to publish two additional volumes in this series. An anthology on the history of recreation and entertainment in Missouri, to be edited by Dr. Alan Havig, professor of history at Stephens College in Columbia, will be available in April 2008, and a collection of essays on the history of St. Louis, to be edited by Dr. Louis Gerteis, chair of the Department of History at the University of Missouri-St. Louis, will be published in October 2008.

While many people have assisted in bringing *Kansas City, America's Crossroads: Essays from the Missouri Historical Review, 1906-2006* to publication, we would like to acknowledge the contributions of two persons in particular. Editorial staff member Paul Dziuba helped to copyedit and design the volume. The idea for this volume originated with Society trustee Brent Schondelmeyer of Independence, Missouri. To him, we owe a special debt of gratitude.

The editors have modernized and standardized punctuation, capitalization, and endnote style and supplied any first names in brackets. Unless otherwise credited, all illustrations are from the State Historical Society of Missouri.

Lynn Wolf Gentzler
Gary R. Kremer

Introduction

In May 1968, Vice President Hubert H. Humphrey arrived in St. Louis to dedicate what would become Missouri's most famous landmark, the Gateway Arch. Designed by Finnish architect Eero Saarinen, the soaring steel arch rises more than six hundred feet above its foundation on the bank of the Mississippi River. The outline of the arch, immortalized on postage stamps and commemorative state quarters, is ubiquitous within Missouri. The landmark was built to celebrate the contribution of St. Louis to the development of the American frontier. In linking the arch to the opening of the West, its architects incorporated America's tallest monument into a powerful national mythology.

From Thomas Jefferson forward, generations of American citizens had long dreamed of an expansive empire of liberty and democracy anchored in lands of the far west. A product of the Atlantic world, Jefferson himself would never venture more than a few dozen miles west of his Virginia home. But of the West he remained a man obsessed. In his travels he scoured libraries and personal estates, eventually amassing one of the largest private collections about the peoples and geography of the American West.[1] It was his faith in the western promise that prompted his sponsorship of Meriwether Lewis, William Clark, and the rest of the Corps of Discovery, an ambitious reconnaissance of America's newest acquisition, the Louisiana Purchase. Lewis and Clark were agents of national greatness as much as they were explorers. They mapped and catalogued the bounty of the region, but they also laid claim to a territory that Jefferson, and many like him, believed would fulfill the destiny of the young United States. And within this weighty mythology, St. Louis stood at the heart of it all—the jumping-off point for settlers, swindlers, and dreamers who looked to the West as the future of the republic.

But greeting Humphrey on this spring day was not a multitude of flag-waving Jeffersonians, but a heavy rain, so much rain that event organizers cancelled a planned regatta and gathered crowds remained smaller than expected.[2] The rain did not dampen Humphrey's enthusiasm, however, as in the middle of his presidential campaign, he tied himself and the nation to the promise and potential embodied by the arch. "Let the Gateway arch stand," Humphrey declared, "as a symbol of America's determination to have beauty with utility, quality with quantity, and humanity with progress."[3]

As soggy St. Louis residents applauded, in Kansas City, 250 miles to the west, Humphrey's visit to the arch met with a resounding thud. The *Kansas City Star*, the city's main newspaper, devoted only a few lines to the vice president's speech, and that within a larger story about a local convention of dairymen. A busy political calendar might explain this lukewarm reception. Fighting for headline space in Kansas City newspapers were European capitals aflame with student protest, an escalating war in Vietnam, and an intense presidential race. But perhaps the reaction to Humphrey's speech should be viewed in more straightforward regional terms. At the celebratory opening of the Gateway Arch, the silence of Kansas City residents confirmed what the history of the region suggests: the arch was misplaced.

In the battle for statewide supremacy, St. Louis had the advantages of geography, timing, and opportunity. Located at the confluence of two major waterways and settled by international merchants with connections to worldwide markets, St. Louis was a city almost from its inception. Kansas City, by contrast, sat on the margins. St. Louis in 1820 claimed nearly four thousand residents, Kansas City only a handful. St. Louis was a commercial center looking to the markets of the East Coast, the future Kansas City a collection of outposts and cabins struggling to establish trading relationships with local natives. Even more significantly, the same mythology giving St. Louis pride of place within the American narrative conveniently placed Kansas City on the edge of the largely hostile and uninhabitable "Great American Desert." Explorers like Zebulon Pike and Stephen Long spoke with federal authority when they repeated the mistaken claim that there was little of value to the American empire in the lands of the Great Plains. Even William Clark, who, unlike many of his early nineteenth-century contemporaries, recognized the potential of the region that would become Kansas City, still bemoaned its separation from the rest of the "Sivilised world."[4] Others in literature, high culture, and business also emphasized Kansas City's position within—to use a modern colloquialism—the "great flyover zone."[5] The staying power of these perceptions is remarkable. Despite census numbers pushing Kansas City past St. Louis in size and population, contemporary opinion still considers St. Louis urban and urbane, Kansas City rustic and provincial.[6]

A closer examination of the history of Kansas City, however, reveals a more complicated story. Not only should Kansas City be granted a larger space within the national creation story, but with respect to St. Louis and its most celebrated monument, Kansas City remains the true gateway to the West. Although rarely the history that survives in the popular imagination, few places in the region can claim as diverse a history as Kansas City. In the essays that follow, we uncover part of the rich history of this city and its peoples.

The explorers who moved through the region in the first decades of the nineteenth century may not have immediately recognized the ingredients needed to build a successful community in Kansas City, but they would be among the last to overlook its possibilities. From its beginnings as a fur-trading outpost in the 1820s, the city was marked by the distinctive rolling energy of a frontier community. Adventurers like Jim Bridger and Kit Carson joined French and Canadian trappers as well as American businessmen such as John Sutter (soon to start a frenzied rush to the California gold fields) to create a small but vibrant multiethnic enclave on the bank of the Missouri River. Typical of the growth of other frontier towns, missionaries—often seeking Native American converts—followed. French Catholics, Methodists, Baptists, and Quakers each established a strong presence in young Kansas City. In the early 1830s, Mormons too arrived, not to save native souls, but to build a model community, a midwestern version of the "city upon a hill." Religious opportunity was just one of many magnets drawing people west. Farmers from the upland South, attracted by the fertile soils of the Missouri valley, moved into the region, laying the foundation for a heartland agricultural empire. In a portent of future trouble, many brought their slaves with them. Conflict was the inevitable result of this social exchange. Indian groups of the region battled other tribes pushed westward by white expansion, Native Americans resisted white encroachment, African American slaves defied their owners, and early white settlers resented the new influence of the Mormon bloc in western Missouri.[7]

The violence coloring early nineteenth-century Kansas City would never completely disappear, but that did not lessen the flow of migrants into the city. The population of Kansas City remained small in the first half of the century even as many thousands more poured through the region on their way to all points west. In Independence, Westport, and the other satellite communities of present-day Kansas City, first caravans to New Mexico, then later settlers to Oregon and California and eventually Colorado and Nevada bought supplies and readied for their transcontinental trek. Few other cities, including St. Louis, could bear witness to such a steady stream of movement and migration in the nineteenth century. In the early decades of the century, it was as Jefferson had envisioned: Kansas City became the portal to the nation's future.

In the 1850s and 1860s, the city was swept into the bitter sectionalism of the era. Long before the Confederate firing on Fort Sumter, the eyes of the nation watched as the citizens of the region attempted to resolve the question of slavery and its place in the republic. Political debates degenerated into bitter feuds that in turn became open hostilities along the Missouri-Kansas border. During the Civil War, federal evacuation orders, local skirmishes, guerrilla raids, border attacks, and, eventually, a major battle rocked the stability of the still-growing community. In the end, the city, like much of the region, was saved by the railroad. Efforts to build a rail line to Kansas City predate the war, but it was not until after the fighting stopped that the riverboat age began its slow decline and the railroad boom began. By 1870 seven major railroads flowed through the city, with many more soon to arrive. Rail lines brought access to markets, and the city responded by transforming itself into a leading grain and livestock production hub.[8] The railroad would, however, bring more than money. The rail connections tied city to hinterland and, in the process, helped forge a common regional sensibility based on a progressive faith in agricultural development and, unfortunately, support for racial segregation and inequality.

In the closing decades of the century, even as the city continued to serve as a commercial center for extractive industries, Kansas City also attracted the traditional markers of metropolitan America. First came a professional and progressive city government and then the outward symbols—including museums, theaters, and opera houses—of cultural sophistication. The City Beautiful Movement replaced narrow streets with wide boulevards, parkways, and fountains and brought a distinctive aesthetic sensibility to the city that continues to the present.[9]

This period of rapid growth also led to the rise of one of the strongest political machines in the nation. For nearly four decades in the early twentieth century, the Pendergast machine controlled many aspects of the city's political and business life. Equal parts benevolent city father and ruthless mob boss, Tom Pendergast helped transform the city from a nineteenth-century cow town to a modern urban community.[10] In wide-open Kansas City, leisure became serious business as the city flouted prohibition restrictions. Downtown joints jumped to the distinctive sounds of Kansas City jazz played by greats like Count Basie and Charlie Parker. Before its inevitable collapse, the Pendergast machine would produce one more distinctive regional product—Harry Truman.[11]

In the postwar years, all aspects of the downside of urban development, including racial tension, crime, unregulated annexation, white flight, sprawl, and blight, impacted the maturing city. The decline of the manufacturing sector, a still-continuing trend, removed one of the city's main economic engines and contributed to the decline of the established urban core. In recent decades, however, Kansas City has turned around. A brief economic boom in the 1970s, followed by a more prolonged period of development in the 1990s, led to downtown revitalization and, finally, a population increase. Home to a growing number of Fortune 500 companies and a thriving cultural and recreational scene, Kansas City is once again a city of national standing.

This thumbnail sketch of Kansas City is, obviously, far from complete. Much of it reads like a chamber of commerce publicity pamphlet rather than a scholarly review of urban growth. But completeness was never our goal. Similarly, the essays that follow do not provide a full history of the city. Readers interested in that narrative are encouraged to look elsewhere. Rather, the reprinted articles accomplish two different but related goals. The first is to illuminate key moments in the history of the city and the surrounding region. Many essays of note about Kansas City have appeared in the pages of the *Missouri Historical Review*; the essays we included in this anthology, however, reflect significant points in the city's development and maturation. And secondly, this volume serves a more academic purpose. In reading the essays, one can learn about the history of Kansas City as well as how the writing of history changed (and continues to change) over time.

Look, for example, to the first essay in this collection, H. C. McDougal's "Historical Sketch of Kansas City From the Beginning to 1909," which appeared in the October 1909 issue. This article fails to reach nearly every benchmark required for a well-written academic essay. Yet we include it as an ideal representation of twentieth-century booster literature. McDougal begins his essay with an overview of early Kansas City, *really early* Kansas City. He reminds readers that the history of this place began when "God created the heaven and the earth" and moves from there to discuss Columbus and Coronado.[12] We will leave it to readers to find the connection between a sixteenth-century Spanish conquistador and the growth of Kansas City, but the article provides a revealing glimpse into the shape, and especially the perception, of early city life.

During the first half-century of its existence, the *Missouri Historical Review* devoted many of its pages to chronicling the rise of prominent white men, the growth of their influential industries, and their impact on statewide development. It was typical of historical society publications of the era to celebrate the men and their professional acumen contributing to the commercial growth of the region. Not surprisingly, then, most of the early vignettes of Kansas City were celebratory accounts of community leaders. Early Kansas City settlers—like the famous Boone family—were described in one representative 1929 article as "the bone and sinew of the frontier life," "virile men [who] wove the warp and woof of the epic of the West." Their history, the authors continued, was as fabled as that of Greeks who "sailed the Aegean Sea in quest of the storied golden fleece." Their tale "will live and echo down the centuries, and will be appreciated after a thousand years as we now esteem the heroic men and deeds depicted by Homer, Virgil and Caesar."[13] Lofty praise to be sure.

Although we do not reprint an example of this kind of laudatory biography, two of the many articles trumpeting important Kansas City industries are included in this collection. Published in October 1960, G. K. Renner's "The Kansas City Meat Packing Industry Before 1900" outlines the history of an industry synonymous with Kansas City. Renner describes in detail both the development of the Kansas City stockyards and the meat packing industry, the first major economic stimulus for the city. In a similar vein, James W. Leyerzapf's January 1972 article, "'Nearest by Air to Everywhere': Aviation Promotion in Kansas City: 1925-1931," reviews the rise of Kansas City as a base for transcontinental flight, a national obsession in the 1920s. Leyerzapf tracks the civic effort behind the construction of the Municipal Airport and the development of Trans-World Airlines into a regional, national, and, eventually, international company. TWA and the Municipal Airport are both victims of the ever-changing fortunes of America's transportation network, but their presence was critical to the city becoming a player in national affairs.

Another important, although recently underused, function of the *Review* is to print edited and annotated versions of original manuscript documents, many of which are housed in the archives of the State Historical Society. The edited version of "From Virginia to Missouri in 1846: The Journal of Elizabeth Cooley" is an excellent example of this valuable contribution. Elizabeth Cooley migrated from Virginia to Jackson County in 1846, where she and her husband worked as schoolteachers until her premature death just eighteen months later. By providing a first-hand perspective on life in Kansas City, Cooley's journal, edited by Edward D. Jervey and James E. Moss and published in January 1966, continues the *Missouri Historical Review* tradition of promoting significant primary documents, but it remains even more important as one of the few articles about Jackson County women to appear in the *Review*.

Starting around 1960, articles published in the journal reflected changes occurring in professional historical scholarship. By considering the experiences of everyday people, historians turned to previously neglected actors like women, the working class, and African Americans. Scholars illustrated how ordinary Americans were historical agents—how they structured their lives, how historical forces influenced them, and how they, in turn, affected historical change. Incorporated under the broad umbrella of "new social history," this investigative approach continues to enrich the traditional understanding of the past.

Pivotal events in the nineteenth-century history of Kansas City are especially ripe for this kind of reexamination. David Boutros, for example, reexamined the early days of Kansas City in his article, "Confluence of People and Place: The Chouteau Posts on the Missouri and Kansas Rivers," which appeared in October 2002. This essay combines contemporary scholarship with original historical accounts to better understand the contributions of the Chouteau family to the first settlements that would become Kansas City. Warren Jennings published a series of articles in the *Missouri Historical Review* about the Mormon experience in western Missouri, including the October 1969 essay, "The Expulsion of the Mormons from Jackson County, Missouri." This essay examines the violent response of Jackson County settlers to the newly constructed Mormon Zion. Jennings seeks to illuminate both the experiences of Mormon families who settled in the area and those of the Jackson County residents who forced them out. Ann Davis Niepman's January 1972 article, "General Orders No. 11 and Border Warfare During the Civil War," chronicles one of the most devastating events in Jackson County history. She outlines the circumstances behind General Thomas Ewing's infamous order to depopulate the Missouri-Kansas border, but her focus remains the harrowing experiences of the men and women displaced by the decree. Although produced in different decades and in different styles, each of these essays bears the hallmarks of social history, including a commitment to a "bottom-up" approach to deciphering the past.

Another trademark of social history is the use of local experiences to interpret and understand large national trends and events. In his April 1962 article, "Beginning of the Park and Boulevard Movement in Frontier Kansas City, 1872-1882," William H. Wilson tracks the motivations behind the creation of the city's well-known park and boulevard system. Kansas City's effort to reorder public space within the urban core became a model emulated by many other American cities in the late nineteenth and early twentieth centuries. Scholars have also examined important national and international events through the lens of the Kansas City experience. In "The 1918 Kansas City Influenza Epidemic," printed in October 1968, Kevin C. McShane follows the reaction of the local medical establishment and municipal government to what became a worldwide public health crisis. The essay reveals how political squabbling, including deference to local business interests, led to an ineffective public health response to the epidemic. A staggering city death rate was the end result. Similarly, Tom N. McInnis connects the story of Kansas City's workers with those of unionizing laborers throughout the nation. At the heart of his April 1990 essay, "The Kansas City Free Speech Fight of 1911," is an examination of the radical Industrial Workers of the World (IWW) and their efforts to maintain worker rights in a political and business climate hostile to any challenge to authority.

By bringing workers into the historical spotlight, McInnis's article highlights individuals often left out of the canon, but few groups were as ignored as Kansas City's African Americans. The historical investigation of black America intensified with the advent of the civil rights movement, but little scholarship on Kansas City's vibrant black community was published in the *Missouri Historical Review* until the 1990s. Again reflecting the effort to understand local events against a national background, Joel P. Rhodes chronicles Kansas City's explosive race riot in his April 1997 article, "It Finally Happened Here: The 1968 Riot in Kansas City, Missouri." Rhodes explains the causes of, as well as the response to, the riot within both the local African American community and the Kansas City establishment. Gary Kremer's January 2004 article, "'Just Like the Garden of Eden': African American Community Life in Kansas City's Leeds," describes a neighborhood that grew up on the eastern edge of the city. In Leeds, African American homeowners practiced a way of life resembling their rural roots while establishing institutions to facilitate their entrance into urban life.

Recent articles written about Jackson County's infamous political boss and presidential native son also reflect these broad trends in historical research and writing. In January 1997, Lawrence H. Larsen and Nancy J. Hulston contributed to the understanding of Kansas City's political boss, Tom Pendergast, in their article, "Criminal Aspects of the Pendergast Machine." Larsen and Hulston not only highlight the colorful crime history of the machine, but also explore how it operated with the neighborhoods of Kansas City. Scholarship about Harry S. Truman too reveals more about his relationship to the Kansas City community than about the man himself. In October 1993, Thomas D. Wilson published an article about the long-standing friendship between Truman and

African American businessman Chester Franklin. In "Chester A. Franklin and Harry S. Truman: An African American Conservative and the 'Conversion' of the Future President," Wilson weighs in on the historical debate about Truman's often conflicted views on civil rights. He argues that along with Truman's personal and practical experiences working with African Americans in the Pendergast machine, it was the future president's interaction with black community leaders like Franklin that profoundly influenced his understanding of race. Franklin, the editor of the African American newspaper *The Call*, held a conservative "accommodative approach to civil rights" and a belief in "equality of opportunity, not equality of condition." Truman initially shared this ideology with his friend and frequent correspondent but, in the end, embraced a New Deal philosophy of "fiscal liberalism with government intervention on behalf of African Americans."[14]

These collected *Missouri Historical Review* essays paint a portrait of a significant American community. These articles, and the nearly sixty others we were unable to include, have done much to expand our understanding of this region, yet they reveal only a slice of the broad impulse that is Kansas City history. For a community of this size and significance, many topics of historical importance await further study.

Issues of political and economic growth rightly garner significant interest, but nuanced social histories of the unexpected contributors to this city's uniqueness need more attention. It is very revealing, for instance, that the only essay on women in this volume comes from a nineteenth-century diary. A gendered examination of city institutions such as schools, hospitals, and benevolent organizations, to name only a few, would illuminate the often hidden, yet critical, contributions that women made to the growth of the city. Kansas City's prominent theater and opera companies are popular topics of study while the city's dynamic jazz community, so often overshadowed by those in Chicago and New Orleans, has largely escaped scholarly notice. Kansas City jazz pioneers created a thriving cultural milieu that impacted the nation's musical tastes as well as a larger debate on American race relations. Kansas City's black-white divide dominates our understanding of race and ethnicity, but much more work could be done to recognize the role of the region's many immigrant groups—Italian, Irish, eastern European, and Hispanic—on city politics, economic development, and social life. Individual Kansas City case studies abound, yet lacking is an explanation of how diverse community constituencies lived, worked, and interacted with one another. Finally, following another trend in American historiography, Kansas City's natural and built environment, both significant elements of the city's profile, need further examination. To study rivers and parks as well as neighborhood formation and housing patterns would expose the intimate relationship between nature and culture in the city.

The Missouri Historical Review remains an ideal venue to pursue these lines of inquiry. For more than a century, the *Review* has steadfastly illuminated the importance of regional events within a national context. Fickle historical fashion often denigrates the analytical power of regional stories, yet in these narratives, and hopefully in this volume, the value of local study emerges clearly. It is our hope that this anthology will encourage young scholars to revitalize community study as an appropriate, even dynamic, tool for understanding our nation's past.

Diane Mutti Burke
John Herron

NOTES

1. The scholarship on Jefferson and the West is huge, but for a very good overview, see James P. Ronda, *Finding the West: Explorations with Lewis and Clark* (Albuquerque: University of New Mexico Press, 2001).

2. *New York Times*, 26 May 1968, 58.

3. *Kansas City Star*, 25 May 1968, 2.

4. James P. Ronda, "The Objects of Our Journey," in Carolyn Gilman, *Lewis and Clark: Across the Divide* (Washington, DC: Smithsonian Press, 2003), 29.

5. A. Theodore Brown, *Frontier Community: Kansas City to 1870* (Columbia: University of Missouri Press, 1963), 3-5, 10-13.

6. Census data is for the city population, not the metropolitan population. For the 2005 population estimates for Kansas City (444,965) and St. Louis (344,362), see www.census.gov/popest/cities/files/SUB-EST2005-01.csv.

7. For more information on early city history, see A. Theodore Brown and Lyle W. Dorsett, *K.C.: A History of Kansas City, Missouri* (Boulder, CO: Pruett Publishing Co., 1978), and R. Richard Wohl and A. Theodore Brown, "The Usable Past: A Study of Historical Traditions in Kansas City," *Huntington Library Quarterly* 23 (May 1960): 237-259.

8. Brown, *Frontier Community*, 115-156.

9. William H. Wilson, *The City Beautiful Movement in Kansas City* (Columbia: University of Missouri Press, 1964).

10. A. Theodore Brown, *The Politics of Reform: Kansas City's Municipal*

Government, 1925-1950 (Kansas City, MO: Community Studies, 1958).

11. Robert H. Ferrell, *Truman and Pendergast* (Columbia: University of Missouri Press, 1999).

12. H. C. McDougal, "Historical Sketch of Kansas City From the Beginning to 1909," *Missouri Historical Review* 4 (October 1909): 1.

13. Virginia Hays Asbury and Albert N. Doerschuk, "The Boone, Hays and Berry Families of Jackson County," *Missouri Historical Review* 23 (July 1929): 548-549.

14. Thomas D. Wilson, "Chester A. Franklin and Harry S. Truman: An African-American Conservative and the 'Conversion' of the Future President," *Missouri Historical Review* 88 (October 1993): 71, 75-76.

Historical Sketch of Kansas City from the Beginning to 1909

H. C. McDOUGAL

Beginning. "In the beginning God created the heaven and the earth." Science often attempts to fix this at some particular period, but as no one knows certainly, this imperfect sketch of the history of Kansas City, Missouri, commences just where the Book does—"in the beginning."

Indians. From the Creator of the universe, this part of the western hemisphere must have passed to the original proprietor of our soil—the Indian. For when the white man here first set his foot, at the dawn of our known history, the copper-colored Indian was here with his squaw, his papoose, and his pony and in the actual, open, and undisputed possession and control of all that country which is now known as North America.

1492. The earliest successful European discoverer, explorer, and adventurer of this continent was Christopher Columbus of Spain in 1492. After his party, there came hither first his many Spanish successors, then the subjects of sunny France and still later the English.

1540. It is more than probable, however, that the followers of the great [Francisco Vázquez de] Coronado were the first white visitors to this part of the country and the time about 1541.

The historical facts relating to this ill-fated expedition in brief are: That following earlier reports which had already come to him, Charles V of Spain and his viceroy in Mexico (New Spain), [Don Antonio de Mendoza], directed Coronado to explore and subdue for the Spanish crown the city of Quivira and the seven cities of Cibola (buffalo) without knowledge as to the precise location of either; that [Pedro de] Castenada, who accompanied the expedition

12

as its historian, twenty years later wrote out his story thereof for the king, and from his writings, as well as from many subsequent publications, the world today has all its information as to the success and failure of that undertaking; that Coronado first organized his forces at Compostela, Guadalajara, in Old Mexico, in February 1540, but made his actual start from Culiacán on the Pacific Ocean in April of that year, with 350 Spanish cavaliers and 800 Indian guides; that during his two years' quest, either the entire or detachments of this expedition wandered onward east and north through (now) Old Mexico, Arizona, New Mexico, Colorado, and into the northeastern portion of Kansas, encountering en route and with strong arm subduing many recalcitrant Indian towns and villages and treating with others who were more friendly; but that finally, disappointed and humiliated at his failure to find the gold, silver, treasure, and cities for which he sought, Coronado and his surviving followers returned to the city of Mexico and thence on to Old Spain about 1542.

It is also historically certain that about fifty miles northwest from White Oaks, in New Mexico, may be seen today, still mutely bearing the ancient name of "Le Grande Quivira," the ruins of a once-great city, which Coronado sought and found not, but which present-day archaeologists say must have contained a population of from 150,000 to 300,000. The dwelling houses, as now shown by these ruins, were constructed with mathematical accuracy of blue trachyte and limestone, while the two ruined temples stand far above all others, with nothing to mark their uses other than that which now appears as the form of a Portugese cross in their front doors. Still traceable in this desert waste, irrigating ditches indicate that this people once obtained their water supply from the adjoining mountains, but for more than one hundred years past, no water of consequence has been found within many miles of the ruins. Skeletons of the human, as well as of the lower animals, are there found; old mining shafts and crude smelters of ages ago are also found in that vicinity but no mines of either gold or silver. The prehistoric ruins of other once populous cities in widely differing points in New Mexico and Arizona furnish persuasive proof that these were once among the famed "seven cities of Cibola."

Among the many traditions and legends respecting the causes which led up to the wanderings of this expedition, and today believed by many Spaniards, Mexicans, and archaeologists of the Southwest, are at least two that are worth preservation: The one is that on their eastward journey, Coronado and his party, almost famished for water, finally reached the big spring near the Indian pueblo in Tagenx which is now Socorro, on the Rio Grande in New Mexico; that these Indian guides then knew that the city of Le Grande Quivira, the main object of Coronado's conquest and expedition, was only about ninety miles northeast of this point, but instead of guiding him there, they then purposely misled him and carried the expedition northward and up on the west bank of the Rio Grande del Dorte and on into Kansas.

The other is that, concealing their abiding place for many long years from some remote country in the far north, mysterious sun worshipers voyaged in their own ships to and quietly purchased rich and abundant supplies of merchandise from the traffickers of the city of Mexico and of Old Madrid, in Spain, and that they were ever laden with gold and silver and precious stones, and the merchants assumed that they must represent a powerful and wealthy people who were skilled in the arts and sciences and lived in many-storied stone houses, with temples of wonderful magnificence, all enclosed within the walled city of Le Grande Quivira. However this may be, it is quite certain that the second Spanish expedition to that country, about 1549, did capture and subdue this ancient prehistoric city and people and then compelled all the residents of that vicinity to change their religion from worshipers of the sun to catholicism. When the Toltecs, Aztecs, and Spaniards first came to the great Southwest, they found there, as elsewhere, the Indian. Through their priests and monks the Spaniards controlled all these natives in that country from about 1549 to 1680, at which later date the natives arose in their might and majesty, drove the foreign oppressors from their soil, and curiously enough, after this lapse of about 130 years, at once resumed the dress, habits, customs, and religion of their fathers and for many years thereafter held the undisputed possession of their native land. When the Spaniards returned to that country about 1740, they found this once happy, flowery, and fertile valley a howling wilderness or barren waste, the once populous city of Le Grande Quivira deserted and with no trace of its former greatness beyond human skeletons and the ruins, while the shifting sands of the desert had covered the habitations of the people.

Between 1680 and 1740, it is probable that every form of man and beast capable of doing so escaped that country before some impending calamity and was gradually swallowed up and lost in the adjacent country, but that all unable through age or disease to so escape perished through the sulphurous fumes of the then-recent volcano at the Mal Pais (bad country), then and now just south of these ruins on the desert plain. An extinct crater, visited by the writer in 1892, is still seen while the lava beds extend thence over fifty miles down that valley. Just who these people were, whence they came, whither and when they went, how they perished, are all questions which can not be accurately answered this side of the river called death, but the lover of the mysterious and unknown, the student, archaeologist, and thinker of the future will stand amid these ruins and will lament the fact with uncovered head, that so little of it all is known to man.

But the precise point now of especial interest to the people of Kansas City arises upon an analysis of the circumstantial evidence which points to the historical fact that at the eastern terminus of their long wanderings in search of the Quivira country, Coronado and his followers were the first white men to visit the very spot whereon now stands Kansas City.

There is a half legendary story to the effect that from the historic spot upon which he once stood in northeastern Kansas, Coronado and the forces under his command passed on to where Atchison, Kansas, is now located, thence down the Missouri to the mouth of the Kansas and thence sixteen miles up the latter to Coronado Springs, later called Bonner Springs, in Wyandotte County, Kansas, where they spent the winter of 1541-1542. It is known that Coronado's Spanish cavaliers, among other weapons, then carried and used an implement of war, halberds similar to the metallic Roman halberd, and in excavations in our Missouri River bottomlands within the past few years, there have been discovered and unearthed, in splendid state of preservation, beneath many feet of alluvial soil, the metallic heads of two such halberds in this vicinity. The first is now in the possession of Professor John Wilson, a distinguished archaeologist at Lexington, Missouri, and was found just northeast of Kansas City in this (Jackson) county, while the other is in the hands of a Catholic priest at Leavenworth, Kansas, and was discovered just across the Missouri River from that city, in Platte County, Missouri. These late discoveries point to the conclusion that Coronado and his men once wandered over these hills and prairies and that at least two of his cavaliers lost their lives in this immediate neighborhood through either savage Indians or wild beasts, in both of which this country then abounded.

1584. Many scholars claim and few dispute the historic proposition that from the voyage and discovery of Columbus in 1492, the crown, as well as the statesmen, of Great Britain longed to explore and own all the territory which later became America, and that Queen Elizabeth, "in the sixe and twentieth yeere" of her reign, and on March 25, 1584, attempted to grant all this vast domain to her then-trusted follower, Sir Walter Raleigh. To those of the present day it is a trifle curious to note the fact that in this patent the Virgin Queen described the grantee thereof as "our trustie and welbeloued seruant Walter Ralegh, Esquire, and to his heires and assigns forever" and also designated this country as "remote, heathen and barbarous lands, countries and territories." This was the first step in the work of the English colonization of America, and while under the grant of this authority, five different voyages were here made, yet that country did not then succeed in making a permanent settlement upon American soil.

1607. In establishing a starting point known to all, it is well to here pause, look backward, and reflect: that whether descended from cavalier, Puritan, or Huguenot, the average American citizen has inherited and today holds, either consciously or unconsciously, many of the thoughts and theories of his remote ancestors, and that heredity, environment, and education largely determine and fix our political and religious faith. And it should be remembered that the United States was originally founded and the first permanent settlements were here first made by peoples of widely divergent views on both politics and religion under the authority conferred by three Royal English grants to American colonists, as follows: Jamestown, in Virginia, in 1607; Plymouth, in Massachusetts, in 1620; and Charlestown, in South Carolina, in 1660.

1609. In the seventh year of his reign, James I, then king of England, by his royal patent dated May 23, 1609, granted to "The Treasurer and Company of Adventurers of the City of London, for the first colony of Virginia" (the same sovereign made the first cession to that colony in 1606) "all those lands, countries and territories situate, lying, and being in that part of America called Virginia," from Cape or Point Comfort, a strip of land four hundred miles in width and therein designated as being "up into the land throughout from sea to sea." This cession from the Atlantic to the Pacific oceans sought to make this part of the territory not only English, but within and part of the colony of Virginia, for Kansas City is located on this four-hundred-mile-wide tract of land running from "sea to sea."

The subsequent European claimants were as follows:

1682. Ceremonious possession was taken of all that country which afterward became the Louisiana Purchase by, for, and in the name of Louis XIV then king of France, at the mouth of the Mississippi River on April 9, 1682, and this portion of the country was then given the name of that sovereign. While that claim was made and thereafter maintained, yet the undisputed possession thereof did not actually begin, nor was there here made any permanent settlement, until the year 1699. New Orleans was founded in 1718, and permanent seat of the French government was there established in 1722. In the meanwhile, Louis XIV first granted this entire province to one Anthony Crozat in 1712 and his occupancy being a failure, later and in 1717 granted a similar charter to John Law. This too proved a failure, and in 1732 both charters were cancelled and all this country reverted to the crown of France. But in history, song, and story may yet be read and studied with profit the final failure of the John Law scheme under the name of the "Mississippi Bubble."

1763. Then in that stormy struggle between England and France to settle and adjust their conflicting claims to this territory and their international disputes growing out of the French and Indian wars, by the Treaty of Fontainebleau,

At the price of $15,000,000 for the roughly 530 million acres of the Louisiana Purchase, the United States paid only three cents per acre of land.

duly ratified by the crowned heads of France, England, and Spain by the Treaty of Paris on February 10, 1763, all the claims and possessions of France in all this country lying to the eastward of the Mississippi were ceded and granted to England while all other portions of this country were then and thereby ceded to Spain.

This treaty fully made the ground upon which Kansas City stands again Spanish. Without apparent knowledge of this Treaty of Paris, the city of St. Louis, in Missouri, was laid out, founded, and named in honor of Louis XV of France in 1764, but in the following year, Louis St. Ange de Bellerive there assumed the reins of government. Then came Count Don Alexandro O'Reilly, under the authority of the king of Spain, with an armed force and formally took possession for the Spanish king on August 18, 1769. From this date on and in fact up to 1804, this territory was subject to and under the command of the Spanish lieutenant governor of Upper Louisiana, whose seat of government was the city of St. Louis.

1800. But Europe was in turmoil, the great Napoleon was in the saddle and disarranging the map of all that country. No one seems to have known just what was coming next. So after many conferences and negotiations, the two countries of France and Spain at last got together, and the result was the terms and conditions of the definitive Treaty of St. Ildefonso entered into on October 1, 1800, by Napoleon, who was then the first consul of the French Republic, on the one side, and the king of Spain on the other, by which all this country was retroceded to and again became a part of France.

1803. Immeasurably greater in all ways than any other land transaction of earth, either before or since, and of vaster direct personal concern to the people of America than all other treaties combined, in this year came the purchase and cession of Louisiana. The war of the revolution had been fought and won; by our treaty of peace and cession concluded with England in 1783, the United States had been granted all public lands east of the Mississippi River (except in Florida) not owned by the original thirteen colonies; the federal Constitution had been proclaimed adopted in 1789; George Washington and John Adams had been and Thomas Jefferson then was the president of the United States of America. Then it was that almost unaided and practically alone, Robert R. Livingston, as our principal representative at the French court, concluded with Napoleon Bonaparte, still first consul of France, on April 30, 1803, the treaty of cession under and by the terms of which the French ceded and granted to the United States all that vast empire since known in history as the Louisiana Purchase. For a period of more than one hundred years, one of the illusions of our history has been that as our president, Thomas Jefferson, then was and today is entitled to all the credit, honor, and glory of this great transaction. But a free people may always consider the truth of history. Jefferson was a cautious and conservative statesman. The historical facts, then well known, in brief are: that under the uncertain and somewhat contradictory instructions from our government at Washington, our diplomatic representative who mainly negotiated this great treaty was authorized and directed, not to acquire this empire, but "only to treat for lands on the east side of the Mississippi." In other words to acquire (among other rights) that part of the purchase then known as the city and island of New Orleans.

The government at Washington did not, at first, dream of acquiring one foot of the unknown land west of the Mississippi River. The scheme to sell and cede to the United States all French possessions on this side of the waters originated in the fertile brain of that marvelous man Napoleon Bonaparte, who proposed to dispose of it all because, as he then said, France "had to sell." Livingston had no authority to negotiate for the purchase of anything save the city and island mentioned, indeed to do so was beyond and in practical violation of the instructions of our government. Yet with farsighted statesmanship, rare courage, and sagacity, he saw the tremendous advantage of the purchase to our country, wisely and bravely assumed the responsibility, closed the negotiations, and concluded this treaty.

Hence to Napoleon's offer to sell and Livingston's wisdom and courage in buying, we are today indebted for the Louisiana Purchase. Livingston then said, "This is the noblest work of our lives."

When the treaty reached Washington in that summer, the administration was astounded at the audacity of Livingston as well as with the immensity of the transaction. President Jefferson at that period inclined to the opinion that our government had no lawful right to buy or hold the purchased territory, talked and wrote about making "waste paper of the Constitution," and even went so far as to formulate, with his own hand, an amendment to the federal Constitution providing for the government of the purchase in the event that the Senate ratified the treaty. Great Livingston again went to the front and so strongly urged its ratification that the president finally yielded and duly submitted the treaty for ratification, but suggested that but little be said about the constitutional question involved, but little debate be had, and that the Congress should act in silence.

Notwithstanding the doubts and fears of the executive and the fierce opposition, the Senate wisely took the broad national view that the right to acquire territory by conquest or purchase and govern it was inherent in every sovereign nation, that ours was a sovereign nation, and accordingly the Senate, by an overwhelming majority, ratified the treaty, and the Congress soon passed laws for the government of the purchase, thus vindicating the sagacity, wisdom, and statesmanship of Livingston as well as [the] sovereignty of the United States.

Thus it came about that for the consideration named and about $15,000,000 of money, the United States purchased and France ceded to this government all the land that had been theretofore retroceded by Spain to France. Of this cession Napoleon then said, "This accession of territory strengthens forever the power of the United States; and I have just given to England a maritime rival that will sooner or later humble her pride." And in his message transmitting this treaty to Congress, which caused it proclaimed on October 21, 1803, in noting the possibilities of this purchase, President Jefferson then said, "The fertility of the country, its climate and extent, promise in due season important aids to our treasury, and ample provision for our prosperity and a wide spread for the blessings of freedom and equal laws." All this occurred before the days when steam and electricity were harnessed and working for the use of man and is therefore not so strange. Then the average American had no adequate conception of the West, the bulk of our population lived east of the Alleghanies, and the people of the Atlantic seaboard knew even less then than they now know of our country lying west of the Father of Waters. This cession included almost all of the now states of Louisiana, Arkansas, Missouri, Iowa, Minnesota, Nebraska, Oregon, Oklahoma, Kansas, the two Dakotas, Idaho, Montana, Washington, and Wyoming. Of late, maps have been published and books written to prove that this purchase did not extend beyond the crest of the Rocky Mountains, but a study of congressional debates upon this question will convince the scholar and thinker that all the states named, and parts of others, were intended to be included. On October 31, 1803, the Congress duly authorized the president to take possession of and occupy this territory, and on December 20, 1803, formal possession thereof was duly delivered by the republic of France, through [Pierre Clement de] Laussat, its colonial prefect, to the United States through W. C. C. Claiborne and James Wilkinson, as commissioners of the republic.

1804. For a few months after this purchase, all this country was known and designated as the Territory of Louisiana, but this was changed by our Congress on March 26, 1804, the now state of Louisiana and a part of that which is now Mississippi was designated the "Territory of Orleans" and all the remainder of the purchase was then called the "District of Louisiana," and that Congress then further provided that the executive and judicial power of the Territory of Indiana should be extended to and over this district and "the Governor and Judges" of that territory were therein given the authority to enact laws for and hold their courts therein. So in May 1804, Governor William Henry Harrison, from the seat of justice of Indiana Territory at Saint

Although Upper Louisiana was transferred to the United States in March 1804, the Spanish officials did not leave St. Louis until the following November.

Vincennes on the Wabash River, rode over on horseback to the city of St. Louis to ascertain the wants of our people in the way of laws and courts. Having satisfied himself on these scores, this territorial governor returned to his home, and during that and the following year, "the Governor and Judges" of that territory enacted and here enforced such laws as they deemed were needed by this "District."

In the spring of this year, too, the great Lewis and Clark expedition started from the city of St. Louis and came up the Missouri River and passed the site of Kansas City on its way to the Pacific Ocean. The wondrously strange history and vaster possibilities of this expedition of 1804 and 1806, under the title of *The Conquest*, has recently been well written and printed by Eva Emery Dye of Oregon.

1805. On March 3, 1805, the Congress of the United States enacted a law which not only changed our official name from the District of Louisiana to the Territory of Louisiana, but provided for our first local territorial self-government. That congressional act conferred upon the governor of this territory full executive authority, while the legislative power and powers to enact and enforce all laws was therein granted to that "Governor and the Judges or a majority of them."

1808. The most important and far-reaching Indian treaty that was ever made anywhere, affecting early Missouri, was that treaty which upon its face recites the fact that it was "made and concluded at Fort Clark, on the right bank of the Missouri about five miles above Fire Prairie" on November 10, 1808, and that this fort was then located "on the south side of the Missouri, about 300 miles up that river" from the city of St. Louis.

This treaty was between the Big and the Little tribes of Osage Indians and our government, and by its terms, those tribes, then being in actual possession, ceded and granted to the United States all lands lying eastward of a line drawn due south from Fort Clark and running from the Missouri River to the Arkansas River. This then left as Indian lands and country all westward of the line so drawn.

Upon their slow voyage up the Missouri River on their way to the Pacific Ocean in 1804, Lewis and Clark had first established this fort and then named it in honor of the junior member of their exploring party.* After the ratification of the great Indian treaty of 1808, and as a tribute to the memory of the Osage

---

*Editors' Note: William Clark noted the site in 1804, but the fort was not established until 1808.

Fort Osage, abandoned by 1827, was recreated in the 1940s-1960s and is now a National Historic Landmark. [Walker - Missouri Tourism]

tribes of Indians, the name of the place was changed from Fort Clark to Fort Osage, and still later was again changed to Sibley, to perpetuate the name and fame of George C. Sibley, who was at one time the U.S. government agent at that point.

If any archaeologist is now curious to know just where to locate the site of ancient Fort Clark, the task is easy: set up a compass anywhere on the Missouri-Kansas line, run due east twenty-four miles and thence due north to the Missouri River, and there may be found today the city of Sibley in Jackson County, Missouri, once Fort Osage and still earlier Fort Clark.

1812. By an act of Congress, which commenced "to have full force" on the first Monday in December 1812, the name of this portion of the country was again changed from the Territory of Louisiana to the Territory of Missouri, and executive, legislative, and judicial powers were then for the first time vested in and conferred upon our own peoples. Although the fathers then knew all about the Missouri River from near its source to its mouth, yet this was the first federal recognition of the name now so well and highly honored—Missouri. This act did not change our boundary lines, and the Territory of Missouri then embraced and had jurisdiction over all the Louisiana Purchase, excepting only the extreme southern portion thereof, as stated. All general laws governing this territory from 1803 to 1821, both congressional and territorial, may be found in print in volume 1 of the *Territorial Laws of Missouri*.

1820. The enabling act of the Congress of March 6, 1820, was passed to authorize the people of this territory to form a state and adopt a constitution for their own government. The boundaries of the future state were then first fixed as they today remain, the "Platte Purchase" of 1837 excepted. Our delegates thereupon duly formed, adopted, and on July 20, 1820, sent to that Congress a state constitution, which was not satisfactory to our national lawmakers.

Upon the questions raised in the discussion of the enabling act was fought the most terrific political battle that had ever been waged in this country up to that time. It is known in history as the "Missouri Compromise of 1820," and for length, intensity, and bitterness, this struggle then had no parallel in American history.

1821. The final result was that on March 2, 1821, the Congress by resolution provided for the admission of this state into the Union, with slavery but "upon the fundamental conditions" named in the act. On June 26 following, our legislature entered its protest against that condition but gave its reluctant assent to its terms, and lastly, on August 10, 1821, James Monroe, as president of the United States, proclaimed the historic fact that on that day Missouri became, and it has ever since been, a state of the American union.

The organization, constitution, and admission into the Union of the State of Missouri then left all the remainder of the Louisiana Purchase lying westward and northward of this state as unorganized territories, possessions of this government, then subject to congressional legislation, but having no laws of its own, excepting those heretofore passed by the several sovereigns named.

1825. The original proprietors, known as the Big and Little tribes of Osage Indians, having relinquished their titles to all lands lying east of a due south and north line drawn from old Fort Clark to the Arkansas in 1808, as stated heretofore, this left a strip of land twenty-four miles in width, lying due eastward of the west line of this state and running from the Missouri River to the Arkansas River. The Indian title to this strip of land was relinquished by them and ceded to the government of the United States by the terms of the Treaty of Nampawarrah, or White Plume, of date June 3, 1825.* From these Indian tribes the government then derived its title to them, and not until then did the United States, as a part of the public domain, come into full and complete possession, ownership, and control of the lands upon which Kansas City now stands. This strip of land was soon opened up for entry, purchase, and settlement. Hundreds of hardy pioneers with their wives and

---

*Editors' Note: The treaty name and date are incorrect. The treaty was signed in St. Louis on June 2, 1825.

The first Jackson County Courthouse was built in 1828 and served as the seat of justice until about 1831. This photo, taken in 1951, shows the former courthouse when it was being used by the Community Welfare League.

children were waiting on the border line, and when the day came that they could lawfully do so, these men here made the first great "rush" on record for Indian lands.

1826. Jackson County was organized under the General Assembly act of date December 21, 1826*, and the first session of its county court was held at Independence on July 2, 1827. But prior to this time, the lands now embraced within the limits of this county had by law been theretofore included within the borders of the counties, successively, of St. Louis, Howard, Cooper, Lillard (name later abolished), Lafayette, and finally Jackson.

1828. When the title to this strip of land was fully vested in the United States by the extinguishment of the Indian title in 1825, the eastern portion of Jackson County had been settled for some years; as early as 1821 a number of French Canadian trappers, traders, and huntsmen had squatted upon and occupied lands along the Missouri riverfront; but the first white American to

---

*Editors' Note: The date is incorrect. Jackson County was organized on December 15, 1826.

make a permanent entry of and settlement upon lands now included within the boundaries of Kansas City was James H. McGee, whose patent for his 320 acres of this land bears date November 14, 1828.

1833. Under a grant of legislative authority, the town of Westport, now within and a part of Kansas City, was established in 1833, and for many a long year thereafter, the few people who lived in the straggling hamlet along the Missouri riverfront and at the steamboat landing here were known only as citizens of Westport Landing.

1839. In the report of his explorations of 1673, Jacques Marquette first mentions the Kansa tribe of Indians as being "on the Missouri, beyond the Missouris and Osages," and from that tribe the Kansas River derived its name. The name of tribe and river were both spelled and pronounced in very different ways by the explorers, but Kansas City was originally so named to perpetuate both and was first platted as the "Town of Kansas" in 1839.

1850. On February 4, 1850, the Jackson County Court, by its order of record entered at Independence, first formally and duly incorporated "The Town of Kansas" and then gave to the people near the mouth of the Kansas River their first local self-government.

1853. By a special act of the Missouri legislature, duly adopted on February 22, 1853, the name of the "Town of Kansas" was changed to the "City of Kansas," and on that day we first became an incorporation under the laws of this state. Various amendments were later made to that charter, and by the first freeholders' charter adopted by our people under grant of constitutional authority in 1889, the name was again changed from the "City

Kansas City in 1855

of Kansas" to "Kansas City." But for many long years now this city has properly and proudly borne its present name of Kansas City, Missouri.

1854. It may again be here noted in passing that all that country from the westward line of Missouri to the crest of the Rocky Mountains was and officially remained unorganized "Indian country" up to 1854. Repeated efforts had been theretofore made by the Congress of the United States to segregate it from the state of Missouri, and bills had been introduced at Washington to make it all into one territory under the name of Platte and Nebraska, but finally on May 30, 1854, the Congress adopted an act, known throughout the English-speaking world as the "Kansas-Nebraska Act," under which these two were created and erected into territories on the same day. Kansas became a state of the American union on January 29, 1861, and Nebraska on March 1, 1867.

In the "Historical Sketch" of Kansas City, printed as a preface to our annotated charter and revised ordinances in 1898, appear in full the facts relating to two amusing incidents of that which might have been: The one is that at the first platting and naming of this city in 1839, one of our early and wealthy settlers, who always signed his name as "Abraham Fonda, Gentleman," because he was not a working man, earnestly desired that the future city be named in his honor as "Port Fonda." He was about to succeed in this when, unfortunately for his fame, he became involved in a fierce quarrel with another part owner named Henry Jobe. The combined efforts of the old "Town of Kansas" company and Jobe's threats of fist and shotgun finally prevailed and are responsible for our present name. The other is that in 1855 a concerted effort was ineffectually made to cede and grant all lands lying west and north of the Big Blue River, from the point at which that historic stream crosses the Missouri-Kansas line near the ancient town called "Santa Fe," down to its mouth on the Missouri, to the then Territory of Kansas. Had the former scheme won out, Kansas City would now be "Port Fonda," and had the second won, we would now be in and a part of Kansas.

1909. Through all the seething and roar, the bustle and the hurry, the buying and building, the enlarging and progress of the years intervening between 1839 and 1909, Kansas City has ever pursued the even tenor of its way, the Kansas City spirit pervading city and country alike; nothing save an invisible line divides the two great municipalities near the mouth of the Kansas, and the stranger within our gates would not dream of its existence; while between the two combined cities and their suburbs, we now have a population of half a million of happy and prosperous people, all hopefully confident that the future of Kansas City will be even more glorious than its past.

Confluence of People and Place:
The Chouteau Posts
on the Missouri and Kansas Rivers

DAVID BOUTROS

Francois Gesseau Chouteau neither envisioned a city nor platted a town, but he reasonably may be called the "father of Kansas City," the place where he put down roots and made the location a landmark. In old St. Louis, merchandise sent up the river was marked "Chouteau's Town," steamboat captains told their crews to dock at Chouteau's Landing, the log church atop the rugged hill behind Chouteau's warehouse was called "Chouteau's Church," and the street running on the south side of the church lot (present-day Twelfth Street) was known as "Chouteau Street." Members of the original company forming the Town of Kansas had known Chouteau; the fact that, in the end, the name they chose honored the Kansa, predecessors of them all, in no way diminishes the stature of Francois Chouteau.

In a like manner, early historians often claimed that Francois's wife, Thérèse Berenice Menard Chouteau, was the first white woman to live in western Missouri. While that distinction almost certainly belongs to another, Berenice's move to western Missouri is significant in that she was one of the first white women to make a real commitment by bringing her "life" to the frontier—babies, slaves, furniture—in short, the trappings for permanent residence.

Researchers exploring the history of the Chouteau family and enterprises in western Missouri are confronted by a wealth of legend wrapped around a few truths. Much of their effort involves peeling back the myth and testing each seed of fact against information within contemporary documents and oral traditions. In this process, some cherished tales do not withstand examination while new stories are uncovered.

Nearly thirty years after Francois Chouteau established his frontier fur trading posts, Kansas City was promoted as an idyllic spot, destined to become a great city.

Critical to most of the traditional stories of the Chouteaus coming to the western frontier was the nineteenth-century historians' desire to find a history for Kansas City. Those writers sought to prove that the founding and growth of the city were predetermined by its location and, secondarily, by the vision and energy of its founders. From their perspective, "where the rocky bluffs meet" at the great river's bend was destined to be a great metropolis. One piece of proof was the fact that a son of Missouri's renowned city-founding family, the Chouteaus, was the first to choose the south bank of the Missouri River at the confluence of the Kansas River as the center of a mighty commercial enterprise.

Until recently most of the information about Francois and Berenice Chouteau had its roots in the "Tales of an Old Timer" by John Calvin McCoy. A talented storyteller with a deep interest in the history of the region—to which he personally contributed in significant ways—McCoy arrived in western Missouri in 1830 to assist his father, Isaac, with missionary work and the removal of Indian tribes from east of the Mississippi to the territory west of the state of Missouri. Calvin, as his friends knew him, was also eager to make a success of his life and engaged in a variety of ventures that earned him both money and status. He is credited with being the founder of Westport and the first to offload goods onto a natural rock landing that would become the heart of the Town of Kansas. Many of McCoy's stories may have come from firsthand knowledge and observation, into which he heavily sprinkled interpretations and assumptions. Writing for a variety of local newspapers and magazines beginning in the late 1860s, he entertained and educated his readers with colorful memories of old times. He filled his tales with coarse and refined characters alike, graphic images of frontier hardships, and descriptions of primitive places and practices. A skilled writer, he used biblical and classical allusions with case.

It is hard to tell exactly where McCoy collected his information, beyond what he knew from personal involvement. Regarding the Chouteaus, he would have known Francois and claimed to be friends with Berenice and with Francois's brothers, Frederick and Cyprien. In fact, McCoy lived across the road from Berenice on Pearl Street for about fifteen years. That Calvin "interviewed" old settlers, gathering their memories for his own, is a certainty. The question is the accuracy of the data he collected and the skill he used to integrate divergent facts into a single narrative—a question that must be asked about any researcher/historian.

McCoy's account of Francois and Berenice Chouteau, reported in numerous articles, is full of contradictions but has a common premise—the couple was the first to realize the importance of the place that would become Kansas City. It is this theme and its attending "facts" that were accepted and included in later histories. Several passages provide a taste of McCoy's style and an outline of his Chouteau story:

> I said there were a few relics of the genesis still with us; aye, the first white woman that ever had a home west of Fort Osage lives here in her venerable old age of 85 years, still blessed with uncommon vigor of mind and body. She first saw the place in 1819, when on her way from St. Louis to the frontier trading post of the Black Snake hills (St. Joseph). It was her bridal tour with her husband on a keel boat, requiring about six weeks to make the trip. She is the daughter of the first territorial governor of Illinois—Colonel Peter Menard, of Kaskaskia. In 1821 she came again with her husband, Colonel Chouteau, when he established a trading post on the south bank of the river, opposite Randolph Point, which was at the time a noted crossing place for the Sauks [Sacs], Iowa and Kickapoo tribes, inhabiting the north, and the Osage and Kansas, of the south side, in their interchange of courtesies, whether friendly or otherwise. Six buildings and other valuable improvement was made, and this was her home until 1826, when the great flood in the Missouri of that year compelled a hasty retreat to the hills of Clay county, and every vestige of the improvement and post were swept away. Again, in the flood

Ironically, the founder of Westport, John Calvin McCoy, did not embrace Kansas City's growing population in the latter half of the nineteenth century. He yearned for the solitude of the area's frontier days. [Kansas State Historical Society]

of 1844, a similar calamity befell her valuable and costly homestead, warehouse and large farm, being utterly obliterated and ruined by the deposit of from 2 to 6 feet of sand left over a large portion of the land. Having in the early years of the settlement and city abundant means, she was noted for her good works and generous charity to the poor and her church. I doubt not our city has many noble, self-sacrificing, generous women, but without disparagement of their merits, I beg to say that this worthy old pioneer is the noblest Dorcas of them all, and will go up to the Master with an offer of sheaves that will be as generous as any. A sketch of the first twenty years of her residence near the Kaw's mouth and her clear recollection of the events and persons of that earliest period would be not only interesting, but would be a valuable starting point in our city's history.

The limits allowable in a newspaper article, however, will admit of only this brief mention, pleasant as the task would be to extend its interesting details.

Late in the fall of 1820 five persons arrived at the point just mentioned, Randolph Point, in a pirogue, (an extra large canoe or double dugout) from St. Louis. The leader of the party was Louis Bertholet, a large swarthy looking French and Iroquois half-bred [*sic*], his wife and step-son (Louis Preu); a youth and two French employees constituted the others [*sic*]. They were sent up by the American Fur company to make preliminary cabins and arrangements for the establishment of a trading post at that point in the following spring.

They had built one log cabin and commenced another when a party of migratory Sauk Indians came along and tore them down and with hostile threats and demonstrations ordered the party to leave instanter; this order was complied with, the party betook themselves again to their pirogue floated a mile or so down the river, and waiting until the Sauks had left, the plucky half-breed returned and landed on the Clay county side near the mouth of the creek at the upper Randolph landing. Selecting a favorable site for defense, in a secluded bend of the creek he there constructed a small temporary shelter and fort wherein to pass the winter while waiting the promised arrival in the following spring of Colonel Chouteau with his large outfit of men and supplies.

These consisted of two keel boats loaded with goods suited for the Indian trade and general use and thirty-five men nearly all of them French of Canada or St. Louis. Indeed this class were almost exclusively employed by the early Indian and rocky mountain fur traders of the upper Missouri.

Mrs. Chouteau accompanied the expedition with her two children, Gesso and Menard.

[Author's note: a break in the article jumps the story to events after the 1826 flood.] She remained six weeks at the Randolph bluffs waiting for the flood to abate and then went with her children and two employees in a pirogue to Ste. Genevieve, Mo. I should have stated that fifteen of the men were sent back to St. Louis with the empty keel boats and twenty were retained; most of whom were at the date of the flood, (which occurred in April) out with trading parties. As soon as the stage of water would permit, Chouteau moved what goods and other valuables were saved from the flood up to about the north end of Harrison street, at the foot of the river hills, built several log houses and remained there two years, at that time three others were located at this point, viz., Daniel Morgan Boone, a son of the famous pioneer, Gabriel Phillibert, and Beneito Vasguez [*sic*]—the latter was sub Indian agent for the Kansas Indians. Boone was farmer and Phillibert, blacksmith, by government appointment, for that tribe. These, however, the next year, (1827) went up westward and established the Kaw agency on the Kansas river, eight miles above Lawrence, but quite a little village grew up at the new Chouteau location, at Harrison street.[1]

Another McCoy article repeats some information, adds other, and also contradicts key dates and places.

There was no other military or trading post above Fort Osage in 1819. Some years after, (in 1825), a trading post was established by Col. Francis Chouteau . . . on the South bank of the river, about four miles below the city, opposite the Clay county bluffs. But the great flood in the Missouri in April, 1826, made a clean sweep of all his buildings and he never rebuilt them at that point, but removed to the South bank of the Kaw river, about six miles above its mouth. He afterwards (about 1830) opened a large farm with costly buildings, about one mile below the lower limits of the city, upon what is now known as the Guinotte tract. He owned about 1200 acres, and the only warehouse and steamboat landing up to 1839 between Wayne City and Fort Leavenworth. Every vestige of improvement on this last place was again swept away by the flood of 1844, leaving a deposit of sand from two to five feet deep over the whole farm.[2]

A third article yields additional data.

About two years before this (1820) a trading post was established on the north bank of the Kansas river, about twenty five miles up that stream which was named "The Four Houses" being four log houses so built as to answer the purpose of a fort and security from possible attacks of savages. That post was occupied only two years and then abandoned.[3]

The workable narrative compiled from all of McCoy's writings contains a wealth of information that rings true when compared to other independent sources and many details that fail when put to the same test. Of particular interest are the locations of the Chouteau posts and the time frame of the events. What follows is not intended to debate Calvin McCoy on the truth of his story, but to lay out the plausible history of the Chouteaus as can be pieced together from the variety of sources now available.

Nearly 400 miles from St. Louis via the serpentine Missouri River, a traveler in the first quarter of the nineteenth century would arrive at the mouth of the Kansas River. At the convergence of the two rivers, the Missouri turns north toward its upper reaches, and the Kansas, fed by many streams and creeks, has flowed east from the plains. It was in the region of the confluence that the Native American inhabitants found crossroads of trade and war. When the first explorers and settlers came from the East, they established forts and trading posts in the area. By the time Francois Chouteau came to the Kawsmouth with his cousin Gabriel Sylvestre (Seres) Chouteau in 1816, a network of independent traders and trappers already occupied the land, along

With poles and men pulling from land, keelboats allowed fur traders to travel upriver with their cargo.

with wandering bands of Indians hunting the forests and engaging in exchange with these traders.

A major tributary of the Missouri River, the Kansas River's first surveyor, Angus Langham, observed in 1826 that its mouth was almost 600 feet wide and its channel often 900 feet wide in its shallow, sandy bed.[4] The two rivers created a small lake, and the turbulence at their juncture determined that encampments and settlements be at least a half-mile upstream or downstream.

Francois and Seres Chouteau may have established the Four Houses post as McCoy suggested, "on the north bank of the [Kansas] river one mile above the mouth of Cedar creek, near the P.R.R. [Pacific Railroad] station of Lenape. It was called 'Four Houses,' being four log houses arranged in a square, answering the purpose of a fort."[5] Its exact location, however, is not as definitive as McCoy related, but it was in place probably as early as the summer of 1819. In October of that year, Major Thomas Biddle noted that the Chouteau cousins "have a trading-house not far from the mouth of the river Kanzas, and their capital is about $4,000."[6]

Competition for trade in the area was fierce, coming primarily from the posts of Andrew Woods, Cyrus Curtis, and Michael Eley located on the right (west) bank of the Missouri, a half-mile to a mile above the mouth of the Kaw. McCoy erroneously asserted that these were short-lived and unsuccessful ventures surviving only a year or so.[7] In fact, these vigorous operations eventually forced Seres Chouteau to seek his fortunes elsewhere. As early as April 1820, Francois's half-brother, Pierre (Cadet) Chouteau Jr., and Jean

Baptiste Sarpy in the Berthold, Chouteau, and Pratte Fur Company's St. Louis office were writing to Seres that the Woods-Curtis-Eley threat was "doing all that is in their power to crush you." Two years later the situation became more complicated because Francois Chouteau was asserting his independence from his older partner/cousin, Seres. "Gesseau [Francois Chouteau] wanted to take the merchandise for his own account, because he alleges, with reason, that the profits are so limited that it is not worth the trouble to increase the number of partners in a small operation." Cadet offered Seres the option to move elsewhere and turn over his Four Houses operation to Cyprien (Chouteau?)— which he apparently did.[8]

The location of Francois's post at that time remains unclear. Tradition (e.g., McCoy) stated that by mid-1822, Francois had established his Randolph Bluffs post. It is troubling, however, that a year later, in July 1823, explorer Prince Paul Wilhelm of Wuerttemberg did not find him there.

Prince Paul's journal recounted the toil of pushing and pulling keelboats against the Missouri's current, the challenges of snag-filled channels that needed to be hacked clear before the boat could progress, and the problems of storms, floods, and ravenous insects. He gave details of where he went, what he saw, and to whom he spoke. He stayed several days at the home of "Grand Louis" Bertholet, situated where McCoy placed it, on a small creek at the Randolph Bluffs landing on the Clay County side of the river. The prince hunted on the south bank, met with a band of Kansa Indians there, and visited at a temporary camp of voyageurs who came to talk with him. Nowhere in his writings does he mention Francois Chouteau, his home, or post.[9]

Berenice, however, remembered that she came to Jackson County in 1822—not 1821 as McCoy wrote.[10] One may wonder if she was correct about the year or if she was somewhere other than across from Randolph Bluffs in Jackson County. At that time, Bates County, the location of an Osage trading post at which Francois held a license to trade in November 1825, was technically part of Jackson County.[11] Alternatively, perhaps Berenice's "Jackson County" should be interpreted more broadly to mean the western frontier.

The year 1822 was significant for other reasons. As mentioned, Seres Chouteau departed the Kawsmouth region that year, leaving Francois and his younger brother, Cyprien, as the reigning Chouteaus in the area. Fort Osage, the westernmost station of the failed United States government factory system, closed and left trade in the West essentially unregulated except for the licenses granted by Superintendent of Indian Affairs William Clark and his subordinates. Lastly, serious interest was increasing in the overland trade with Santa Fe, and new faces and opportunities were beginning to appear.

Frederick Chouteau had four wives and at least ten children. He lived along the Missouri-Kansas border until his death at age eighty-two. [Kansas State Historical Society]

Lacking evidence one way or the other, some researchers, including this author, have retained the traditional establishment date of 1822 for Chouteau's Randolph Bluffs post. Another reasonable theory, however, is that Francois brought Berenice and their children to Four Houses in 1822 and did not build the Randolph Bluffs warehouse until the following year. This would explain why Prince Paul did not mention the Chouteaus and would be consistent with a later point about retailer's licenses Chouteau purchased in Clay County.

Regardless, Francois Chouteau did operate a post at Randolph Bluffs, whether or not it was in place as early as 1822. Frederick Chouteau, who, unlike McCoy, was on the scene before the 1826 flood washed away the post, clearly remembered it being on the north bank of the river, not on the south bank in Jackson County as McCoy believed.[12] A comparison of Francois's contemporary letters and Frederick's later account of the sinking of the keelboat *Beaver* shows that Frederick was remarkably accurate in his reminiscences.[13] Moreover, evidence and interpretation support Frederick's recollections.

First, as McCoy intimated in the above quotation, the south bank was off-limits to white settlement prior to the Kansa Treaty of 1825. Francois Chouteau, as revealed in his letters, was a stickler for following the rules, and though he could have gained permission to build on Indian lands, there was no particularly good reason for him to do so.

Moreover, the south bank was lowland, unprotected, and opposite the main channel of the river. It would have been a more difficult place to land and unload goods and would have presented problems of exposure and flooding.

Also, a curious incongruity exists in McCoy's tale. In comparing the floods of 1826 and 1844, he commented, "The first was caused by a great accumulation of snow on the western plains, which was suddenly melted by a sudden change of temperature and assisted by heavy rains."[14] This would suggest that the warning of disaster was short. Moreover, McCoy also stated that Chouteau made "a hasty retreat to the hills of Clay county" when the 1826 flood came. While it is reasonable to assume that Clay County may have been closer than high ground on the south side of the river, this still seems an odd response to the disaster. Short of hands and time, why would Francois carry his goods across the rising river?

Sometimes evidence is what is unsaid: Major Stephen W. Kearny wrote in his diary for October 12, 1824:

> Started [from near Liberty, Mo.] at day break; morning cool, frosty & a heavy fog on the water. made 3½ [miles] to breakfast came up to Mr. Chouteaus Trading House to dinner, where we found the *Kickapoos*, & the *Kansas* were expected to-morrow[;] made some purchases: In the afternoon passed the *Kansas River* & halted one mile above it, on the left Bank, opposite to *Curtis & Ely's* Trading House, having made 16 miles.[15]

Did Kearny cross the Missouri River to reach Chouteau's post? If so, why did he not mention it, particularly since he would need to cross again to be on the left bank opposite from Curtis and Eley's house? The more reasonable assumption is that Kearny was touring Clay County. As discussed below, Chouteau had built his post at the crossing (a ford and later a ferry) of a major north-south trail used by the Indians to conduct commerce across the Missouri River. Kearny was following established roads improved from the Indians' paths.[16] Support for this theory also comes from tracing a journey from Liberty to the Chouteau Bridge, then along the river to the north end of the Downtown Airport—a distance very close to the sixteen miles Kearny reported.

Lastly, Francois Chouteau paid $22.50 to the Clay County collector for a retailer's license on November 10, 1823, and $23.61 for another license on February 15, 1825.[17] There would have been no reason for the financially careful Chouteau to purchase such licenses unless his business resided in Clay County.

Regardless of what has been written in previous Kansas City histories, Francois Chouteau's 1822-1826 post on the Missouri River was not in Jackson County, but rather in Clay County.

Where was the post located? In the 1950s, historian James Anderson, along with descendants of the Chouteaus and other French families of Kansas City, argued successfully that the city's newly acquired Milwaukee Bridge should be renamed the Chouteau Bridge in honor of its proximity to the site of the early trading post. They were, in fact, correct, but instead of being close to the south end of the bridge, the post had been located about a half-mile west of the north end. The key to determining this location is the site of the Randolph settlement in the early nineteenth century.

According to McCoy, "Randolph Point was, previous to the advent of the white man, a famous crossing place for the Indian tribes of the north and south sides of the Missouri river in the interchange of visits, peaceable and otherwise, and that fact was the inducement with Francis Chouteau, in 1820, for selecting that point for a trading post of the American Fur Company.[18]

Landscapes change, towns and rivers move, but ravines and bluffs were more resistant to change until big earthmoving equipment became common. To find nineteenth-century Randolph required locating old landmarks, one of which McCoy cited: "the mouth of the creek at the upper Randolph landing." The site of "Grand Louis's" cabin is the landmark for finding this creek. *The History of Clay and Platte Counties* placed Bertholet's home in section 18, township 50 north, range 32 west. Prince Paul stated that the cabin was near the river on the west face of a chain of bluffs and on the road south from Liberty.[19] Only two natural cuts through the bluffs in section 18 have a west face—the first at a small unnamed creek about a half-mile west of the Chouteau Bridge and the second at Rock Creek about a quarter-mile farther west.[20] Also, in 1826, Calise Montardeau purchased from Richard Linville a ferry operating across the Missouri River, which was reportedly located where "Grand Louis" Bertholet lived at Randolph Bluffs. Montardeau afterward patented land on the south bank immediately opposite the Randolph community.[21]

Shielded below the bluffs, Randolph was not so much a town as a settlement of between six and twelve families. After the Civil War, the town was moved away from the river to the top of the bluffs, then to its current location near the intersection of I-435 and Highway 210.

The flood of April 1826 washed away Chouteau's warehouse, which surely lay close to the riverbank to facilitate the loading and unloading of goods. McCoy's statement that Berenice resided in the Clay County hills until the waters receded and then went downriver to St. Louis and Ste. Genevieve

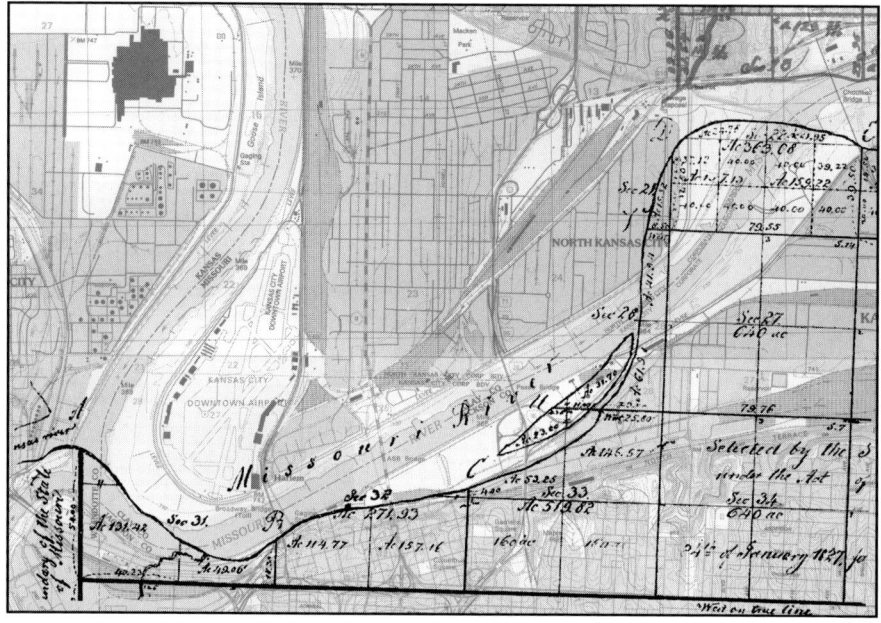

In the early nineteenth century, floods dramatically changed the course of the Missouri River's channel. Overlaid on a current U.S. Geological Survey map are the 1827 Jackson County survey and part of the 1819 Clay County survey. [Western Historical Manuscript Collection-Kansas City]

seems reasonable, since her third son died and was buried in St. Louis on October 25, 1826, and her fourth son was born there in March of 1827.[22]

Francois quickly recovered from the catastrophe of the flood and by October 1826 had settled on the south bank near the present junction of Harrison or Gillis Street and the Missouri River. Traveler John Glover noted in his journal, "Traveled on and came to Shotoes [i.e., Chouteau's] Trading house 1 mile below the Kaw river on the Missouria."[23] It was there too that Subagent Antoine F. (*dit* Baronet) Vasquez established the Kansa Agency, though McCoy also disagrees with Frederick Chouteau as to where the agency was located prior to the flood. Frederick stated that Vasquez had been at Randolph at his brothers' post.[24]

Francois Chouteau built the Vasquez home at Harrison Street and, after Vasquez's untimely death in August 1828, purchased the house from his widow. Unfortunately, though he owned the buildings, Francois was unable to secure rights to the land on which they stood. By 1829 he moved his family farther east near Olive Street, where he developed a farm, warehouse complex, and, later, a steamboat landing.

The migration of Native Americans from the East began in the late 1820s, and Chouteau understood the value of that trade, particularly with the Shawnee and the Delaware who would occupy lands in present-day Johnson and Wyandotte counties in Kansas—lands from which the Kansa Indians had been displaced by their 1825 treaty. Various references and the channel of the Kansas River give clues to the location of the Shawnee post that Francois and his brothers built in November 1828. Francois's letter of December 2, 1828, to his father-in-law and business partner, Pierre Menard, made clear his circumstances:

> Now I have three good houses [posts] made. My situation is not very comfortable but I believe that for the business that I could not choose a better location. I am exactly across from the Shawnee village, [a] distance of about six or seven miles, near the Kansas River.[25] It is a very elevated point. Water has to rise more than 40 feet to endanger us. There is a good port and a good place for the barge. On the other side across from our establishment, it is a beautiful side, rolling low land where we gather stone when we are in need. Major Graham tells me that Colonel Leavenworth has the intention of cutting a road from the fort all the way to the Kansas River.[26] And he believes that at our establishment will be the best spot suitable to cross over. I am almost in a straight line with the fort and the landing on the two sides of the river is very good. And if the transaction is completed, that could be an advantage for our place.[27]

Francois, true to form and experience, positioned the trading house near established Indian trails, which would be improved for the military and new settlers. McCoy reliably reported from a surveyor's firsthand knowledge that there were two ancient, well-beaten Indian trails through the Kawsmouth area. The first route, as already discussed, "continued south [crossing Brush Creek near Troost Avenue] toward the Osage [in current Vernon and Bates counties], and north from the river to the country occupied by the Ioways, Sauks and Kickapoos in Northern Missouri and Iowa."[28] The second trail came from Fort Osage westward through Independence, crossing the north-south trail near Prospect and Linwood, then to the state line near Westport, "and continuing westward up the Kaw valley *ad infinitum.*"[29] Francois anticipated the new military road south from Fort Leavenworth would ford the Kansas River at the site of his post. He and Cyprien built their Shawnee trading house on the right (south) bank on Shawnee land, across from the abandoned "half-breed establishment on the Kanzas, about 12 miles from the mouth" on the left (north) bank of the river.[30] The Kansas River surveyor, Angus Langham, identified this village at between the eleventh and twelfth miles from the mouth.[31] His map, which corresponds closely to the current river channel, noted a rise on the south bank in that vicinity—the likely spot for what would be called Cyprien's Post.

A quote from Father Benedict Roux, the first Catholic pastor of the Kawsmouth French community, has caused confusion about the location of Chouteau's home: "I am at present at the trading house of Messrs. Chouteau. . . . I cannot . . . speak too highly in praise of Mr. Gesseau Chouteau and of his wife and brother. . . . But I do not expect to remain long with them, as they are right in the Indian country and too far away from the Catholics for me to carry on my ministry with convenience."[32]

One interpretation of this statement suggests that the Chouteau family resided at their Shawnee post in November 1833 when Reverend Roux wrote to Bishop Joseph Rosati in St. Louis. Perhaps this is true, but it is more likely they were at Chouteau's Landing—the headquarters post on the Missouri River. Father Roux was a scholarly man, slight of build, who was not suited to missionary work on the frontier. The main body of his Catholic parishioners was located well away from the Chouteau plantation. In fact,

Below is a segment of Angus Langham's 1826 survey map of the Kansas River. The notations for the "half-breed" settlements are still visible. [Kansas State Historical Society]

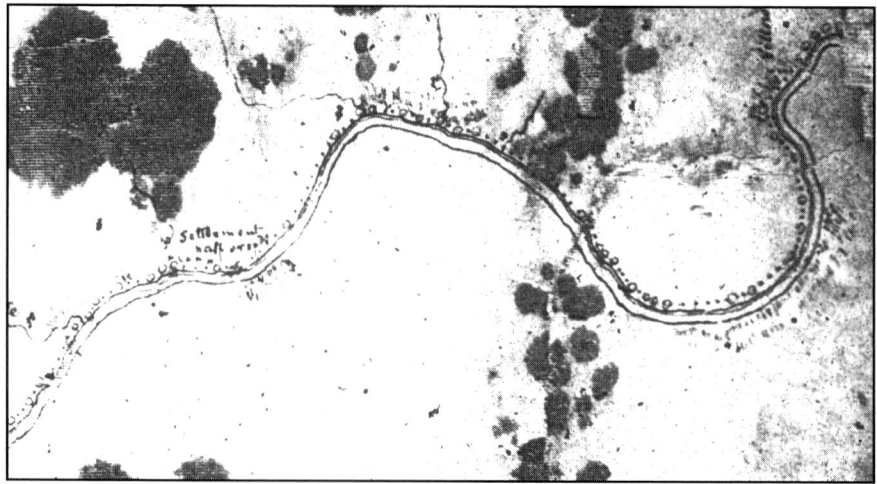

when "Chouteau's Church" was constructed in 1834 on top of the bluffs near what would become Eleventh and Pennsylvania, it was very nearly three miles over rugged terrain from the Chouteau home and landing. Moreover, the post, surrounded by visiting Indians, would have seemed to be "right in the Indian country." Lastly, Francois's letters of the period do not suggest an extended stay at the Shawnee post.   Early in 1831, Francois began to experience weakness and chest pains, which worsened in 1832-1833 and plagued him until his death in 1838, most likely from a massive heart attack. During this period, Francois gave over greater responsibility for his outlying posts to his brothers and limited his journeys from his home post on the Missouri River.

The location of Francois Chouteau's trading house developed in the late 1820s on the Missouri River was roughly a half-mile east of the present-day Paseo Bridge. Its main landmark was a mile-long island, once called Chouteau's Island, but more commonly known as Mensing's Island after a farmer who built his home there in the late 1850s. Now completely attached to the mainland, in the early 1830s when Chouteau built his steamboat landing, the island was a fifty-five-acre scrub-covered grazing pasture. The main channel of the Missouri passed between the island and the south shore—a 100 to 300-foot wide "slough."[33] Here, Francois Chouteau "died suddenly while down on the river bank watching some cattle swim across the slew [slough]."[34]

Descriptions of the place suggest that it was a well-developed farm, warehouse operation, and steamboat landing built in the early 1830s as steamers became more common. The Chouteau farm was large, perhaps patterned after Berenice's father's plantation, which fronted the Kaskaskia River to the east of the town of the same name.[35] Unfortunately, no photographs or drawings of the establishment and farm have been located. The best description of the plantation is found in an 1872 interview with Francois's son, Pierre Menard Chouteau, concerning the devastation of the 1844 flood.

> The flood of 1827 [*sic*] . . . was quite moderate in dimension as compared with the one that followed it seventeen years later. The Harlem bottoms were totally submerged, and all of the bottoms immediately below this city, with the exception of the Guinotte bottoms farm. The mere fact that these Guinotte bottoms were above high water-mark in 1827 caused it to be purchased by the Chouteau family, and in due time the rich, loamy bottom lands, now an almost barren sand-bar, became a fine, large plantation, with hundreds of acres of fertile fields surrounding the fine old homestead of the Chouteaus.

The residence of Mr. P. M. Chouteau (now City Collector) was a spacious double log house with two wings, all covered with weatherboarding. The house had three heavy chimneys built at the ends and one in the centre. There were numerous barns, ware houses, hemp and tobacco houses, besides the negro quarters, clustered around the large house, hundreds of head of stock, horses, cattle and hogs, roamed at will in the quiet bottoms, and all seemed as peaceful and prosperous as could be. . . . The winter of 1844 was somewhat like the present one, deep snows fell in the mountains and very little in this valley. The "June Rise" of 1844 came booming down the river, the channel of which ran down just west of the north end of the railroad bridge and struck fair against the rocky bluff at the foot of Broadway, and then ran along the south shore of the river bank down to Randolph bluffs, where it crossed over and washed the base of the Clay county bluffs. A large island covered with heavy timber existed where now only a low sand bar is seen opposite the gas works.

The plantation of P. M. Chouteau, below the city, was gradually submerged. Inch by inch the angry, muddy stream crawled upon the fertile face of the fields: the slough soon became filled with water, but the wealthy planter remained with his family, expecting every day that the water would go down. One morning the family awoke to find themselves surrounded by four feet of water. Cattle, horses, and hogs were wading and swimming about in the stream; a hundred acres of fine hemp standing in shoals in the field was nearly covered. Upon nearly every every [sic] shock were perched chickens, turkeys, or little pigs. The family had barely time to escape to the main shore when the current became quite rapid, and raised to the second story of the house. While a party of young men were endeavoring to save some of the furniture from the upper story, the steamer Missouri Mail hove in sight up the river. The boys, eager for a joke, dressed up in female apparel, and got upon the roof of the house and hoisted a signal of distress. The steamer rounded to and came to the house. The boys went on board, took a drink, and were taken by the boat to the bluffs, where Chouteau shipped a few tons of water-rotted hemp to the St. Louis market.

The flood was about two weeks going down but when it left it had changed the face of the low lands. In many places the sand had been piled up ten feet deep, in others it had taken off the rich top soil and left only the sandy subsoil. The Choteau [sic] plantation was worthless. What had been rich land was now poor. No one would buy it at five dollars per acre. It was nearly twelve years before the bottom land would sell at any price. It finally sold at $ 12 [?] per acre. The old house stood against the flood until the chimneys were fairly battered down by the huge trees that were hurled against them. When the chimneys went down away went the house. The stream was dotted with floating houses and barns, some surmounted with chickens, dogs and pigs, all alive and taking an involuntary ride.[36]

At the height of his career, Francois Chouteau supervised five trading houses: the Kansa post operated by his brother Frederick, the Shawnee post run by Cyprien, and posts for the Weas and the Kickapoos. The fifth was the large Kansas City warehouse and steamboat landing. He also established a landing at the point of land on the right bank of the Kansas where it joined the Missouri—literally on the state line. Other places associated with, and abandoned by the Chouteaus as circumstances demanded, included the Randolph Bluffs post, the Harrison Street home, Four Houses, and various Kansa post locations.

The French and later settlers who arrived in the Kawsmouth region built the first community upon a network of family and friendship, linking people in a barter of services and goods. An amazing fact of the frontier was the ability of people, and through them, information, to travel long and rugged distances through the wilderness. Rivers and streams joined most destinations, and primitive roads and paths connected other places. The scattering of homes and pastures and trade buildings were transitory landmarks. Nevertheless, the people, regardless of their place or role, created the geography of the community.

This drawing of Pierre Menard's home suggests how the Chouteau plantation may have appeared before the 1844 flood.

NOTES

1. John C. McCoy Scrapbook (KC296), 31, Western Historical Manuscript Collection, University of Missouri-Kansas City (hereinafter referred to as WHMC-Kansas City).

2. Ibid., 3.

3. Ibid., 27.

4. William Clark to Thomas McKenney, 29 April 1828, *St. Louis Superintendency, 1827-1828, Letters Received by the Office of Indian Affairs (OIA), 1824-1881* (National Archives Microfilm Publication M234, roll 748).

5. McCoy Scrapbook, 45.

6. *American State Papers: Indian Affairs* (Washington, DC: Gales and Seaton, 1834), 2: 202. Captain (Brevet Major) Thomas Biddle served as military attaché to a battalion of the rifle regiment, which in 1818 ascended the Missouri River to the mouth of the Yellowstone to establish a post. He was the journalist-historian of the expedition, who at the request of his commander, Colonel Henry Atkinson, reported his personal observations of the Indian tribes and their trade. Albert Watkins, "First Steamboat Trial Trip Up The Missouri," *Nebraska State Historical Society Collections* 17 (1913): 164-165.

7. Louise Barry, *Beginning of the West* (Topeka: Kansas State Historical Society, 1972), 99-100; "Fur posts at Kawsmouth," Chouteau's (Topical) Scrapbook (KC395), 17.1, WHMC-Kansas City; McCoy Scrapbook, 42. The right and left banks are determined while facing downstream.

8. John B. Sarpy to G. S. [*sic*] Chouteau, 6 November 1820; Pierre Chouteau Jr. to C. G. Chouteau, 30 April 1820; 19 July 1822, all in Chouteau Family Collection, Missouri Historical Society, St. Louis. A transcription of the last letter appears in Dorothy Brandt Marra, *Cher Oncle, Cher Papa* (Kansas City: Western Historical Manuscript Collection, 2001), 205-206. Contradicting McCoy, the Chouteau letters in *Cher Oncle, Cher Papa* suggest that Four Houses continued to be used until the new Kansa and Shawnee posts were built in 1827-1828.

9. Paul Wilhelm, Duke of Wuerttemberg, "First Journey to North America in the years 1822 to 1823," *South Dakota Historical Collections* 19 (1938): 299-318.

10. Berenice F. Chouteau, affidavit, 26 October 1887, recorded 28 May 1890, County Deed Book B423: 404 (150360), Jackson County Recorder of Deeds Office. The affidavit related to the church land acquired by Reverend Benedict Roux.

11. Francois Chouteau, license, 20 November 1825, *St. Louis Superintendency, 1827-1828, OIA*, roll 747, frames 439-441. The license reads, "At the or near the old Fort on the Marais des Cygne with the Osages." The old post was a short-lived extension of Fort Osage.

12. "Reminiscences of Frederick Chouteau," *Kansas Historical Collections* 8 (1904): 423. "I came to Randolph, Clay County, Missouri, about two miles below Kansas City, on the opposite side of the Missouri river, in the fall of 1825, October or November." Some historians have suggested that Frederick was misquoted, but this ignores an additional statement later in the paragraph that Kansa Subagent Baronet Vasquez took "goods in my brother's boat across the Missouri river and up to the yellow banks, just above where Wyandotte is" as the first annuity payment for the Kansa.

13. Marra, *Cher Oncle, Cher Papa*, 54-56.

14. McCoy Scrapbook, 45.

15. Barry, *Beginning of the West*, 103.

16. Prince Paul Wilhelm of Wuerttemberg followed this route from Liberty to the cabin of "Grand Louis." Paul Wilhelm, "First Journey," 299-300, 311-312.

17. Clay County Record Book 1, 21, 42, Clay County Archives, Liberty, Missouri.

18. McCoy Scrapbook, 6. Randolph Point was the lowland in Jackson County across the river from the Randolph Bluffs in Clay County. The curve of the river shaped the point.

19. *History of Clay and Platte Counties, Missouri* (St. Louis: National Historical Co., 1885), 113; Paul Wilhelm, "First Journey," 311.

20. Newspaper articles from the *Liberty Tribune* (21 April 1899, 22 June 1906, and 22 May 1908) support this location. An interesting article in the June 12, 1885, *Liberty Tribune* told about D. B. Moreland unearthing an "old fashioned frying pan, a peculiar tin can, and a lot of shreds of decayed wearing apparel, [and] . . . a lot of decayed papers" in the vicinity of Old Randolph.

21. Barry, *Beginning of the West*, 148-149. Certificate of Patent 9031 was issued on September 7, 1838, to Callice Montardeau [*sic*] for the southwest fractional quarter of section 22, township 50 north, range 33 west. U.S. Department of the Interior, Bureau of Land Management, "The Official Federal Land Records Site," www. glorecords.blm.gov/. The discrepancy in dates between occupancy and filing likely meant little. Possession was ownership until someone challenged the claim. As new settlers came to the frontier, older residents often filed to legitimize their holdings.

22. *Guide to the Microfilm Edition of the Pierre Menard Collection in the Illinois State Historical Library* (Springfield: Illinois State Historical Society, 1972), 30. Others suggested that the family moved to Four Houses after the flood. *History of Jackson County* (Kansas City: Union Historical Co., 1881), 378.

23. Marie George Windell, "Westward Along the Boone's Lick Trail in 1826, The Diary of Colonel John Glover," *Missouri Historical Review* 39 (January 1945): 195. Glover, from Mercer County, Kentucky, traveled to this area seeking land opportunities but did not move to Missouri until the mid-1830s. He settled in what

was then Lewis County. Ibid., 185.

24. "Reminiscences of Frederick Chouteau," 423. The letters in Marra's *Cher Oncle, Cher Papa* indicate that the Chouteaus resided there until 1829, and perhaps also at the new post for the Shawnee and Delaware on the Kansas River.

25. The three trading posts were on the Missouri River near Harrison Street, the Kansa Post most likely at the Four Houses location, and the new Shawnee Post described in the letter. Both the Shawnee village and the trading post lay on the south side of the Kansas River. The "six or seven miles" apparently referred to the distance from the Shawnee village to the post that was "near the Kansas River."

26. Richard Graham was the agent for the Shawnee tribe. Henry Leavenworth, of the Third U.S. Infantry, founded Cantonment (Fort) Leavenworth in 1827. The fort is located twenty-nine miles northwest of present-day Kansas City on the Missouri River. All cantonments became forts in 1832.

27. Marra, *Cher Oncle, Cher Papa*, 38-40.

28. McCoy Scrapbook, 25.

29. Ibid., 11.

30. *St. Louis Superintendency, 1829-1831*, OIA, roll 749, frame 1285.

31. Ibid. The mouth of the Kansas River in 1964 (the year of the Kansas City quadrangle topographical map) was about 900 feet west and 1,100 feet south of its location in 1826. This reflects significant changes that have occurred, including the 1844 flood that caused Turkey Creek to flow into the Kansas River rather than the Missouri. The current channel of the Kansas is substantially the same as in 1826 until about twenty-five miles from the mouth.

32. Gilbert J. Garraghan, *Catholic Beginnings in Kansas City, Missouri* (Chicago: Loyola University Press, 1920), 47-48.

33. Joseph S. Chick, "Kaw River, Recession of at Kansas City," in *Encyclopedia of the History of Missouri*, ed. Howard Conard (New York: Southern History Co., 1901), 3: 510. Chouteau Landing was probably closer to the center of Chouteau's Island, with the Chouteau home located farther east near the end of the island. Neither of the sites was on the island.

34. "Joseph S. Chick interview," 19 October 1908, Indians History Collection, General, Kansa, Kansas State Historical Society, Topeka.

35. The Pierre Menard home survives today as a historic site and museum managed by the Illinois Historic Preservation Agency.

36. "High Water," *Kansas City Times*, 7 January 1872.

The Expulsion of the Mormons from Jackson County, Missouri

WARREN A. JENNINGS

As October frosts transformed the green summer foliage into golden hues in Jackson County, Missouri, in 1833, across the border to the west the Indians commenced their fall hunts by firing the prairies. A murky cloud drifted eastward on the autumn winds, filling the valleys with blue haze, making what the settlers termed the "smoky days."

There was a new stir of activity in the county after the quiet which followed the outbursts of violence the previous July. Irate Jackson Countians had demolished the Mormon printing establishment at Independence, tarred and feathered Bishop Edward Partridge, and committed other depredations against the unwelcome Mormons who had been attempting for two years to build up a religious Utopia known as Zion. The Mormons had created much antagonism among the original settlers with their talk of the Second Advent, which they believed would take place soon on the temple site dedicated two years before by Joseph Smith on a plot located a half-mile west of the village of Independence. The Mormons were not indifferent to the feelings of others, but they were filled with a sense of urgency which permitted them little time or energy with which to concern themselves about the attitude of their "Gentile" neighbors. Their rapid migration into the county (they eventually numbered about 1,200) caused the original settlers to feel threatened. The latter had dealt with the violent problem in the forthright manner of the frontier. Under duress the Mormons were forced to sign an agreement that no more of their number would settle in the county, that one-half of those already within the county would remove by January 1, 1834, and that the remaining half would vacate the area by April 1, 1834.

In the ensuing period, the Mormons sought assistance from Governor Daniel Dunklin and counsel from Smith, who was residing in Kirtland, Ohio. It was determined, partly on the governor's advice, to try to settle the matter through legal process. Four lawyers from Liberty, Missouri, were consulted. These included Alexander W. Doniphan and David Rice Atchison. They recommended that the Mormons arm themselves for protection against any future attacks. This the Mormons determined to do.

When the Missourians learned that the Mormons would now stand on the defensive, they were incredulous. They felt that the Mormon promise to be gone by April 1, 1834, had been broken. They were further provoked when informed that the Mormons had appealed to the governor and were even contemplating taking some of their assailants to court to answer for past conduct. One resident of the county wrote, "It was found not only that the Mormons did not intend to move according to agreement, but that they were arming themselves, and threatened to kill if they should be molested. This provoked some of the more wild and ungovernable among us to improper acts of violence, such as breaking in upon Mormon houses, tearing off the covering, &c. On this the Mormons began to muster, and exhibit military preparations."[1]

The original settlers lost no time in responding to this challenge. About fifty of them met on Saturday, October 26, and voted to move the Mormons. All day Sunday they rode over the county spreading the word. Monday, court

day, came, and "fewer people were seldom seen at a Circuit Court."[2] A few Mormon families arrived during the week from Ohio and Indiana. They were threatened by the Jackson Countians, but none were injured. In Independence the citizens began stoning Mormon houses and intimidating individuals. At this the Mormons were not greatly alarmed. They felt that the agreement would protect them until January 1.

On Thursday, October 31, the first concerted action was taken. This was the day following a decision by the Liberty lawyers to take charge of the Mormons' legal affairs. That night a group of forty or fifty men, "without other warrant than their own judgment of the requirements of the situation," attacked a Mormon colony eight miles west of Independence.[3] This was just over the Big Blue River and was known as the Whitmer settlement. Ten houses were unroofed, and several men were whipped. Philo Dibble remembered:

> I was aroused from my sleep by the noise caused by the falling houses, and had barely time to escape to the woods with my wife and two children when they reached my house and proceeded to break in the door and tear the roof off. I was some distance away when the whipping occurred, but I heard the blows of heavy ox goads upon the backs of my brethren distinctly.[4]

In truth, the Mormons were short of weapons. The raid took them completely by surprise, and in the confusion, no force could be organized. Many of the men, along with their families, fled into the fields and forests. The marauders finally completed their depredations and dispersed "after having threatened to come again in a more violent manner."[5] No injury had been done to the women and children. As they withdrew, they boasted of their intention to tear down the gristmill owned by the Mormons at the Colesville settlement three miles away.

The next morning the fugitives came out of hiding to find their homes and furniture destroyed. The sight made a vivid impression on three-year-old John Brackenbury, the son of a widower. He had spent the night in a cornfield. He testified later:

> In the morning when we came back to the house I remember that the house was torn down to the eaves, and the rafters were all off of it, and I remember going into the house, and there was a table sitting in the middle of the room, and a big large pan of honey sitting on it. Then they took us away from there off into the woods to a schoolhouse, and there were the women, children, and an old man there, but I do not remember

the old man's name. We staid there all day, women, children, and the old man were there all day, crying, and in great distress.[6]

The news of the raid soon spread among the settlements, causing great consternation. The Mormon prospects were not bright, "houseless, and unprotected by the arm of civil law in Jackson county—the dreary month of November staring them in the face."[7] Parley Pratt walked the three miles from Colesville that morning. He wrote that he was "filled with anguish at the awful sights of houses in ruins, and furniture destroyed and strewed about the streets; women in different directions, were weeping and mourning, while some of the men were covered with blood from the blows they had received from the enemy; others were endeavoring to collect the fragments of their scattered furniture, beds, &c."[8] Some of the citizens pitied the Mormons, but they dared not offer help.

Until this time the Mormons had not mobilized for defense, though it appears that a number of them had guns. None, apparently, had joined the local militia regiment. Mormon leaders met near Independence to discuss the situation. At first it was suggested that they gather all the people together into one group. This would have meant leaving their settlements to the prey of raiders, and so large a number could not be supplied with food and shelter. It was, therefore, concluded that each settlement would organize its own defenses and muster its own men. The men would assemble in small bodies

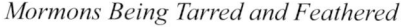

Mormons Being Tarred and Feathered

in the different neighborhoods and take up guard duty. They were, however, to be prepared to march anywhere on a moment's notice. At this time the men felt little compunction about leaving their families, since "women and children were considered safe, they seldom being abused."[9]

In an effort to protect the gristmill, Pratt took charge of approximately sixty men from the Colesville settlement who had armed themselves as well as possible. On Friday night (November 1), Pratt was posting guards when two Missourians, Robert Johnson and a man named Harris, came walking by. Pratt hailed them "and commanded [them] to advance and give the countersign."[10] A fight immediately broke out. Johnson cracked Pratt over the head with the barrel of his rifle. Pratt was momentarily stunned, but help came from the guardhouse, and the two men were taken prisoners. After being detained the remainder of the night, they were released in the morning.

Jackson Countians, in bands of ten to twenty members, began stoning the Mormon structures in Independence on the same Friday night. A number of Mormons, including John Corrill, were gathered on the Temple Lot. The night was clear, and the clatter of stones against the houses was plainly audible. It was decided not to intervene as long as nothing more destructive took place. Finally, a party was sent into the village to survey the situation, and they discovered that the citizens had "commenced pulling down the dwelling house of brother A. S. Gilbert."[11] The damage was mainly to a brick annex.

About midnight, other parties of Mormons marched into Independence where they surprised a group attacking the store owned by the Mormons. When the raiders saw the Mormons, they fled. Richard McCarty, however, who had broken in one of the doors, was captured. All the doors into the store were smashed, and some of the goods strewn in the streets. Gilbert, accompanied by several others, took his prisoner to Samuel Weston, justice of the peace, to obtain a warrant for his incarceration, but Weston refused to issue one. The Mormons reluctantly set their prisoner free and returned to their homes, where they discovered that long, ragged rails had been thrust through the windows and shutters of many of their houses. No longer could they feel that the women and children were safe at home.[12]

The next morning (Saturday, November 2), a council was held by the Mormon leaders to discuss this latest development. It was determined to move all the families which resided in the village to the Temple Lot. Hiram Rathbun, who was twelve at the time, testified later: "Finally the women and household goods of the members of the church were taken to the Temple Lot, and piled up there on the Temple Plot in the woods; and we were there, I think it was three days. . . . They were yelling and hollering and swearing and shooting around there night and day."[13] About thirty Mormon men were

Parley P. Pratt

formed into an irregular military unit to guard the refugees on the Temple Lot.

That night another party of Missourians raided a settlement on the Big Blue River about six miles west of Independence. They tore the roof from one house and wrecked the furniture. The party then divided. One group pulled the roof from another dwelling while the other attacked the home of David Bennett. The owner was sick in bed, but they beat him anyway. One attacker drew a pistol and swore that he intended blowing out Bennett's brains. The gun discharged, and the ball cut a deep gash in the top of the Mormon's head. There is some disagreement about what then transpired.[14] A party of Mormons was nearby and, hearing the noise, came up to investigate. In the ensuing confusion, firing commenced. Who fired first is still in doubt, but one of the marauders, the son of Justice of the Peace George Manship, was shot in the thigh.[15] These were the first shots fired by the Mormons, and word raced through the county that the Mormons had shot a man.

The Jackson Countians were busily engaged the next day in organizing their forces. The retaliation had incensed them still further. The rumor spread that a six-pounder would be used against the Mormons in an open engagement the following day. Some of their Gentile friends warned the Mormons that "Monday would be a bloody day" and that they would be massacred if such an engagement took place.[16] This greatly alarmed the Mormons, and they prepared for the worst. According to Corrill, "Two or three branches west of the Blue gathered together as well as they could, leaving their houses and property to the ravages of the *mob*."[17]

On Sunday night, Parley Pratt, Thomas B. Marsh, Hiram Page, and Joshua Lewis set out to see Circuit Judge John F. Ryland at Lexington, forty miles away, to get a warrant for the arrest of the leaders of the mob. Taking the back roads and cutting through the woods to avoid interception, they lost their way and had to wait until it grew light. A heavy rain drenched men and horses. They made no halt for food or rest, however, until their arrival in Lexington. Stopping first at a friend's house to breakfast and refresh, they then went to Ryland's home. Here they made [a] statement "but were refused a warrant," Pratt later claiming that the judge "advised us to fight and kill the outlaws whenever they came upon us."[18] Deeply disappointed, they returned to their friend's house to spend the night. The next day they headed back to their settlements in a dispirited mood.

On Monday, November 4, a large party of citizens gathered on the Big Blue River, captured the ferry owned by the Mormons, and threatened some of those present. Moses C. Wilson, a member of the raiding party, testified that their purpose was "in expectation of having a fight with the Mormons."[19] Tired at last of this sport, they returned to Wilson's store a half-mile west of the river. In the meantime, the Mormons who had assembled at the Colesville branch were apprised of the escapade. They were informed that the citizens were doing damage and that their brethren needed their help. Accordingly, nineteen men, among whom was David Whitmer, volunteered to give assistance. Corrill wrote, "But when they had proceeded a part of the way, they learned that the *mob* were not doing mischief at that time, but were at Wilson's store, so they turned about to go home."[20]

At this point, two small boys—one of them Wilson's son—happened to pass along the road on their way to the store. They were detained and questioned by the Mormons. When the boys finally arrived at their destination, they told those assembled about the band of Mormons. Thirty or forty armed and mounted men set out at once in pursuit. After riding about two miles, they overtook the Mormons, who fled and dispersed. A few hid in the woods; others, including Whitmer, sprinted to the Colesville branch. According to Dibble, Whitmer was the first to bring the news, and he took charge, saying, "Every man go, and every man take a man."[21] Thirty men with seventeen guns hastened back toward the river.[22]

Meanwhile, the Missourians were still seeking those who had fled. They searched a cornfield which belonged to Christian Whitmer, a cripple who had not left his home, and "fed their horses freely upon his corn."[23] They bullied Christian, attempting to coerce him to tell the whereabouts of his brethren. They were engaged in this manner for about an hour, and the sun was just setting when Whitmer's group came up after having jogged the three miles. It will probably never be determined who fired the first shot, but a hot engagement ensued. The Missourians soon fled the field, followed in close pursuit by the Mormons. The fire must have been heavy, for when the battle was over, two of the citizens and a number of their horses were dead on the field. Dead were Thomas Linville, who had his jaw shot away, and Hugh L. Brazeal, an attorney, who had received two balls in the head. Several others were wounded.

The Mormons also suffered casualties. Andrew Barber died the following day, and it was not expected that Philo Dibble would survive.[24] He had received "an ounce ball and two buck shot" in the bowels,[25] claiming later that it was from "the first gun that was fired."[26] He remained a lifetime cripple. Abigail Leonard later asserted that her husband, Lyman, had returned from the affray with fourteen bullet holes in his garments and two slight wounds, one on the hip and the other on the arm.[27]

Wilson's boy, who had gone out to show the Jackson Countians where he had seen the Mormons, may also have been wounded in the encounter. Lieutenant Governor Lilburn W. Boggs, a resident of Independence, wrote:

> The information which reached [Independence] about eight o'clock on Monday night, the 4th instant, by an express, giving intelligence of the aforesaid battle, stated that the Mormons, to the number perhaps of sixty, well armed, attacked a party of the citizens, numbering about twenty; that he had left them fighting, and bore off the body of a small boy, who was shot in the back; that he could not tell the extent of bloodshed that had taken place.[28]

That same day, Gilbert, Corrill, Isaac Morley, William McLellin, and William Phelps, Mormon leaders in Independence, had been arrested for assault and battery and false imprisonment on warrant of McCarty, the man they had taken prisoner at the store. Late that evening these men were being tried in the courthouse in Independence when news of the skirmish arrived. Corrill wrote that it was rumored "that the mormons had gone into the house of Wilson and shot his son."[29] Those present were enraged, and the prisoners were in a precarious situation. All doors out of the courtroom were barred, and there was no possible escape. But Samuel C. Owens, seeing that the Mormons were without counsel and in imminent danger, advised them to request imprisonment as the only alternative for saving their lives.[30] Corrill noted, "The courthouse being filled, a rush was made upon us by some to kill

John F. Ryland

us; but the court esteeming it too dishonorable to have us killed while in their hands, on our request shut us up in the jail to save our lives."[31] Guns were brandished, and there was a vocal demonstration.

That night mounted horsemen were dispatched in all directions to call out the Jackson County militia. Lieutenant Governor Boggs stated that "the information of that battle having taken place, produced the call of the Militia." He noted further that this was "for the purpose of suppressing the insurrection."[32] Rumors were rife: one that the Mormons had taken Independence, another that they were allied with the Indians. Alexander Majors observed that "every citizen, as soon as he could rim bullets and fill his powder horn with powder, gathered his gun and made for the town; and in a few hours men enough had gathered to exterminate them had they approached."[33]

In the jail, according to Corrill, the prisoners were "frequently told that night . . . by men of note, that without any doubt many lives would be lost the next day; for now not only the *mob*, but the whole county were engaged and greatly enraged against us and that nothing would stop them short of our leaving the county forthwith."[34] Even this might not calm the cry for vengeance. The leaders in prison talked it over and then sent word to some of their brethren "that they might not expect anything the next day but a general slaughter of our people."[35] It was decided that in view of the rage of the Missourians, they should agree to evacuate the area. One elder wrote his brethren in Kirtland, "We saw plainly that the whole county were enraged, and preparing for a general massacre the next day. We then thought it wisdom to stop the shedding of more blood, and by agreeing to leave immediately we saved many lives; in this we feel justified."[36]

Their sentiments were conveyed to Sheriff Jacob Gregg. He and two others took Gilbert, Corrill, and Morley to discuss their decision with some of their brethren. A short consultation was held in which the leaders persuaded the others to agree to leave the county. When the prisoners were being returned to jail after midnight, they were hailed by a party of men with guns. Six or seven citizens were seen standing near the jail. The sheriff called out his name and the names of his prisoners. Some hostile moves were made, and the sheriff shouted, "Don't fire, don't fire, the prisoners are in my charge."[37] Corrill turned, ran, and was fired upon. Morley also made his escape, but Gilbert stood his ground. The citizens came up to him, pointed two guns at his chest, and fired. Fortunately, "one snapped and the other flashed in the pan."[38] Gilbert was then knocked to the ground by Thomas Wilson, but was not seriously injured. Upon the arrival of another group of citizens, the affair came to an end. Gilbert was then placed in jail. He and the remaining prisoners were freed at sunrise, probably because of their promise to vacate the county. Edward Partridge, the bishop in charge of Zion, Gilbert, and others promptly went across the Missouri River and sent an affidavit to Governor Dunklin.

On Tuesday, November 5, the militia, called out by Lieutenant Colonel Thomas Pitcher, in the absence of Colonel Samuel D. Lucas, the commanding officer, assembled in Independence. Corrill wrote that the ostensible purpose was "to quell the *mob*: but it would have been difficult for one to have distinguished between the militia and *mob*, for all the most conspicuous characters engaged in the *riot* were found in [its] ranks."[39] Boggs had given his approval to this action.[40] Most of the Missourians, like most of the Mormons, had not as yet been informed of the elders' intentions of leaving. As the ranks formed and the citizens were told of this agreement, a strange quiet descended over the town. Stores were closed, and business activity was suspended completely. More than two hundred men were standing in the ranks when alarming news was carried into town by persons riding in from the west. They had seen a large body of Mormons, "well armed," marching toward the village. It was reported that they were "coming on with a view to attack and destroy the place."[41] It was around nine o'clock in the morning.

One of the members of the militia was Josiah Gregg, who had returned only a few days before from Santa Fe, Mexico. He reported:

> I had often heard the cry of "Indians!" announcing the approach of
> hostile savages, but I do not remember ever to have witnessed so much

Alexander Majors

consternation as prevailed at Independence on this memorable occasion. The note of alarm was sounded far and near, and armed men, eager for the fray, were rushing in from every quarter. Officers were summarily selected without deference to rank and station: the "spirit-stirring drum" and the "ear-piercing fife" made the air resound with music; and a little army of as brave and resolute a set of fellows as ever trod a field of battle, was, in very short time, paraded through the streets. After a few preliminary exercises, they started for a certain point on the road where they intended to await the approach of the Mormons.[42]

The Jackson Countians erroneously believed that the objective of the oncoming force was "to kill or drive out all the inhabitants, and to destroy the Village."[43] Pitcher later asserted that the Mormons had the "avowed intention of burning the town and to kill Col. Sam Owens, Gen. S. D. Lucas, myself, and several other leading citizens."[44]

At the same time the Missourians mustered, the Mormons united their forces. Approximately 150 men from west of the Big Blue River volunteered to march to Independence under the leadership of Lyman Wight, a veteran of the War of 1812.[45] They were poorly armed; only about one in three had a gun. The others had improvised weapons; some made spears by fastening chisels to poles while others found clubs.[46] They had not been informed that their leaders had agreed to leave. Word had come to them that several of their

Lilburn W. Boggs

brethren were in prison, "and the determination of the mob was to kill them."[47] They had heard also that the branch in Independence was in imminent danger since the main body of Missourians was gathering there.[48] Leaving early in the morning, they hastily covered ten miles. They intended making a stand on the Temple Lot, but before reaching that objective, they were advised that their leaders had promised to leave the county and that the militia had been called out. Wight directed his men off the road into the woods, a move the Missourians interpreted as a military movement for the purpose of forming lines.[49]

Lieutenant Colonel Pitcher dispatched a Mormon as a messenger "with this information, that the militia were raised to quell this insurrection, and that they must come forward, surrender their arms, and return to their homes."[50] Negotiations then began between the leaders of the two forces. Boggs was present, acting as intermediary between the two groups.[51]

The Mormons, faced by a superior military force, were at a considerable disadvantage. Their elders had already come to an understanding with the Missourians. Pitcher, according to Corrill, "would not give us peace only on the conditions that we should deliver up those men who were engaged in the battle the day before, to have them tried for murder; and also, that we must deliver up our arms, and then, he said, we should be safely protected out of the county."[52] Pitcher remembered that "they were to surrender their arms and leave the county within ten days."[53] Later the Mormons contended that they understood that the Missourians also were to be required to give up their weapons.[54] According to Smith, "The fear of violating the law, in resisting this pretended militia, and the flattering assurances of protection, and honorable usage, promised by Lieutenant Governor Boggs, in whom they had reposed confidence up to this period, induced them to submit."[55] It was late in the afternoon before the negotiations were terminated. The Mormons understood that their weapons would be returned to them after they had left the county.[56] Both units were marched into town where a committee was appointed to receive the arms. The weapons, fifty in all, were stacked around a white oak stump standing in the public square. Afterward, they were placed in the jail for safekeeping where they "were eaten up with rust."[57] Those Mormons who were present and had participated in the battle gave themselves up. Who these were is unknown, but it seems that only three were turned over to the authorities and imprisoned.[58] According to Boggs, the militia men—weapons still in hand—were dismissed, "with the exception of a small guard intended to guard the Mormons."[59] The Mormons, Wight recorded, "returned home, resting assured . . . that we should not be further molested."[60] In celebration of their victory, the Missourians fired a number of rounds from their cannon that night.

Orson Hyde and John Gould, two Mormons who had been present when McCarty was taken before the magistrate, had completed their business in Jackson County and were prepared to return to Kirtland. They boarded the *Charleston* at Liberty Landing on Tuesday, November 5, and during the night, they heard the cannon fire. The next morning before the steamboat cast off from its moorings, "a messenger rode by, saying that he had just come from the seat of war, and that the night before, another battle had been fought, in which Mr. [Russel] Hicks, Attorney at Law, fell, having three balls and some buck shot, through his body, and about twenty more of the mob."[61] As the steamer proceeded downriver, Hyde prepared a report of all that he had seen and heard in Jackson County. This statement was given to the editors of the papers in the river towns at which the steamer stopped. It was printed widely throughout the nation and was responsible for an impression that more blood had been shed than actually was. Gould and Hyde arrived in Kirtland on November 25 "and brought the melancholy intelligence of the riot in Zion."[62]

On Wednesday, November 6, Pitcher, acting in his civil capacity as constable, released the remaining Mormon prisoners. According to the Mormons, he first warned them and then took one of their watches "to satisfy costs." Leading them out to a cornfield, Pitcher released them and told them to "clear."[63]

At first the Mormon leaders planned to move south into Van Buren County. They discussed the matter with some of the more prominent Jackson

Countians, who gave their approval. At a meeting of the citizens, however, it was resolved that the Mormons could go neither to the south nor the west, but must move north of the river. It can only be surmised that the motive behind this was fear—fear that the Mormons might establish contact with the Indian tribes to the west and encourage the savages to attack the Jackson Countians.

The Mormons later accused "Lt. Gov. Boggs, Col. Pitcher and Col. Lucas, of practising a stratagem upon them, and thereby depriving them of their arms."[64] In the light of that which followed, it appeared to the Mormons that they had been deliberately deceived into giving up their weapons so that the citizens might torment them without fear of harm or retaliation. Without arms, the Mormons were helpless and the Missourians had "full power to come upon [them] when they pleased."[65]

On Wednesday, November 6, a systematic policy of harassment began. Companies of from fifty to eighty men, mounted and with guns on their shoulders, visited the Mormon settlements. Many of the Mormon men were away making arrangements for departure. Homes were broken into and searched for weapons. Some of the Mormon men were caught and whipped, and others were fired upon. A few were chased for several miles into the woods. As the aggressors passed through the Whitmer settlement, "they swore that if the people were not off by the time they returned at night, they would massacre the whole of them."[66] They rode on to the Colesville branch. Emily Austin recalled that one of these was a man named Campbell, who drew a horse pistol on a woman.

> "Madam, where is your husband? tell me the truth; do you see this weapon, which is only waiting for your heart's blood?" My sister-in-law calmly replied that she knew nothing as to his whereabouts, and could not tell anything more about it. "Well, can you tell us when the Yankee's intend to leave this county?"[67]

After intimidating the inhabitants, "they rode off, with their broad-brimmed hats and blanket overcoats, which costume was in those days characteristic of a fully developed Missourian.[68] Consternation and confusion swept the settlements. Women and children fled to the woods; others hastily packed what they could and headed for the Missouri River.

Lyman Wight was one of those who had been chased "by about 60 of these ruffians five miles." He later recorded:

> I fled to the south and my wife was driven north to Clay County, and for three weeks I knew not whether my family was dead or alive. . . . At

one time I was three days without food. When I found my family I found them on the banks of the Missouri River under a rag carpet tent short of food and raiment. In this deplorable situation, on the 27th of December, my wife bore me a son.[69]

Mrs. Wight and her three small children had made their escape in a skiff which they rowed down the Big Blue River for fourteen miles to the Missouri River.

Typical of the experience of many might have been that of Parley Pratt. On Tuesday afternoon he and Thomas Marsh had ridden within four miles of Independence on their return from Lexington. They stopped at a farmhouse and passed themselves off as strangers. The farmer asked them where they were from, and they replied from Lexington. "Have you heard?" he asked. "The Mormons have riz, and have killed six men."[70] Circling the town, Pratt came upon some of his brethren about sunset and was informed of the surrender. Walking his horse through the woods in order to avoid the main roads, he arrived home about the middle of the night. After resting a few hours, he arose before daybreak and rode off into the forest.

That afternoon Pratt headed for the river. On his way he came across a Mormon, John Lowry, who was moving his family in a covered wagon. Lowry had a permit to pass in safety, and he concealed Pratt in his wagon. They made it safely to the Missouri River, "although frequently meeting armed men, who were pursuing our brethren." When night came they were still on the south side of the river, where they were forced to camp since the ferry did not operate after dark. Pratt found a cave in which to sleep in the limestone ridge which overlooked the river. Later in the night, he was joined by Isaac Morley and several others bringing rumors that "the mob were driving and probably butchering men, women and children."[71] The next morning Pratt crossed over without mishap.

Return I. Holcombe, who gathered his information from old settlers, wrote, "Affrighted and almost terror-stricken, the Mormons crossed the river and sought safety in Clay county." When the crossing began, "the weather was cold and rainy; and the plundered, half clad women and children suffered severely."[72] In their hurry to depart, many had taken no extra clothing or bedding. They were ill prepared to face the rigors of the coming winter. Those encamped on the Temple Lot appeared to have fared better than most since they already had their possessions packed and loaded.

Just north of Independence on the Missouri River was located the Wayne City landing where the steamboats and Everett's ferry operated. This was the place where the major portion of the Mormons congregated to cross the river. Pratt described the scene as it appeared on Thursday, November 7:

> The shore began to be lined on both sides of the ferry with men, women and children; goods, wagons, boxes, provisions, etc., while the ferry was constantly employed; and when night again closed upon us the cottonwood bottom had much the appearance of a camp meeting. Hundreds of people were seen in every direction, some in tents and some in the open air around their fires, while the rain descended in torrents. Husbands were inquiring for their wives, wives for their husbands; parents for children, and children for parents. Some had the good fortune to escape with their families, household goods, and some provisions; while others knew not the fate of their friends, and had lost all their goods. The scene was indescribable, and, I am sure, would have melted the hearts of any people on the earth, except our blind oppressors, and a blind and ignorant community.[73]

Not all groups crossed over to Clay County. One wandered on the southern prairies for several days. A large number of women and children, approximately 130, had been collected at the Colesville School. On Wednesday when the harassment began, a party of 75 to 100 men rode through the area, ordering every Mormon out of the region within two hours. Most of the Mormon men were absent, looking for wagons or in hiding, and only six were present— among them young John Brush. Only four wagons were available, and the group, in a state of near panic, loaded these with bedding and provisions.

Everything else was left behind. The party, under the leadership of Solomon Hancock, then headed south with no apparent objective other than to flee from the raiders. The first day they covered six miles. When night fell, they made camp as best they could and after prayers retired.[74]

The following day, still drifting southward, they debouched upon an open plain and trudged fifteen miles. The prairie had been burned over, and the bunch grass left sharp stubs above the surface of the earth. Very few of the children had shoes, and by night their feet were torn and bleeding.[75] The next day another fifteen miles were covered without meeting a single traveler or passing a farm site until evening, when they stopped near a small house owned by a single man. He offered them the use of his home. The rain commenced to fall, and the women and children huddled together in the one room of the house while the men and larger boys leaned against the house and wagons until morning with the rain streaming down their backs.[76]

After breakfast they again took up their journey, but the land was inundated. When the party came to a slough, they found the water from ankle to waist deep for a distance of over a mile, and across this they were compelled to wade. Nearly every adult had to carry a child the entire distance without resting. That evening they finally found a dry camp site under a bluff. When they awoke in the morning, the earth was covered with two inches of snow. They ate their last morsel of food for breakfast. With no apparent place to go, and without food, resignation swept the group. After prayers they remained inactive to await further developments. About mid-morning a man came riding up and offered them assistance if they would come to his place five miles away. He had some potatoes to be dug and fence rails to be split. He promised them, in return for their labor, an ox and half the potatoes. The man was David C. Butterfield, and he and his neighbors collected clothing and provisions for the Mormons and took families into their homes. They also gave them work. But word soon came to the refugees that their brethren had crossed over into Clay County. Desiring to be reunited with their families and friends, many of the Mormons packed up and set out for the Missouri River. They circled around Independence, took Williams's ferry across the river, and camped above the northern bluffs until spring.[77]

On the night of November 13 there occurred a singular phenomenon. According to Mormon eschatology, one of the signs of the end would be: "The sun shall be darkened, and the moon shall be turned into blood, and the stars fall from heaven."[78] That night the stars "fell." There was by all accounts a very remarkable meteoric display, probably the greatest Leonid shower ever observed and recorded in the United States. Parley Pratt remembered:

About two o'clock the next morning we were called up by the cry of signs in the heavens. We arose, and to our great astonishment all the firmament seemed enveloped in splendid fireworks, as if every star in the broad expanse had been hurled from its course, and sent lawless through the wilds of ether. Thousands of bright meteors were shooting through space in every direction, with long trains of light following in their course. This lasted for several hours, and was only closed by the dawn of the rising sun. Every heart was filled with joy at this majestic display of signs and wonders, showing the near approach of the coming of the Son of God.[79]

Judge Joseph Thorp, a Clay Countian, also observed this spectacle. "The saints," he wrote, "looked at it as being a sign from heaven that the Lord would in some miraculous manner enable them to overcome the ungodly Gentiles who had so recklessly driven them from their homes and exposed their wives and little ones to the cold and chilling blasts of winter without shelter."[80]

It was not alone the Mormons who saw this as a portent. Josiah Gregg wrote that many of the citizens in Jackson County "began to wonder whether, after all, the Mormons might not be in the right; and whether this was not a sign sent from heaven as a remonstrance for the injustice they had been guilty of towards that chosen sect."[81]

At first, of course, the hardships were cruelly difficult for the Mormons, especially the women and children. Babies were born those first nights in the cottonwoods, and the exposure to the chill and dampness apparently ruined the health of some of the elderly Mormons. Many had sold their cattle and personal effects at a very low price before leaving Jackson County.

The initial response of the Clay Countians to the plight of the Mormons was warm and friendly. One reason, perhaps, was that their county had been settled longer than Jackson County. Liberty, the county seat, was six years old when Independence was founded, and it was "one of the proudest towns in the West, with its aristocratic families."[82] There was considerable difference in the political sentiments of the two counties, too, as their names would imply. Clay Countians tended to be Whigs; those from Jackson County were generally Jacksonian Democrats. The citizens of Clay very hospitably opened their homes to the refugees, providing them with shelter, provisions, and work. This irritated the Jackson Countians, and for years thereafter, they stigmatized persons from Clay County as being "Jack Mormons."[83]

Some of the Mormons moved into abandoned slave cabins or built huts in the woods, while others lived in tents or even in the open. Every vacant cabin in the southern half of the county was occupied by the fugitives. In the spring, some of the Mormons rented unimproved land in the southeast corner of the county, where they again built homes and put in crops. The harvests were generally good, and by fall some began to enjoy a degree of comfort. A number of the Mormons hired out to work. Judge Thorp, who employed several of them, observed:

> The Mormons, in the main, were industrious, good workers, and gave general satisfaction to their employers, and could live on less than any people I ever knew. Their women could fix up a palatable meal out of that which a Gentile's wife would not know how to commence to get half a dinner or breakfast. They had the knack of economizing in the larder, which was a great help to the men, as they had mostly to earn their bread and butter by day's work, and wages about half what they are now.[84]

Considering the implacable hostility that had been created by the Mormons in Jackson County, perhaps they should have abandoned their efforts to build Zion. This they did not do. While it was reported by the *Missouri Republican*, as early as November 22, 1833, that the Mormons had ceased all resistance and were leaving Jackson County "with intention of forming another community elsewhere," they did not abandon Jackson County as the chosen site. They made several efforts to obtain reinstatement onto their lands by legal process and the display of armed strength. These efforts failed, but the dream did not die. Though violently expelled, the Mormons still adhere tenaciously to the belief that Zion will yet arise on the prairies and hills of Jackson County.

NOTES

1. B. Pixley to *New York Observer*, 7 November 1833, quoted in *Washington (DC) National Intelligencer*, 24 December 1833. See also Isaac McCoy to editor, 28 November 1833, *St. Louis Missouri Republican*, 20 December 1833.

2. See "Extract of a letter dated, Independence, October 30, 1833," *Kirtland (OH) Evening and Morning Star,* December 1833. Hereinafter cited as *Kirtland (OH) Star.*

3. *History of Jackson County, Missouri* (Kansas City: Union Historical Co., 1881), 255.

4. *Early Scenes in Church History* (Salt Lake City: Juvenile Instructor Office, 1882), 82.

5. Ibid.

6. *In the Circuit Court of the United States, Western District of Missouri, Western Division, at Kansas City. (Complainant's Abstract of Pleading and Evidence) In Equity. The Reorganized Church of Jesus Christ of Latter Day Saints. Complainant vs. The Church of Christ at Independence, Missouri* (Lamoni, IA: Herald, 1893), 232. Hereinafter cited as Temple Lot Suit.

7. Parley Parker Pratt, *Late Persecution of the Church of Jesus Christ of Latter Day Saints* (New York: J. W. Harrison, 1840), 32.

8. Ibid., 33.

9. *Nauvoo (IL) Times and Seasons*, December 1839.

10. *Washington (DC) National Intelligencer*, 24 December 1833.

11. Corrill to Oliver Cowdery, December 1833, in *Kirtland (OH) Star*, January 1834.

12. *Nauvoo (IL) Times and Seasons*, December 1839.

13. Temple Lot Suit, 217.

14. Isaac McCoy claimed that "a company approached a house, about five miles from Independence, with a view no doubt of injuring it; and as they approached the Mormons fired upon them." McCoy to editor. "Some shots were exchanged, the Mormons having given the first fire and wounded one man." Pixley to *New York Observer* in *Washington (DC) National Intelligencer*. Compare: "A party of the saints were collected nearby, who hearing the disturbance went to the place. The mob began to fire upon them." *Nauvoo (IL) Times and Seasons*, January 1840. Orson Hyde wrote the editor of the *Boonville Herald* on November 8, 1833, that after the citizens "had fired five or six guns upon the Mormons without effect, the Mormons fired upon them, and one of the mob screamed, 'O my God; I am shot.' The mob then dispersed in much confusion." Reprinted in *St. Louis Missouri Republican*, 12 November 1833.

15. Letter, 6 November 1833, in *Kirtland (OH) Star,* December 1833.

16. *History of Jackson County*, 255.

17. Corrill to Cowdery.

18. Parley Parker Pratt, *Autobiography of Parley Parker Pratt* (Salt Lake City: Deseret Book Co., 1950), 98. Compare: "I wish to know whether Joshua Lewis and Hiram Page handed the writ to the sheriff of Jackson county, that I made and issued on their affidavit against some of the ringleaders of the mob in Jackson county, dated the sixth of this month." John F. Ryland to Robert W. Wells, 24 November 1833, in "History of Joseph Smith," *Nauvoo (IL) Times and Seasons*, 1 June 1845.

19. Testimony at a court of inquiry into the conduct of Colonel Thomas Pitcher in Liberty, in *St. Louis Missouri Republican*, 20 January 1834. This ferry was operated by Orrin P. Rockwell who was later charged as being the attempted assassin of Governor [Lilburn] Boggs. See Monte B. McLaws, "The Attempted Assassination of

Missouri's Ex-Governor, Lilburn W. Boggs," *Missouri Historical Review* 60 (October 1965): 50-62.

20. Corrill to Cowdery.

21. *Early Scenes*, 83. David Whitmer headed the disciples, according to "John Whitmer's Manuscript History," 44, Historian's Office, Community of Christ (RLDS), Independence, MO.

22. "History of Joseph Smith," *Nauvoo (IL) Times and Seasons*, 15 May 1845.

23. *Kirtland (OH) Star*, January 1834.

24. "He was the first to give his life in the cause of the Church, the first modern martyr for the truth," *Salt Lake City Deseret News*, 13 June 1959.

25. *Early Scenes*, 83.

26. *Nauvoo (IL) Times and Seasons*, January 1840.

27. Edward W. Tullidge, *The Women of Mormondom* (New York: Tullidge and Crandall, 1877), 163.

28. Boggs to editor, 26 November 1833, *St. Louis Missouri Republican*, 6 December 1833; also reprinted in *Jefferson City Jeffersonian Republican*, 21 December 1833.

29. Corrill to Cowdery.

30. "History of Joseph Smith," 15 May 1845; *History of Jackson County*, 256.

31. Corrill to Cowdery.

32. *St. Louis Missouri Republican*, 6 December 1833.

33. Alexander Majors, *Seventy Years on the Frontier: Alexander Majors' Memoir of a Lifetime on the Border*, ed. Prentiss Ingraham (Chicago: Rand, McNally and Co., 1893), 47.

34. Corrill to Cowdery.

35. Ibid.

36. Letter, 17 November 1833, *Kirtland (OH) Star*, December 1833.

37. Pratt, *Late Persecution*, 42.

38. Corrill to Cowdery.

39. Ibid.

40. "The Militia were ordered into service by Lieut. Colonel Pitcher, (the colonel being absent,) for the purpose of suppressing the insurrection. I approved of the course adopted by Col. Pitcher, as the only means of saving bloodshed, and of restoring order." Boggs to editor.

41. Ibid.

42. Josiah Gregg, *Commerce of the Prairies*, ed. Max L. Moorhead (Norman: University of Oklahoma Press, 1954), 220.

43. McCoy to editor.

44. Thomas Pitcher, interview, *Kansas City Journal*, 17 June 1881.

45. The number of men in this force has been estimated variously. Pitcher, McCoy, and Corrill claimed there were 150, while Smith asserted there were 100. Wight alleged he had 200 men with him.

46. Pitcher, interview; *Nauvoo (IL) Times and Seasons*, January 1840.

47. "History of Joseph Smith," 15 May 1845; John Corrill, *A Brief History of the Church of Christ of Latter Day Saints* (St. Louis: by the author, 1839), 20.

48. *Nauvoo (IL) Times and Seasons*, January 1840.

49. Pitcher, interview; McCoy to editor.

50. Boggs to editor.

51. Ibid.; "History of Joseph Smith," 15 May 1845.

52. Corrill to Cowdery.

53. Pitcher, interview.

54. "History of Joseph Smith," 15 May 1845; Lyman Wight, testimony before Municipal Court of Nauvoo, Illinois, 1 July 1843, in *Liverpool (England) Millennial Star*, 6 August 1859.

55. "History of Joseph Smith," 15 May 1845; Pratt, *Late Persecution*, 44.

56. Corrill, *Brief History*, 20.

57. Majors, *Seventy Years*, 49

58. *St. Louis Missouri Republican*, 6 December 1833. "I am sorry to add that such was the ungovernable and unmanly conduct of some in our community, that it was with the utmost difficulty that the civil authorities could protect their prisoners from being massacred on the spot." Pixley to *New York Observer* in *Washington (DC) National Intelligencer*.

59. *St. Louis Missouri Republican*, 6 December 1833. It appears that a group of the more prominent citizens of Jackson County formed a guard to see that the Mormons were protected and that the provisions of the agreement were carried out. Clearly, they were not always effective. See "Isaac McCoy's Manuscript Journal," 7-9 November 1833, Kansas State Historical Society, Topeka.

60. *Liverpool (England) Millennial Star*, 6 August 1859.

61. This letter was first printed in the *Boonville Herald*, 7 November 1833. It appeared subsequently in *St. Louis Missouri Republican*, 12 November 1833; *Columbia Missouri Intelligencer*, 16 November 1833; *Washington (DC) National Intelligencer*, 30 November 1833; and *Kirtland (OH) Star*, December 1833.

62. "History of Joseph Smith," 1 June 1845.

63. Ibid., January 1840.

64. On December 12, 1833, Pratt, Corrill, and Newel Knight issued a handbill stating the Mormon position on the events in Jackson County. See *St. Louis Missouri Republican*, 30 January 1834.

65. Corrill to Cowdery.

66. Ibid.

67. Emily M. Austin, *Mormonism: or, Life Among the Mormons* (Madison, WI: M. J. Cantwell, 1882), 70.

68. Ibid., 69.

69. "Lyman Wight's Journal," in Joseph Smith and Heman C. Smith, *History of the Church of Jesus Christ of Latter Day Saints* (Lamoni, IA: Board of Publication of the Reorganized Church of Jesus Christ of Latter Day Saints, 1897), 1: 335.

70. Pratt, *Autobiography*, 98-99.

71. Pratt, *Late Persecution*, 45-46.

72. Walter B. Stevens, *Centennial History of Missouri* (St. Louis: S. J. Clarke Publishing Co., 1921), 2: 104.

73. Pratt, *Autobiography*, 102.

74. This trek is covered in "Elder John Brush," *Autumn Leaves* 4 (January 1891): 23-24, 64.

75. Ibid., 23; Tullidge, *Women of Mormondom*, 164-165; *Liverpool (England) Millennial Star*, 6 August 1859.

76. "Elder John Brush," 23.

77. Ibid., 64; Tullidge, *Women of Mormondom*, 165.

78. *A Book of Commandments, for the Government of the Church of Christ* (Zion [Independence, MO]: W. W. Phelps, 1833), 62, 107.

79. Pratt, *Autobiography*, 103. "And let others think as they may, I take it as a special manifestation to fulfill the scriptures, and to rouse our drooping spirits, by a fresh memorial, reminding us of a coming Messiah." Pratt, *Late Persecution*, 50. The Leonid meteor shower occurs annually around November 14. It is so named because it appears to originate in the constellation of Leo.

80. Joseph Thorp, *Early Days in the West: Along the Missouri One Hundred Years Ago* (Liberty, MO: I. Gilmer, 1924), 76.

81. Gregg, *Commerce of the Prairies*, 220. This meteor shower was seen all over the United States. That night in Virginia the wife of a strolling actor gave birth to a son, and the midwife told her that he would be a great man since the heavens proclaimed his birth. The baby grew up to be one of America's greatest actors, Edwin

Booth. The *Washington (DC) National Intelligencer*, November 21, 1833, reprinted a report from the *Columbia (PA) Spy* that many persons assumed that "the last day had arrived," and that only one drink was consumed at a public house the next day "and no charge was made for that." The *Washington (DC) National Intelligencer*, December 9, 1833, took notice of the death of a young woman in New York whose mind had given way from fear that the meteors portended the speedy dissolution of the world.

82. William Larking Webb, *The Centennial History of Independence, Missouri* (Independence, MO: by the author, 1927), 70.

83. *History of Clay and Platte Counties, Missouri* (St. Louis: National Historical Co., 1885), 133.

84. Thorp, *Early Days*, 76-77.

From Virginia to Missouri in 1846:
The Journal of Elizabeth Ann Cooley

Edited by EDWARD D. JERVEY and JAMES E. MOSS

. . . I have employed myself reading the pilgrims of the Rhine. It has some very interesting pieces in it. I feel as I have read today that I have many Poetical sentiments but have not language to express them. I have ever desired to see Towns & Rivers and people—but if I think of going if I had the chance it makes me shudder at the Thought of leaving a home so dear to me. I feel like I wanted to love and something to love me—but stop I have went too far. There is danger in the thought."
[May 1, 1842]

When Elizabeth Ann Cooley left her Virginia home in 1846 and traveled west to Texas and finally to Missouri, she joined the course of the empire and participated in an emigration movement that has become an important part of our cultural heritage. In our national history, 1846 was a remarkable and exciting year, infused with the spirit of Manifest Destiny and marked by the settlement of the Oregon question, Frémont's explorations, the Mexican War, and especially by the vast overland emigration from Missouri to California and Oregon. It was a year of decision for the United States as it expanded to the Pacific and emerged as a continental nation. It was also a year of decision for Elizabeth Cooley, signaling a turning point in her destiny.

On February 20, 1842, Elizabeth began a journal recording those events and thoughts which were important to her. In the first part of her journal, 1842-1846, Elizabeth wrote of her life in Virginia in the early nineteenth century and of her approaching marriage to James W. McClure on February

25, 1846. In the latter portion, 1846-1848, she described her journey to Texas and ultimately to Missouri and her life in Missouri thereafter.

Elizabeth was born July 21, 1825, in Grayson County, Virginia. Her father, Benjamin F. Cooley, the son of an English emigrant who had come to America in the eighteenth century, moved with his family when he was seven years old from New York to North Carolina, and five years later finally settled in Grayson County, Virginia. Benjamin became a landowner of some means and an officeholder, serving as a member of the state legislature and sheriff of the county. He was also an expert clockmaker and invented a cutter for making brass wheels for clocks. Elizabeth's mother was Jane Dickey and married Benjamin when she was not quite seventeen years of age.[1]

In her first journal entry, Elizabeth announced that she would "endeavor to tell where and what all of the family is and what they are doing." Through her account of the family activities as well as her own, she succeeds in presenting a fine insight into rural Virginia life. Her personal observations and conjectures enliven her narrative and reveal her character as she writes of her hopes and dreams, her boredom and despair, her joys, hardships, frustrations, fears, and indecision. Elizabeth was an introspective young woman possessing strong religious beliefs. She also was eager to broaden her horizons, to develop her intellect, and to know and enjoy all of the fullness of life.

The Cooley family was close and affectionate, and Elizabeth's love for her home becomes evident as she contemplates marriage and meditates upon the uncertainties of moving west. At the same time, she expresses her desire "to live and be loved by someone special" and fears that she may never marry. When James McClure comes into her life, at first casually, and then firmly, with more and more visits to her home, Elizabeth becomes vibrant with happy expectations which are tempered by thoughts of leaving her family and friends.

Elizabeth's reaction to the relative isolation and tedium of her rural living is reflected in her journal. Whenever her day is not filled with activity, it is obvious that she becomes morose and dissatisfied. [March 13, 1842] "I have went to school all the last week. It is raining at this time. I feel tolerably smart but weary of doing nothing." [August 26, 1842] "I have been sick by spells all last week. I don't expect to see anything of much interest, the world has but little or but little I can get to enjoy. . . . Heaven have mercy on me and all the rest of us." [September 4, 1842] "For some time I have not wrote any. During that time I have seen but little for I have not went anywhere much—though I went to meeting last Sunday and to Coxes the Sunday before—and nobody has been here. I feel like an isolated being living alone and neglected by all but those I live with." Sometimes, however, Elizabeth could be content with inactivity: [February 11, 1844] "It has been very cold last week. At this time I am as me and Amanda used to say, having a good time without anybodys knowing it. We learn nothing, make nothing, so we are all most completely dormant in every sense of the word."

Usually Elizabeth's days were busy with spinning and other household chores, most of the evenings spent in visiting friends and relatives, and many Saturdays and Sundays taken up with camp meetings. [October 29, 1843] "For the last week we finished our dresses, dipped candles, 30 dozen. We made Ika's blue jeans coat and brown jeans pantaloons.[2] Mama packed. I began my flax stockings. . . . Today is meeting but none of us went. Perhaps some of us will go to Aunt Mary's this evening."[3] [March 10, 1844] "We spun a little tow, trimmed up some carpeting. Malinda Moore and Mahala Hanks came here and got their dresses cut out. I made a pot of soup, done the cooking. Frank Edwards has left here. Tomorrow we are to have a log rolling. We have baked pies, killed two turkeys, stewed apples, etc. . . . I have been reading in the U. S. Philadelphia Post." [July 28, 1844] "Last Monday we worked on Amanda's white dress; I spun wool the rest of the time, and Julian too. . . . All of us are at home as usual, but James as usual has gone today to J. Hankses. The garden is full of flowers, the field full of blackberries, the house full of work, my head full of romance, my heart full of love, (but nobody in particular), my tongue uttering folly. They are all good humored, all busy, and all do plenty of work. . . . Today there is meeting at the schoolhouse and next Sunday campmeeting."[4]

Elizabeth loved her schooling, and she had ambitions of being a good teacher: [August 6, 1843] "Now I have a plan to learn to cypher as far as discount and learn English Grammar so as to teach it and to write a shining hand. . . . I wish for Mr. R. E. Campbell to come and teach a school. Now I have told what I wish and hope for, and pray to God for assistance in a task to be finished in 2 years. [October 22, 1843] "Another week is passed, another Sunday passing and I am still here longing and constantly desiring something to enlighten my contracted and perplexed mind, for what can I do? My only and best chance is to hoard up learning sufficient to allow me to teach a school, and I lack so much it perplexes me to think of it, to get Grammar and Arithmetic and how to govern a school &c."

As her marriage approached, her schooling became more intense: [November 30, 1844] "I went to school all last week, and weary and bitter it is to try to study Grammar and my mind so agitated as it is now. I study Grammar all day and marrying all night until my nerves become feeble and trembling. Good Lord, do brighten my ideas and temper my mind to that study. Oh, could I learn it with more ease without my head aching and temple throbbing and perplexed to despair." [January 11, 1846] "I went to school by sunrise of a morning and late in the evening. I enjoy myself tolerably well now. I think I get along right smart. I expect to go to school until it is out four weeks from now. We had a little debate . . . last Friday for the first of my undertaking it. We are to have another next Friday but I don't feel much that way now, though I will try; and may God help me in that and Grammar also, and marriage and all its attending difficulties for I don't know what way to proceed with my affairs."

Throughout her journal, Elizabeth records her hopes and her frustrations, her expectations and reservations on life. She was a young woman for whom life was vital and to whom each day was to be guarded jealously for the new experiences it might bring. [May 14, 1843] "This is a clear windy day, no one has been here but Bill Hill. This looks to me like one of the romanticest days I ever experienced, the most perfect quiet, no fuss agitating the sweet perfumed air, the wind rustles the wild sweet briar by the window—such a place indeed fits my ideas exactly for hours of study, but always to stay in the same lonely spot presses hard on my spirits. But sometimes I have a hope of something more active and busy, but 'Hope deferred maketh the heart sick indeed' but it is only because its brightness is dimmed by the forecast shadow of impending despair, the soul's sorest malady. Wretched indeed would our lot be were we confined to the poor precints of the present, but, blessed be God! we have rich possessions in the storehouse of memory, and bright figures are ever hung before us, drawn by the magic hand of hope upon the dim curtains of the future."

A death in the community often was the occasion for some of Elizabeth's deeper thoughts: [December 10, 1843] "Today Calvin Jones is to be buried. I had liked to have went but Fate, Alas forbade the trip, it bade me do as usual, stay at *home*, read, fret, study, grieve, and journalize. But even now me thinks amidst the gloominess of thought perhaps it is for the best; perhaps it is for some design of the ALL wise Creator that I was born in this lone and solitary spot to accomplish some ends. I otherwise would be unfit; but for all this I have no real proof. No! it is the silent whisperings of prophetic hope, blest consoling word, my staff of life my all is *hope*." In such a passage, and in the one that follows, Elizabeth indicates a deep longing to do something worthwhile with her life or, at the very least, that she wanted to escape the daily routine of her existence: [May 12, 1844] "Julian wanted to go to Nathans but we have not time the present evening but will follow along in the same old channel that we have done a staying at home forever struggling to be something eccentric, something good, smart and happy, but Alas, it is like unto a drowning man catching at straws when all other hope has failed for its weak mortals to ever expect to do anything toward advancing into society from this place of recluse. It is not rational. I live and have not idea what for. I do not know what to do no way nor fashion, for let me do as I will I offend or displease some person."

This last passage, and the next, suggest that at times Elizabeth may have had a desire to rise in the social strata: [July 21, 1844] "This day I am 19 years of age and weigh 117. Last Tuesday A. [Amanda] & Ika and myself went to town a trading. There are proud aspiring haughty souls there. I am poor, humble and innocent. I believe as happy as they are, but reason will not allow me to raise my aspirations of life as high as the dictates of my heart and mind requires, all because I am *poor* and therefore have not had the talents improved that would be suitable to fill the station of life that my restless spirit now longs for. But enough."

Sometimes Elizabeth felt completely hemmed in, uncertain of herself, of the world, of any purpose for anything. [August 1, 1844] "I am here [in] this still, old place, no person coming, no where to go, nothing to divert but read some *borrowed* newspapers. What—Oh! what am I living for, to drag out a few miserable years in solitude, to struggle on from time to time to raise myself in this world, and what for? To be more unhappy? And what am I keeping this tedious old journal for? No purpose—no good, no nothing but the present

past time, the pleasure of pouring out my whole soul, for this journal will never tire of my presence and abruptly leave me like human mortals do, neither will it abuse me for complaining of hard times etc. Sometimes it appears that I ought to be happy, but it is *hard* to be, so confined my body and mind to be lonesome, so odd and so distant from all my fellow travellers in this fantastic world of ours." Or, again, [November 3, 1844] "Such is the theme with me every week—no news—no hopes—no loves, all work on and stay at home. I feel sorter like I was seized by the everlasting wilt." [December 29, 1844] "The old clock ticks mockingly on, our lamp burns pale and sickly. I don't know what to say of myself only to say that I am too high souled and proud to equalize myself with the ornery and too course [*sic*] and inexperienced for quality, so I have to remain as I am."

Elizabeth's thoughts often turned to love, and frequently her hopes and dreams and frustrations were intertwined with this part of life. [February 5, 1844] "I have had a dreamy time for awhile. I know not what to do. I am as it is doing nothing and no one complaining of me, but I perhaps will have to determine something in the matrimonial line before long and I am as wavering as the wind about it. One moment I am ready to give my hopes into the hands of one with character uniformed and no particular way of making a living, but young. More than all I love him, but I know not how lasting circumstances has drawn me in without my knowing it, and has not went far enough to show me the depth of my affection for him. At another moment I think I will marry a man of good living principles, settled, but of a bad family, about 31 years old, but I have no particular love for him at this time, but far from hatred. Some doubt his goodness . . 'so do I.' At another moment I forsake all and fly off to Missouri in a flash of pride and worldly ambition. Therefore I know not myself and will lie silent until I find out."

Eight months later Elizabeth confided that she had no prospect of marriage, adding, "I am as cold as the west winds to all about me." However, her entry for November 3, 1844, notes that "J. W. McClure has come back." Thereafter his name appears constantly, and a change gradually takes place in Elizabeth's spirits. [November 17, 1844] "I do not know what we will do the latter part of the winter not what I ought to do, but I do feel better than I did two weeks ago—for then I was entirely *out* of hope." [December 29, 1844] "Tuesday J. P. W. went home and the same evening J. W. McClure came here.[5] Wednesday we went to the Forge. . . . Night stole on us and then for the dance. The rest all danced and *we* sat off odd as usual. . . . There was one consolation that attended me at the Forge . . that was a pair of sweet *blue* eyes that met my own at times. There was a certain damp on my feelings I could not help also. Concerning J. W. Mc. I do not love him well enough to marry, nor do I hate him so as to intentionally sleight [*sic*] him. He loves me I think and so much the worse he thinks I sleighted [*sic*] him for S. Blair, but not so, although it dampens my feelings."

By the middle of the ensuing year, Elizabeth was wavering: [May 25, 1845] "Elder Hicks delivered a fine sermon on baptism. Mc come back with me and James. We come by J. Hanks's and took dinner, and in the evening Mc went home, and I think! I think! what do I think! I love, I don't." By the fall Elizabeth worried about what McClure was going to do with his life: [October 19, 1845] "James says that Mc talks of coming here today, or tomorrow after his watch before he goes to college, thinking to stay *3* years, but is it possible? Can it be that he too will neglect me like so many others do; but if he does once go to stay three years, all I can say is farewell, farewell, for when he is gone there three years, his love for me will not amount to the weight of three feathers: but if he thinks best for himself, go and forget and bury the childish past in the gay speculations of calculating manhood and the future . . these! these! thoughts, more than these fill and make up the week. But I want to see him and hear from his own lips his plans, and my hopes let them be great or small."

The following month they were committed: [November 9, 1845] "Last Sunday J. W. McClure came here and it was cold and misty, but nevertheless *we* went in the garden and stayed about two hours, and during that time made a bargain between us that is to last forever or during life, a confession . . a bargain that is to seal our happiness or ruin for life. Our fates hereafter will inevitably be linked as one, and I hope, and pray, that nothing but harmony and love will accompany us wayfarers through this life. May no discordant word jar our united hopes and enjoyments in this life and life to come." Elizabeth hoped she was beginning to find the happiness for which she had longed: [December 28, 1845] "I am better contented with myself than before. The case is this: my mind is the most busy, most active at present. I have long sought for one on whose confidence to rely . . to whom I can without restraint, pour out my inmost secrets 'from out their thousand secret cells,' one who can love and confide and bear with me through all the various vicissitudes of life; for such a one I long have sought and now I (think) have found. May such be the case."

Happy now in the love she desired, Elizabeth became excited about the journey to Texas, where she and McClure had decided to go. At last she would cross those horizons she had thought of so often. Still, there were to be moments of reservation; moments flooded with memories of her years past, her home, her family, and her friends, all of whom she soon would be giving up. On the first day of the new year, she speculated: [January 1, 1846] ". . . what will we be about next New Year's day . . perhaps a thousand miles from here. But let me not dive in matters it is not for mortals to know but be contented with the present and also with the future let it be what it may for the Great God the bestower of all things who knows best and is always kind. I know this much, I am better satisfied than at last New Year's day, and may the next be better. May we all be happier and better." Ten days later she wrote: [January 11, 1846] "I wish that we were married and sorter settled for I do dread the undertaking. I want to stay . . but me thinks I want to go away worse, for how can we live here like anybody . . and I had almost as soon not live as to live like a dog."

At one time it seemed as if Elizabeth and her husband might remain in Virginia. Members of the family urged them to buy the "Crawford's Mill place," but Elizabeth thought it undesirable and described it as "a narrow strip of land lying on Coal Creek hemmed in on every hand." With no good land in Virginia available to them, Elizabeth stood firm in her resolution, recording on February 15, 1846, that "Texas is the motto with me now. I expect to start by the last of March and must have a mind of my own and get along the best I can." As she contemplated her future and her western journey, she confessed her trepidations: [February 8, 1846] "I know trouble awaits whither so ever I goeth, but he who tempers the storm to the shorn lamb, who I love and worship will I trust lead me safe and point my wandering foot steps right, and point my lingering soul to heaven, and Oh God, direct us in this crisis, enlighten our mind, show us where to go, how to love and serve thee."

Elizabeth set the date for her marriage and on February 15, 1846, confided in her journal that "James is gone to invite hands to my wedding. What a word! how long have I thought of it . . I dread it . . I would be glad if it was over." Soon it was over and she began a new life. Elizabeth and her husband made one last effort to acquire suitable land in Carroll County upon which they might settle, but their search was in vain. In April they started for Texas to seek a home. Her regrets upon leaving her Virginia home prompted her to write: "Oft will I think of Carroll [County] and its inhabitants with tears of fond remembrance, but may they not be those of bitter repentance."

Editors' Note: Due to space limitations in this anthology, Elizabeth Ann Cooley's journal entries for March 15 to June 22, 1846, have been omitted. These entries described her wedding, the newlyweds' departure from Virginia, and their journey to Texas and then to Missouri.

The account abruptly ends in March 1848. In that month, Elizabeth died of typhoid fever in Independence.[6]

The Journal of Elizabeth Ann Cooley

June 24th, . . . We got to Independence Landing, went to tavern—11 o'clock, went to bed. Tuesday morning William [Cooley] came down there.[7] I was very glad to see him. It rained. We rode up here in a hack; been here two days, raining all the time. Suffer very much of pride. I can't be fine, everything out (of) pocket. Wrote a letter to Matilda Hanks, Mc. [Elizabeth's husband, James] one to Esau Worrell. The Masons (are) eating dinner here tonight.[8] I took ice cream with them. No stands. I look pale, regret leaving home, but the land is rich here. I may do well yet, bad as it is.

June 25th. Today been over to William's shop, saw all his things.[9] He owns a heap. Saw Mr. Mercer and promised to go there tonight. Now wish it would rain for excuse, they are too tippy.

June 26th. We went last night to Mercers. Henrietta came after us but we ate supper here—went there, the prettiest parlor I ever seen. They were friendly and are vastly rich. Mc. was sick, went early to bed. William come home, we stayed for late breakfast. Mc. is shaving. I feel bad, look pale too. I fear I will never be satisfied if I am here. I remember and with regret the good water of Carroll, and if there, I remember the rich productive soil of Mo. I fear my peace of mind is forever shaken.

June 27th, 1846. Warm and dry—looked for D. [Davis] Smith all day . . want to go . . all our things are here. I have been writing today some, feel a little better. We *will* leave here soon if no accident. Mc. brought me some pins today. The air feels fine here.

June 28th. Sunday. Been to meeting in the Methodist church at 11 o'clock, then eat dinner and went to the grave yard where dear Parthena lies—come back drank ice water, then went to Presbyterian church at 4—came back and talked with William. Mc. is getting better and I have hope of real enjoyment. Have enjoyed myself today very well. It is very warm, some cloudy and some sun. I have on black silk . . the people dress very fine and tasty. I can if I wish, go again to church tonight.

June 29th, 1846. Been here all day. Isaac Smith came up here, is gone home to send Davis [Smith] with the buggy. I hate staying here so long. I hate to put them to the trouble of coming after us but I can't help myself . . it is the best I can do in present dependent situation but I do hope ere long to be more independent. It is very warm today. All the ladies out shopping I do know.

July 6th, 1846. At Hezekiah's [Smith], and have been to meeting to Pleasant Hill.[10] Enjoyed ourselves very well . . been doing about here, feel languid and feeble—eat good things, and Hezekiah and wife is good to one another and to us too. I am better contented than I have been for sometime. Mc. is better. The children cry and fret too.

July 10th. Been over to Gorshen's school. Mc. is sick and I feel low spirited indeed. It is such a pity persons should be raised in one climate, then be removed to another. They are so puny and so sickly. Nancy is sick, Davis is gone to Independence.

Sunday July 12th. At Hezekiah's—was in weather. Mc. and Davis went to Lone Jack to meeting and John Snyder come here.[11] They are very good to me here and kind to us. I feel a heap better now. I hope we can pass an examination and make some money and live ourselves.[12] Mc. yesterday took some of Cook's pills and is better . . I think he will get well now.

July 29th. Last Sunday week we went to union meeting house 2 days and stayed two nights at Snyders. Friendly people and felt very well there. Last Sunday we went to meeting at Lone Jack—went home with Miller Easly . . Monday night went home with Galen Cave . . Tuesday come here to H. Smith's. Have generally enjoyed myself tolerably well since I come here. Sometimes feel bad—it is so sickly here now—and warm—I don't feel satisfied and fear I never will. It is too bad a country to think of permanently settling. The extreme heat and cold, ague, fevers, and such bad weather, I can't think of staying here always. Nancy & Davis have gone to Basses. He is sick. Mc. is started to get his certificate *** me one too. I fear, but hope to do well.

Aug. 2nd, 1846. Sunday at Hezekiah's. No one here but Nancy, and the children. I feel but cannot tell how; uneasy, I fear there is something I ought to

The Independence Square as it Looked when Elizabeth Arrived

do but do not know what—but I will try to get religion. Mr. McClure has been sitting by me reading and singing. We love each other well, and have near and good friends here but I do not at present like this country. It is sickly and disagreeably hot. I sweat all the time. I wish we were settled, we could have so much peace. I have been in company so much I am willing to retire and enjoy domestic felicity. Oh! I wish my soul was happy, then perhaps I would not be so uneasy as now. I feel that I am standing on a trembling and uncertain world and subject at any time to be plunged into a dark abyss of futurity . . to leave this tangled hazy world, to be separated from a large number of its inhabitants forever and forever. Great God have tender mercy on us poor and trembling mortals here on earth.

July 30th the thermometer stood at 94 degrees . . hot weather, that. People dying nightly . . hear of more every day . . feel somewhat alarmed—billious fever, ague and so on is raging all over this very sick, sickly and much peopled land!

August 10th, Monday. Yesterday went to meeting at P. [Pleasant] Hill. Wm. [Cooley] was here. Mc. is gone to take him home. Rained last night, now warm and showery, thermometer as high as 90. I am not doing much certain. Wm. Cooley looks cold and spiritless; I am not at all contented. I would not care to live, if my soul was saved. Nancy is sick, Martin is too.[13]

August 19th. Today Mc.'s school commenced. I have been cyphering and spinning &c. Children crying, Nancy sick . . rained this morning. I feel solid and firm bent on learning . . low spirits. I want to return to my native country sometime. We went to Underwoods last week.

Aug. 20. Received a letter from Rebecca and Amanda and Jesse yesterday. Feel bad indeed. Cloudy day.

Friday 21st. Raining . . had a hard rain and it not done. Received a letter from Matilda Hanks—feel bad. Been knitting some and writing some. I will see Mc. tomorrow I hope! My spirit is breaking but sometimes I feel gay and happy.

Sunday, Sept. 7th, 1846.[14] At Hezekiah's but have been teaching school two weeks. Small school, sickly children, sometimes feel very bad, again feel well. Last Sunday we came to P. [Pleasant] Hill to Camelite [Campbellite] meeting and stayed here. They are very kind to us here. We have been writing letters to Harold Smith, S. A. Hill, P. Early, Wm. Long . . cloudy day. I am in a little better health but fear I won't stay so. We have a great many difficulties to encounter. I like teaching tolerably well indeed; I'll write more next time.

Sunday, 13th Sept. 1846. At Keeton's. Was here every night last week. Mr. McClure took the ague and fever Monday and has been very bad—quit his school. I don't feel quite well—headache, I don't know what to do. I wish I was back in Va., I am not happy here. Everything going to destruction, drinking the worst kind of water, breaking our constitutions. There are a few white clouds and very windy and warm.

14th Sept. [This entry was made by Elizabeth's husband.] Very windy though warm. I sitting by myself in my room writing; and thinking whose land in Virginia I will get when & if I go back. Mrs. McClure gone to school. 14th at 8 o'clock. McClure.

Sunday the 20th, 1846. Another school week gone which is 4, and I do little besides study. I sit up at nights and cipher, of days study geography and grammar and get along very well. McClure has regained his health so as to attend to his school. Today has been quite pleasant. No person here but Martha Collins and children last week. Mc. went to Pleasant Hill, got soap, whiskey &c. I have been ciphering in vulgar fractions, squared the cube root. I pray that the Lord will brighten my ideas. I enjoy myself tolerably well at school. If I get leisure time I am restless beyond description I don't know how to content myself.

Wednesday night 9 o'clock, 23rd. In our room. Mc. gone to bed, has toothache; I have bad cold. Been studying grammar very hard. Susan Keeton is in the adjective pronouns. How hard I wish I understood it better. Mc. went to school this evening. He dismissed his school until Monday on account of sickness. I really fear to stay here, I fear death . . I want once more to visit my native land before I die if the Lord will. I really crave to see Father!! and Mother!! again. But these subjects bring gloomy thoughts. I fear Mr. McClure never will enjoy good health in Missouri. I feel very lonesome, so I will prepare for bed.

Sunday 27th Sept. Cold last night, warm today. Been reading John Wesley. My mind is busy and active in many things. Today it is smoky like Indian summer which always has a charm for me. I washed yesterday out of Big Creek.[15] In pretty good health . . have uncontrollable desire to return to Va. Mr. McClure taught Friday for me . . I was there too. The children I think have the whooping cough bad. I have not ciphered any today. I sigh when I think of home and home people. I long to embrace them.

Oct. 4, 1846. Frost this morning for the first time this year. We are still at Keetons. They have brought in complaint against Mr. McClure as unable or unwilling to teach arithmetic. He has adjourned his school, so have I, on account of sickness. Next Saturday to be examined again at J. Moor's.[16] We wanted to go to H. [Hezekiah] Smith's today but can't find the filly. Keetons are most all sick. Hezekiah has been sick. We are now, and intend studying, this coming week, entirely. It is our trade but it is hard. My school is half out now. Tis clear and very smoky today.

Monday the 5th. I have been ciphering all day. Oh! how irksome. Oh, would to God I had a stronger mind so as to comprehend more things at a time. Mc. will be tried Saturday whether he is smart.[17] Certainly I do sincerely pray he may come out victorious; for he is unjustly accused I think.

Tuesday 6th. Have ciphered until my head aches. It has been a very windy day. 8 o'clock in our room at Keetons. The moon looks red in the smoke. I am thinking of Virginia and its inhabitants. It gives me a sick sensation when I think of the *Father* and the kind and tender *Mother* left there. I sigh, my bosom heaves, I long to embrace them again and I do hope I will ere many more years.

Wednesday, 14th. Last Wednesday I took intermittent fever which lasted till Saturday. Sunday Brother William [Cooley] and E.S., I.S., came here. William stayed all night. I then went to school yesterday and the day before. Keeton finished his fire place yesterday.

Thursday 15th. Been to school. I feel fatigued and Mc. has just come from school and talking about going to Hezekiah's next. Friday I had 7 scholars, Mc. 2 today.

Sunday 25th October, 1846. In our room by the fire writing on the box. I have the headache and feel aguish. It is windy and smoky. Friday the fire burned the prarie all up most, and all the Wilmotts and Kennys fence and wheat. It was a sight indeed.

Nov. 4, 1846. Mr. McClure has been examined one time more and come out in flying colors, thank Providence. I have been writing a letter to Amanda today, Journal last Sunday, Mr. McClure is writing in it now.[18] We are writing on the box by the fire. My health is better, so is Mc.'s. Three weeks more and I'll be done on Big Creek.

Nov. 7. Mr. McClure is gone to see Mr. [Hezekiah] Smith who is very like to die. I really fear he never will recover. I was so sick, I could not go. I have a bad Diarea It is a little better today. It is very warm pretty weather, and I think very sickly. Most every person complaining some way—bad colds very common. I don't know what to be about. Mc. has a bad cold. Keeton's all sickly.

Nov. 14. Cold windy day. Mc. has had ague every day this week but 2. He looks aguerish. I feel low spirited and bad though not sick. I intend to try to go back. I am tired of going to school and no scholars, and I am *tired* of this open room and geography Atlas.

Dec. 27, 1846 . . My school is out. I have been here 5 weeks and no where else. The children have all been sick and are still sick. Martin, poor child is dead. We sat up a long time with him and he suffered much. Christmas is come and gone . . I sat up Christmas eve with little James. He is now better. I have had the scarlet fever. Mc. has made up a writing school at the Lone Jack. I expect to go to the geography school next week and then the next to go [to] Keeton's to keep school for three months. I feel a little better than I did though not healthy nor fat.

NEW YEARS DAY. I am at H. [Hezekiah] Smith's. Children are getting better but very cross. It snowed last night 7 or 8 inches deep and snowing and blowing yet. Mc. is teaching a writing school at the Lone Jack. I have been to singing this week but it is too cold today to go. I study here today and work a little. I have often wondered what would be at the next New Years—now I find myself a married woman living in Missouri being a lady, not working but still studying . . enjoy myself tolerably well but a long ways from home.

9 Jan. Very cold . . has been all the week. Mc. is very unwell, had a blister drawn on his breast . . caught cold but is better . . but a pain in his breast yet. I fear it will not get well soon, but hope it will. We went to meeting last Sunday and attached ourselves to the Methodist Church. Glad we did, and Thursday morning agreed to drink no more dram for fun . . I was glad again. I am very well and if Mc. was could enjoy myself very well. I learned a good deal of geography.

January, 24, 1847. Living at Hezekiah's yet—went all last week to the writing school, today been to circuit meeting. I do really enjoy myself very well. I am in good health. Mc. is well too and enjoys life as it flies. Mc. is writing, an article for another school, Hezekiah reading, Nancy reading too—Isaac, Davis singing in the other room—children asleep. We have a heap of enjoyment at school, some anyway.

Jan. 31. Sunday at Hezekiah's in the new room, Mc. writing all the *** Davis gone to "Blue," Isaac going to meeting.[19] I feel well, Mc. is well too and I am so glad, I don't know what I am to do for awhile but in the summer I want to teach a school and make some money.

Feb. 9, 1847. I wrote a letter today to Amanda and Julian. Mr. McClure has gone to meeting out to Phill [Pleasant Hill], said for me to go but I did not want to go, because I wanted to write. We received a letter from Julian and Amanda last Tuesday . . last week I made Mc. 2 shirts, he bought me a pair of side combs, a pocket comb. He has a writing school made at Pleasant Hill to be taught this week. Perhaps I will teach it. If I do, may the Lord help me, keep me from error. It will be a new business to me. I dread it a little, but I must do something to live by.

Feb. 21, 1847. Went last Sunday to Gibson's to meeting and then to T. Franklin's Monday, to writing school at Daniels, Tuesday evening came here to H. Smith's, piddled about sewing and knitting. Mc. came home last night. Froze last night and a little colder. Received a good letter from Uncle Wm. Worrell Friday. Nancy Smith lost her child the 9th of this month, but she is now some better. Mc. and me are both in better health.

Feb. 26, 1847. This is a fast day. The snow fell last night about an inch deep. Mc. is gone to "Blue"—went last Monday. I don't know exactly what he is doing but I hope it is what is right. I have been married 12 months and one day. We are both in tolerably good health though we have been sick a heap. I feel very well satisfied now or as well as I could hope and be so unsettled as we are. I don't know where we will settle yet . . in a healthy country is the presumption.

March 28, 1847. At Mallory Smith's.[20] Been teaching school three weeks—been from Hezekiah's four weeks. I have a very full school, some 24 scholars last week. I am well situated for the summer I think. I go to meeting most every Sunday. I have been 4 times since I came here. Mr. McClure has taught one writing school at the Blue Spring meeting house, one at Barkers near Independence—now he has one made ready to teach over the S . . . Daileys. He came here last night—was not well but is gone again. I went to meeting and rode in Esq. Smith's buggy. Have on black silk, &c. Mallory is very sick of the ague and fever.

[The following undated entry is in the handwriting of Elizabeth's husband]. Old Mr. Harris is sing . . . I think he is going happy. It is awful sickly now. I felt curious. I thought of my old home. I fear sickness.

April 4, 1847. Yesterday I went to singing school and today I went. . . . Mr. McClure came here last night and is sick . . has been sick all the week. I have taught school 4 weeks. This is Easter Day. It rained very pretty shower of rain last night and today. There is no sign of grass until last night. I felt uneasy and restless all last week.

April 9, 1847. Just one year since I left my Father's house—now in Mo. teaching school. It is Friday. I am glad I don't have to teach any more this week. I like to teach better than I have thought I ever would. It is fine practice, it improves my mind much. I long to see my old friends. I enjoy myself very well considering all things. Mr. Mc. is gone to H. Smith's today. I am at Mallory Smith's. It is fine weather now but has not been long.

April 20. I have been to school today, had 13 scholars. Went to meeting and singing yesterday. It was very cool but this evening it is warmer, and tremendous windy from the South. Mc. came here Friday evening. Is and was sick last week . . today he is gone to town. Wm. Cooley got back from Va. 10th this month and come to the meeting house 14th. I started a letter to Caroline Martin this morning, Mc. one to Grandmother. I had trouble last week and prayed until I was relieved, but I begin to feel uneasy again. I wish I could feel easy awhile. What does make me feel so . . I wish I knew . . I fear it is because Father and Mother is grieving for me. Lord help them I pray forever. Could I see them I would embrace them a thousand times over. Elizabeth Smith is dead, she died 17 April. I was very sorry for her.

April 25, 1847. This day got a letter saying my *Dear Father is dead* . . shocking word . . awful truth he is no more, my *own* my dear father is dead. He died 24 March, buried 26. How *dear* and how much lamented. I was at meeting today when I heard it, large congregation. Stayed last night at Hightows . . at Mallory's [Smith] now. Mr. McClure here, been talking over matters and things. He is sick . . pain in his side . . affection of the lungs, spleen or something . . blister on his side—last Monday he went to Independence and got him and me watches . . his silver, mine pretty gold *** both skeleton *** leaves me a breast pin and pen holder from Wm. Cooley. It is pretty weather, grass getting green. I am sorry for poor!! Mother and sisters . . could I relieve them!

May 17. Mr. McClure has a school at Barker's.[21] He has taught one week. He is just now started again. We cried about leaving now, and leaving last spring, our dear native home. We have been to meeting to hear Slone preach. He did it well too. They took the sacrament today. We are getting along very well now I think, I have a very large school, 26 scholars. I have some trouble with them of course, and may the Lord have mercy on us, give me strength both of body and mind, show me how to govern myself, my school, give me knowledge and understanding enough to (do) all that is or will be required of me; guide me, protect me, give me grace, give me good pure religion, prepare me for heaven, make me love thee, love thy works, forever not my will but thine be done, Oh Lord have mercy.

May 27, Saturday. [May 27, 1847, Thursday][22] Been to meeting, Powell exhorted. Mr. McClure came home last night. His horse has gone and left him. I am uneasy about it. I have a good school, get along very well, have some scrimages.

May 31, 1847. I have been to the quarterly meeting at a little meeting house in the brush. I took the sacrament for the first time in life, put our letters in the church again. I rode behind Mrs. Wood. It rained a good deal, raised the creek to swimming so McClure will stay tonight with me. I have been ciphering a little. There is a talk of P. Hawkins and several large boys coming to school. I had rather they would not. Feel well enough.

[June 6, 1847, Sunday] I stayed all last night at W. Burris's, went today to the singing . . met Hezekiah [Smith] and Davis [Smith] there . . came home. Mr. McClure is gone just now; I have my hands full at school and will have them fuller, it has been cold at spells.

June 11, 1847. I have been today to the reformer meeting, heard Mr. Wood preach, stayed last night at Franklin Smith's. Bought me a pair of shoes, McClure hat, pants, droirs [drawers].

Thursday 18, [June 18, 1847, Friday] been to school, Malory's wife gone to Woods . . I by myself going to the Burris'. Small school this week. P. Hawkins like to drive . . I feel bad a little about something. I want to see Mc. bad. There is a letter at Pleasant Hill I want so bad, I need it, but take all things together I do unusually well I think. I am trying for religion.

Sunday 21, 1847 [June 20, 1847, Monday] I have been to Slone's meeting, good many persons. I feel that I need religion. I study about it a great deal. This day we received a letter from Jesse Worrell, one from *James*, Julian & *** and Amanda, and a journal from Amanda. Mr. McClure is gone again— he came last night at dark. Today he wrote a letter to Father McClure.[23] Mc. was at town yesterday, saw the volunteers start and the ladies of Independence present them with a flag.[24] I feel tolerably well this evening. I am so sorry for poor Mother—I suffer a heap about it lately.

June 26, 1847. Small school last week. Mr. McClure lost his horse again, and he went down to H. Smith's and got him a *** came home today by Hightower's, ate dinner there. Mallory and George Burris are started down to Howard Co. Mo. to see John Burris who is sick and we are staying by ourselves tonight. It is cloudy and thundering like it will rain. I feel weary. Mc. is gone away. I was very glad to see Jim and Benja. We had a heap of chat going down and coming back—talked about going to Va. and how we will fix. In about 2 years from now I calculate on being near Carroll, Va. My heart yearns toward there. Oh could I see *Mother* I would be happy as mortals ever are.

July 5, Monday morning. Day before yesterday Mrs. *** went to Independence, I went to Christmase's to fix her bonnet. Yesterday 4, we wrote a letter to James, Julian, Amanda and Mother and then went to the singing—came back to Mrs. Burris'es. It is raining this morning. I feel bad, have the headache, I will sew a little while on Hail's dress.

July 16. Yesterday went to hear Slone preach—heard it good. Stayed Saturday night at Mrs. Burris', last night at Mrs. Burris till after John Wood prayed. Friday was at Mrs. Harris B. quilting, Saturday at meeting. Mc. went to town Saturday to meeting. Mc. is weakly talks a heap about religion—started soon this morning. I must go directly to school. I had above 20 [pupils] every day last week but Friday.

July 26, Monday morning. It is raining. Mc. is just started to his school. Mallory and wife in bed yet. Last Saturday and Sunday I went to meeting. Mc. went to town Saturday to meeting Sunday and in the evening we went to Esyr Smith's. I expect I am going to town Thursday to the dinner there. I feel uneasy—I am afraid it is not right—I don't know. I pray to God to have mercy on me, be with me, keep me from evil, direct us both through this world of trouble, but I am contented as ever I was. I must quit.

July 30. Yesterday I went to the great dinner at Independence.[25] It was pleasant day and the greatest concourse of people I ever saw. I enjoyed myself tolerably well. Mr. McClure is unwell, but is now gone to his school. I soon will have to go to mine. I am tired . . I want time to commune and study things over, to read the bible. O I am tired of the world, I want Religion!!

Wednesday 11, August. Went last Sunday to camp meeting near Independence and Saturday saw William [Cooley]. He has a letter from Jesse [Worrell]. James [Cooley] is sick of white swelling. They are in a lamentable situation. I wish I could do something for them but I cannot. I enjoy myself very well now, but I have to whip the scholars sometimes.

August 15, Sunday evening. Been to meeting . . Cumberlands [Cumberland Presbyterian]. Mc. is gone to try to take Demar and Hill for horse stealing. I wish he was here. I have been at Mrs. Burris's. James is very sick. Dr. Thornton is there and John Wood Christmas. I hear Mc. coming. I am glad. I am doing tolerably well. Very busy.

August *** Monday evening. Been to school, 24 scholars. Butts come there this evening. Day before yesterday I went to meeting, heard White preach—was there Saturday also. Mc. went to town with D. S. [Davis Smith]. I am a bad horse I fear, I feel very bad, but have no reason to complain but I feel a depression of spirits. I know not why but I am getting weary keeping school so long, for it is all the time from morning till night, from beginning to end, all the time. I talk just as much as I can possibly bear to keep order and govern the school as I wish it to be done. Last week I went to Halloway's, to Tatum's, to Christmas's. My mouth is very sore, a little sick since last week but well as common. Mc. is better. My school will be out in 2 weeks. O! I feel so lonesome tonight.

August 28, Sunday evening.[26] Mc. and I have stayed at home all day, fixed out all my speech for next Saturday. I have thought of heaps of things, some about Benaley's land and about my school—where to get another, about troubles in school. Washed and ironed my white dress. Mc. went to town. Wm. [Cooley] has a letter from Amanda [Cooley]. She says they all look badly and have hard times. Mrs. Christmas was here, Dillenhans & *** I have but one week longer [of school].

Sept. 9. At [Silas] Barkers.[27] My school is out, it pleased me very well . . several there, a light shower of rain. They delivered their speeches well, spelled well. I felt bad in the evening. Sunday morning prepared for leaving Mallory's, then I took a chill at 10 o'clock and oh! how bad I was. Mr. McClure went and got some quinine, so, late in the evening I was able to ride to Mr. Halloway's. Stayed all night, in the morning sick again but come on here. Been half sick ever since. I cannot easily get acquainted here but Mc. is with me. I *love* him, he loves (me) and is good to me. It is cool this morning. I am making my calico dress that came from Duncan's. I am upstairs writing but I am going down to warm. My mouth is all fever sores.

Sept. 12th. At [Silas] Barker's. Sitting upstairs with Mc. He is reading our new Methodist discipline bought yesterday. Yesterday we both went to town—went to Dr. Twiman's [Leo Twyman] got acquainted with his wife, went to all the stores, to Wm.'s [Cooley], to Woaland's. My dress is done. There is singing at the school house. I am going I expect.

Sunday evening, 12. Been to the singing, been up stairs talking Christian perfection and keeping ourselves employed always.

Tuesday 21 Sept. Last week I cut out and made Mc. a coat, a shirt, all do well. Saturday we went to the Blue Bottom camp meeting, went to Mr. *** tent. Felt bad at first strove hard to get happy. Saturday evening went to the mourner's bench, prayed and was prayed for and got a great deal happier.

Sunday was baptized and was happy . . and happy yet, feel pure and clear from sin. Mc. is happy too.

Saturday evening Sept. 25. Day before yesterday I had a severe chill and fever. Mc's back is worse than it ever has been though he started to Vanburen yesterday.[28] I hated to see him go and so unwell. Today I went to the singing. I have been ciphering some and have nothing to (do) next week but ciphering. I must do it and prepare myself for school.

Oct. 3, Sunday evening, 9 o'clock. Mr. Mc. has been all the week out at Harrisonville court, gained his suit.[29] I ciphered all the week, got to decimal fractions. We both been studying Algebra, got to substraction in Algebra, 25 pages, began this morning, in a great fiz to be a scholar. Intend to be.

October 9, Saturday. Been ciphering most all the time. I am to Duodecimals. Mc. is ciphering now, is going to town for the singing. I am all of a work thinking of so many things at once.

Oct. 11, Monday evening. Last Saturday we went to town, bought Mc. some pants, a vest, pair of boots, and myself a dress (alpacca) &c. Sunday morning the 10th wrote letter to J. P. Worrell and to Wm. Worrell, then went to the singing and then home with Mr. Saunders, stayed all night. Today I have picked a little cotton and fixed my coats up to quilt. Mr. McClure is some better.

Nov. 27, 1847. At Mr. Lowe's.[30] It has been a long time from my Journal. In that time I went to Blue Springs to meeting, then to H. Smith's. I stayed there a week and made Mr. D's pants and vest coat and my dress. Mr. McClure went and made a school at Mr. St. Clair's for himself and one at Mr. Grumps for me, then come and bought a buggy and swapped horses. We went over the river to Father McClure's, stayed two days.[31] Our expenses there and back was $3. Three of the girls married; went to see all of them; stayed all night with Mr. Carter then come on home; found the neighborhood all in trouble about my school.

*** [no entry date] chills, sprained my ankle terrible. Began my school and not well . . went around seeing patrons most. Been here one week. Went to town Saturday, came and stayed all night at Mr. [Silas] Barker's. I went in at Dr. Twiman's [Twyman]. We are both tolerably well now. I cleaned out the trunk . . put my things in the new large one and Mr. Mc.'s in his. Doubled and twisted some yarn. It is Saturday night 9 o'clock . . Mr. Mc. is here. He has been round today and seen the subscribers. The majority is in our favor and I am going too.

Wed. 1st De. 1847. Just came from school, had 22 scholars, a heap trouble to keep school. I come home each night weary of life itself. I have a good time enough here at Mr. Lowe's but it does pester me to keep school but I see no prospect of ever getting to quit while I have life to enjoy . . but it is best.

Dec. 6, 1847. Monday evening. Been teaching school, had 21 scholars today . . very pretty day. Yesterday we stayed at home all day, had a good Sunday. E. Crump, E A Montgomery come here last night . . we were all weighed, I 126, Mc. 158.

Dec. 24, 1847. I scarcely know how to describe my feelings. Another death to record . . William [Cooley] is dead. His soul left this mortal world and sought a home in heaven. He died happy. I went to town on Sunday, thought him better, then Tuesday evening they sent for me again. It was dark before I got there. He died in the night. I stayed there Sunday, been keeping school all the week.

Jan. 2, 1848. Sunday evening.[32] Yesterday we went to Mr. Little's to a quilting, enjoyed myself very well. Today I went to Mr. Montgomery's. I am not very well. Enjoy myself very well. I have a new dress and shawl.

—9, 1848. Sunday 10 o'clock P.M. [This entry is in the handwriting of Elizabeth's husband.] Now at Lowe's by the fire dreading the time of leaving my wife for school. Snow about 6 inches deep . . very cold. I want to teach school awhile and go to school one year; then myself and wife teach an Academy and live together in some country where we will not have to take pills all the time and the health of the country depend on the skill of

the physicians. Now teaching school, making some $25. per month.—Mc.

Jan. 9, Been ciphering some, had very large school last week, 31 scholars. Andrew in subtraction of vulgar fractions. Feel very well. Am happy now, pretty good health. Been to Mr. Lowe's all day ciphering &c. Andrew is to Double Position.

Jan. 23, Monday morning, fixing to go to school. Had a large school last week—31 scholars . . pretty warm weather, like spring. I stayed at home all day yesterday, ciphered some. Perry Gibson is coming today, a new scholar. I am going to Lowe's tonight. I pray that God will guide, guard and protect me, give me knowledge and strenth to govern my school a right and teach all that is required of me.

— —1848. Now at Joe St. Clair's. Come here last Sunday. School is out at Crumps. I was compelled to whip — —, they kicked up about it, I called a meeting and got — —3 months. Now have no school but want one now. Went yesterday to Mc's school. He had 35 scholars. Last night went to Robert St. Clair's. Been reading natural philosophy . . ciphering in Ray's arithmetic. Fine pretty warm weather—just like spring.

Feb. 27. Last week I went to Mr. McClure's school and Friday I taught school while Mc. went to make a school. Got it to commence Monday week. Friday night we stayed Mr. Billiam's, Saturday went to meeting at the Ish school house, went home with Judge Gray, stayed all night. Went again Sunday . . come back to Dickenson, got dinner, criseneld my silk aplaca dress. Am happy . . fine weather . . little windy. Living at St. Clair's.

March 17, at Mr. Henderson's—got the fever bad. I don't feel like every getting up at all. I am very low. Very good places here to stay but I am among strangers. Must send for Nancy [Smith]. I feel like I should die here but the Lord's will. . . .

March 18, 1848 [This entry is in the handwriting of Elizabeth's husband.] Elizabeth sick of slow typhoid fever—took ten small doses of calomel; operated four times; gave her 40 drops of laudanum. Employed Dr. Gordon. I think she is some better. God of heaven have mercy on her. Mc.

[The last entry by Elizabeth Cooley is in pencil and so faded as to be almost totally illegible. The following is all that can be read]: My best to *** in a terrible *** feel very doubtful of whether *** I can *** well now *** Mc. has dissiness *** his school out on account of go with me along *** through the valley of death *** help James if I die ** and ** if I live.

[The final two entries in the journal are in the handwriting of Elizabeth's husband]: Elizabeth has written some now would to God I was done writing *** I call upon God to have mercy upon her *** Grant she may get well *** tification and have mercy upon me. Mc.

March 29, 1848. This Journal is done! The author being Elizabeth A. McClure died March 28, 1848. Tho happy in Christ Jesus being the only consolation left me!! She was 22 years 7 months and 12 days old.[33]

NOTES

1. In 1842, Carroll County was formed from Grayson and Patrick counties. It was in the newly formed Carroll County that the Cooley family lived. Including Elizabeth, there were eleven children, some of whom are mentioned frequently in the early portion of her journal. Three of the children died before Elizabeth began her journal. Those mentioned in the journal are Martin, William, Nancy, Rebecca, James, Amanda, and Julia Ann. Martin Cooley was born in 1806, went to South Carolina in 1842 and Georgia in 1844. He died while making plans to go to Missouri, and his widow, Catherine Currin Cooley, and children moved to Oregon. William Cooley was born in 1811. He married Parthena Cox and, as a young man, moved to Independence, Missouri, where he died on December 15, 1847. Nancy Cooley, born in 1812, married Hezekiah Smith and moved to Jackson County, Missouri, about 1835. Rebecca Cooley, born in 1815, married Jesse P. Worrell in 1840 and moved to Pleasant Hill, Missouri, about 1857. James Dickey Cooley, born in 1822, was living at home on the Carroll County farm when Elizabeth began her journal. He later married Caroline Higgins. Amanda J. Cooley, born in 1820, married Logan Roberts of Mt. Airy, North Carolina, and died of consumption three weeks after her marriage in 1854. Julia Ann Cooley, born in 1831, married Joseph Price of Spartanburg, South Carolina, in 1869. Both Amanda and Julia Ann were teachers for a number of years. Information on the Cooley family as well as many neighboring families, acquaintances, and friends in Virginia which Elizabeth mentions in her journal may be found in B. F. Nuckolls, *Pioneer Settlers of Grayson County, Virginia* (Bristol, TN: King Print Co., 1914).

2. Ika was the small son of Elizabeth's deceased sister Mary.

3. "Aunt Mary" was Mary (nee Hanks) Cooley, wife of Peter Cooley, who was a brother of Elizabeth's father. Nuckolls, *Pioneer Settlers*, 188.

4. In this journal entry, Elizabeth mentions members of her family by their first names. For identification, see endnote 1.

5. Jesse P. Worrell was married to Elizabeth's sister Rebecca. See endnote 1 and Nuckolls, *Pioneers Settlers*, 161.

6. The editors [Jervey and Moss] are indebted to the Cooley family for their willingness to make the journal public, especially to Mr. S. Bruce Jones of Abingdon, Virginia, and to Miss Linda Sue Bowman of Radford, Virginia. Mrs. Harry F. Jepson, Kansas City, great granddaughter of Rebecca Cooley Worrell, and Mrs. Fleming W. Pendleton, Independence, great granddaughter of William Cooley, have been especially helpful in supplying information about members of the Cooley family who moved to Missouri. To maintain the originality of the journal, the spelling and punctuation, or lack thereof, have not been altered. Elizabeth occasionally used parentheses, which are reproduced as they appear in her journal. She also used two dots to indicate breaks in her thoughts; they do not signify omissions in the journal. The editors use the standard ellipsis and bracket form to denote editorial omissions and additions. Astericks are used to indicate a complete break or an illegibility in the

original journal.

    7. William Cooley, Elizabeth's older brother, was living in Independence.

    8. Information about many of the individuals mentioned by Elizabeth in this portion of her journal may be found in the early histories of Jackson and Cass counties. See *The History of Jackson County, Missouri* (Kansas City: Union Historical Co., 1881) and *The History of Cass and Bates Counties, Missouri* (St. Joseph, MO: National Historical Co., 1883).

    9. William Cooley owned a jewelry shop located on the courthouse square in Independence, where he also repaired clocks.

    10. Elizabeth's sister Nancy (see endnote 1) was married to Hezekiah Smith, who is listed among the pioneer settlers of Cass County. See *History of Cass and Bates Counties*, 226. Pleasant Hill is located in northeastern Cass County (then named Van Buren County), just south of the Jackson County line.

    11. Lone Jack is located in southeastern Jackson County.

    12. Elizabeth and her husband hoped to pass an examination required in obtaining a teaching certificate so that they could teach school.

    13. Martin was Nancy and Hezekiah Smith's son.

    14. Sunday came on September 6 in 1846.

    15. The first settlements in Cass County were made along Big Creek, located west and south of Pleasant Hill in the northeastern part of the county.

    16. Elizabeth refers here to a teacher qualification examination.

    17. Ibid.

    18. It is assumed that Elizabeth meant that her husband was writing in the letter to Amanda Cooley.

    19. Elizabeth presumedly refers here to Blue post office in Jackson County (later called Little Blue), located on the Little Blue River ten miles directly south of Independence and eight miles southwest of Blue Springs.

    20. Elizabeth was now living with the family of Mallory Smith, a farmer who lived near Blue Springs.

    21. This was probably Silas Barker, a well-to-do farmer who lived in Blue Township near Independence.

    22. Beginning with this entry and until the entry of July 5, 1847, Elizabeth's days do not correspond to the correct date.

    23. This may have been James McClure's father, although Elizabeth refers to her husband as a "lone orphan" in an entry dated March 29, 1846.

    24. Elizabeth refers here to the Missouri troops assembling in Independence in response to a call for volunteers to form a battalion of five companies to serve during the war with Mexico. *Liberty Weekly Tribune*, 5, 26 June 1847.

25. The dinner celebrated the return of Colonel Alexander Doniphan and his Mexican War volunteers. Ibid., 17, 24, 31 July 1847.

26. August 28, 1847, was Saturday.

27. See endnote 21.

28. Elizabeth refers here to Van Buren County, bordering Jackson County on the south. In 1849 the name of the county was changed from Van Buren to Cass. Harrisonville was the seat of justice for Van Buren County.

29. Presumedly, Elizabeth refers here to McClure's charges against Demar and Hill for horse stealing. See Elizabeth's entry for August 15, 1847.

30. It is not clear which Lowe family Elizabeth lived with. In later entries, she mentions both Joseph and Robert Lowe.

31. See endnote 23.

32. Sunday was January 1, 1848.

33. Elizabeth's birthday was July 21, 1825. This would have made her 22 years, 8 months, 7 days old.

General Orders No. 11 and
Border Warfare During the Civil War

ANN DAVIS NIEPMAN

During the Civil War, General Orders No. 11 of the District of the Border was unique in that it was a repressive measure used by the United States government against citizens legally a part of the Union. In order to rid Missouri's western border of guerrilla warfare, on September 23, 1863, General Thomas E. Ewing Jr. ordered citizens of Jackson, Cass, Bates, and the northern portion of Vernon County, many of whom were believed to have fed and supported [William] Quantrill's men, to leave their rural homes regardless of their innocence or guilt in aiding the guerrillas. In 1863 depopulation of an area was not an altogether new concept. As Major General Henry Halleck reassured the commander of the District of Missouri, it was a measure within the recognized laws of war. Wellington had adopted such a procedure in Portugal, and the Russian armies had used it in the campaign of 1812. Still it was a procedure which was reverted to only in the case of overruling necessity. Did such a necessity exist in the District of the Border in Missouri in the summer of 1863? General Ewing, the border commander, evidently believed that it did. However, this order and the methods by which it was enforced unleashed a multitude of intense reactions.

Appointment to the command of the Department of the Missouri had not been eagerly sought in the spring of 1863. John Charles Frémont, David Hunter, Henry Halleck, and Samuel R. Curtis had all suffered frustrations in this border state where the political battles proved more exhausting than the military ones. General John Schofield, in assuming this post in May, was stepping into the vacancy created by President Abraham Lincoln's removal of

General Curtis. Curtis had been at cross-purposes with Missouri's Governor Hamilton R. Gamble so often that Lincoln at length realized he could not replace Gamble, but he could remove Curtis. As Schofield stepped into this cauldron of political dissension, he came upon a scene described aptly by his commander in chief:

> We are in civil war. In such cases there always is a main question; but in this [Missouri's] case that question is a perplexing compound—Union and slavery. It thus becomes a question not of two sides merely, but of at least four sides, even among those who are for the Union, saying nothing of those who are against it. Thus, those who are for the Union with, but not without slavery; those for it without, but not with; those for it with or without but prefer it without. Among these again is a subdivision of those who are for gradual, but not for immediate, and those who are for immediate, but not for gradual extinction of slavery.[1]

Missouri represented an area where all of these shades of opinion and more were fervently held.

Under these circumstances, the confusion existing in the state was understandable. Two governments represented Missouri for the duration of the war: the elected one in exile under Governor Claiborne Fox Jackson, who

Refugees at Rolla

Thomas E. Ewing

after failing in his attempts to secure Missouri's secession had finally located the seat of the elected government in Marshall, Texas, and the provisional one sitting at the state capitol in Jefferson City and directed by the appointed governor, Gamble. As General Halleck, in charge of the operations in the Departments of the Missouri and Northwest, had warned, neither faction in Missouri was actually friendly to the president and his administration, and each wished to destroy the other. In their mutual hatred they seemed to have lost all sense of the perils of the country and any sentiment of national patriotism. Halleck instructed Schofield to make every possible effort to allay the bitter party strife in the state.[2] A letter from Lincoln warned Schofield: "If both factions or neither shall assail you, you will probably be about right. Beware of being assailed by one and praised by the other."[3]

Assuming command, Schofield created the District of the Border, which included Jackson, Cass, Bates, St. Clair, Henry, Johnson, and Lafayette counties south of the Missouri River and the adjacent portions of these counties in Kansas.[4] He placed in command of this district Brigadier General Thomas E. Ewing Jr., headquartered at Kansas City. Before the war, Ewing had been a promising young attorney practicing in Leavenworth. In 1861 he was chosen as the first chief justice of the Kansas Supreme Court, resigning in order to become colonel of the Eleventh Kansas Volunteers; he had seen action in Arkansas, advancing in rank when he assumed command of the District of the Border in June 1863. This new command was characterized by savage and vindictive strife along Missouri's western border south of the Missouri River, where the presence of many Southern sympathizers and the active predatory spirit among the Kansas Unionists created supreme confusion. In addition, the Missouri border between the Missouri River and Arkansas was a corridor where opposing forces were constantly moving. Missouri may have been officially in the Union at the time, but to the majority of Missouri border residents, especially those in the counties south of the river, their sympathies lay elsewhere.

In the 1860 election in Vernon County, no votes were recorded for Lincoln although probably there were a dozen or so men in the county who would have voted the Republican ticket had they been allowed to do so. Vote was viva voce, and the people of the county considered themselves lenient enough to let those with abolitionists' views live among them, but they were not generous enough to let them vote.[5] In Clay County just north of the river on the border, with a population in 1860 of 13,023, 9,525 whites and the remainder Negroes, Lincoln's tally was the same.[6] Antislavery men in Bates County discreetly kept quiet, and the ones who allegedly cast the few recorded Lincoln ballots found their names posted at various public places over the county with a broad invitation that they might be happier elsewhere.[7]

For Southern sympathizers it was dangerous to say anything against the depredations and high-handed operations of the Kansas Jayhawkers or Red Legs. Even the "decent Radicals" were afraid to criticize them, for these bands of men were "loyal" to the Union. Those who criticized them in the least were at once denounced for disloyalty.[8]

The District of the Border command was not an enviable one. Ewing began splendidly enough, however, with a speech given at Olathe in Johnson County, announcing his intentions in that capacity:

> I hope soon to have troops enough on the Missouri side not only to prevent raids into Kansas, but also to drive out or exterminate every band of guerrillas now haunting that region. I will keep a thousand men in saddle daily, and will redden with their blood [the Missouri guerrillas] every bridle-path of the border until they infest it no more. . . . I mean, moreover, to stop with a rough hand all forays for plunder from Kansas into Missouri.[9]

The guerrilla excursions into Kansas thus received top priority. But Ewing had also spoken that day of some Kansans as "stealing themselves rich in the name of Liberty."[10] The newspaper reaction he received for this must have exceeded his wildest expectations. The plunder taken from the Missouri border counties supplied a lucrative market in Fort Scott, Lawrence, and

Leavenworth. Kansas Red Legs sold their booty at public auctions on Lawrence streets until that city achieved a distinction of sorts as the "citadel of stolen goods!"[11] Leavenworth was even placed under martial law in July in an attempt to combat the ready market offered there for contraband.[12] Since before the war, Missouri had been infested with thieving bands from Kansas, who, justifying their actions under the guise of being loyal Unionists, made frequent trips into Missouri and "confiscated" what they held to be Confederate property. Missouri guerrillas operated throughout the same territory and also in the eastern counties of Kansas, thus providing two sets of outlaws preying upon one another and both preying upon the residents of the border counties.[13] Moreover, members of the Kansas and Missouri militias were not above such confiscations themselves. There was really little danger, noted the *Kansas City Journal of Commerce* on July 25, 1863, to the officers who were "going into limbo" over attention being directed toward cattle speculations, because it would be necessary for "one without sin to cast the first stone." This was the condition prevalent all along the Kansas-Missouri border.

Earlier attempts had been made to combat these forays by the organization in Missouri of county battalions to guard the border. They also aided the Southern cause by reporting on Union troop movements. But after "sweeps" made by Colonel Charles Jennison and General Jim Lane with their Kansas

Rebels Burning House of Unionists

"troops," these home guards had long since been abandoned as a county effort.[14]

During the first months of his command, Ewing set in motion strategy with primary concern centered on the Missouri guerrillas. Led by William Quantrill, these bands roamed the border in small groups or at times in groups numbering in the hundreds. Two methods were employed to neutralize them. General Orders No. 10 was issued on August 18, 1863, at the District of the Border headquarters in Kansas City.[15] Section II of this order attempted to rid the state of those willfully engaged in aiding the bushwhackers. Their wives, children, and families were ordered to move out of the state immediately; should they be derelict in this, the military indicated a willingness to escort them to Kansas City for shipment south. The guerrillas who would surrender voluntarily were promised protection until banished with their families.

While directly seeking to avert the marauding efforts, Ewing also made provision to thwart guerrilla excursions into Kansas. This was done by a system of defense extending from Westport to Mound City, Kansas, and consisting of the establishment of military posts and patrols. Four cavalry companies were located at Westport, three at Little Santa Fe, two at Aubry, one at Coldwater Grove, and one company each of infantry at Olathe, Paola, and Mound City.[16] Governor Thomas Carney, of Kansas, was told that he might now disband his special force of state troops.[17] This procedure was not intended to accomplish the task completely, but it was believed to offer a good system of alert.

The military abstract sent to St. Louis for the District of the Border for August 1863 reported that Ewing had present for duty 114 officers and 3,073 men, with an aggregate present and absent of 4,430.[18] Apparently this force was not adequate because Lawrence was suddenly attacked August 21, 1863, by more than three hundred of Quantrill's raiders. Many citizens were murdered, and much of the city was destroyed. The raiders may have been driven by their bitter hatred of Jim Lane who lived in Lawrence, by retaliation for the enactment of Orders No. 10, or by fury at the imprisonment and subsequent death of some guerrilla family members in the military prison at Kansas City.[19] Whatever the motivation, the result was tragic.

The hue and cry of the press over this wanton attack centered on Ewing. The *Leavenworth Daily Conservative*, edited by D. W. Wilder, provided a scathing denunciation of the Union general and his policies:

> The know-nothing, do-nothing policy of the General commanding this
> District, who has shown his utter incapacity, with five thousand soldiers
> under his command, in allowing a few hundred guerrillas to get fifty

William Clarke Quantrill

miles into the interior of our State and burn Lawrence, destroying two millions of property is ample proof that we must depend upon ourselves for the defense of our city and State.[20]

Wilder and Leavenworth's mayor, D. R. Anthony, were his severest critics. Smarting from the prolonged weeks of martial law and from the wrong perpetrated against their city, they seized every opportunity to ridicule and denounce Ewing. Editor Wilder continued to voice criticism with the publication of terse comments and questions. He wrote: "There is a remarkable similiarity between general ruin and General Ewing," "The lesson taught by the Lawrence Massacre.—Remove Schofield and Ewing," and asked, "Will President Lincoln think, as he reads the sickening tales of the Lawrence Massacre, that he is in any way responsible? Who appointed Schofield? Who appointed Ewing?"[21]

The *Conservative* took pains to quote newspapers throughout the country regarding the tragedy. Missouri's *St. Joseph Herald* referred to Ewing as "that dull and incompetent man in military cloth."[22] Other papers called for a full explanation from the military officers in charge in Missouri as to just how such a raid was possible.[23] Oskaloosa's *Independent* and the *Kansas City Journal of Commerce* provided Ewing's best defense.[24] The *Independent*, in stating facts on Ewing's behalf, relayed the information that on August 20 he had 2,435 effective officers and men stationed at twenty-seven different camps and posts throughout his entire widely scattered district, extending from Fort Larned and Fort Riley in the west to Lexington, Missouri, in the east, and from Fort Leavenworth in the north to the Trading Post in the south. Thirteen of these posts were in Kansas, and others were just over the Missouri line. Moreover, two companies of the Sixth Kansas had been sent to Brigadier General James G. Blunt and relieved of duty only a few days previously. Summarized the *Independent*: "With such a mere handfull [*sic*] of men as this, scattered over so many hundreds of miles, that man has not lived and never will live who could prevent raids into Kansas under the circumstances[.] Napoleon himself could not have done it."[25]

Schofield and Lincoln also shared the brunt of the incident. Lane and the Kansas Radicals had switched their censure from Ewing to "Skowfield," as Lane preferred to refer to the Missouri commanding general. "Skowfield" was far too moderate to suit Lane's methods. In addition, Schofield recently had issued General Orders No. 86, which the Lane faction criticized severely. This order issued on August 25, 1863, provided that those who voluntarily abandoned the rebel cause and desired to return allegiance to the United States

Lawrence Attacked by Quantrill's Guerrillas

would be allowed to do so. A clause inserted in this directive enabled loyal citizens to bear arms in order to protect themselves. According to the Lane faction, this made it possible for bushwhackers to take the oath and obtain arms.[26] Lincoln, however, reassured Schofield that the massacre was only an example of what B. H. Grierson, John Hunt Morgan, and many others might have done on their raids had they chosen to "incur the personal hatred and possessed the fiendish hearts to do it."[27]

Ewing had been in Leavenworth on business when the Lawrence attack occurred. Consequently, he was not aware of Quantrill's presence in the area until after the damage had been done.[28] Returning to his headquarters, he dispatched the order which he had been considering as a follow-up to General Orders No. 10. This new edict, Orders No. 11, issued on August 25, 1863, was of a different nature, however. It called for the depopulation within fifteen days of the first tier of counties south of the Missouri River, those of Jackson, Cass, Bates, and the portion of Vernon County lying within the District of the Border. Residents living within one mile of the limits of Independence, Hickman Mills, Pleasant Hill, and Harrisonville, and those living in the part of Kaw Township, Jackson County, north of Brush Creek and west of the Big Blue River were exempted from the order. All others were to move from the district.[29]

Schofield was informed of the decree in a dispatch from Ewing issued the day Orders No. 11 was given.[30] Ewing's stated reason for acting on his own initiative was the fear of immediate retaliation upon the Missouri border counties. He had reason for alarm. Jennison was actively recruiting again, and Lane oratorically already was launching the offensive.[31] Ewing saw no censure of himself as valid except the possibility of his being away from the post at the time. Political enemies were "fanning the flames" and wished to sacrifice him as a "burnt-offering," he asserted. At this time he acknowledged a lack of confidence in his own judgment and desired, if Schofield thought it best, for it to be known that he wished a court of inquiry with regard to his actions.[32]

The threat of retaliation was only one of the reasons Ewing took such measures. Although not discussed in his letter to Schofield, he believed the order was a military necessity for suppressing bushwhacking.[33] Also, it was necessary to calm and reassure the people of Kansas. Another reason was of a more personal nature. The severe criticism by virtually the whole Kansas press made it necessary for him to issue such an order to counter the attacks by the news media and his political enemies.[34] Finally, he hoped to retain the political confidence of Lane. The two had met the night after the massacre,

General James H. Lane and Indian Scouts

and Lane's pressure was believed to have been a factor in the decision to issue the order.[35]

Parallel lines of thought existed, for the general pattern of Ewing's order was the same as that which Schofield had contemplated. In a letter dated the same as Ewing's directive to him, Schofield enclosed a draft of an order which he proposed to issue in due time. He asked Ewing to take the necessary precautions and concluded with a warning that, because of the possibility of retaliation, the people from the districts involved should be removed to safety before the execution of the order. His plan, unlike Ewing's, called for total devastation of the area involved.[36]

Apprehension was now mounting in the second tier of Missouri counties, where it was believed the depopulation measure might be extended. Schofield advised Ewing that "they seem to fear as much from the Kansas troops [militia] as from Lane's lawless rabble."[37] The Eleventh Kansas played a major role in assisting enforcement of the depopulation. Schofield believed it prudent at this time to transfer the counties of Lafayette, Johnson, Henry, and St. Clair to the command of General Egbert B. Brown's District of Central Missouri. Ewing was asked to make arrangements for this change as soon as possible, and also to transfer his Missouri Militia troops to Brown's district.[38]

The removal of the citizens from the border counties prompted many individuals to make their views known, either personally or by correspondence, to Ewing, Schofield, and Lincoln. A very direct approach was taken by the artist George Caleb Bingham, serving at this time as Missouri's state treasurer. Bingham was profoundly shocked by the severity of the order and determined to ask that it be recalled.[39] In this effort he was not at all successful and was so incensed by his audience with Ewing, and by what he had observed on a tour of the affected area, that he threatened to paint Ewing as infamously in history as this order had made him appear in Bingham's eyes. On his tour, he had ridden unarmed and unguarded through the depopulated area in order to see with his own eyes the tragedy which he had informed Ewing would occur as a result of the order.[40] Returning to Jefferson City, Bingham reported his observations to Governor Gamble. The scene Bingham presented was one in which men were shot down in the very act of obeying an order; one in which their wagons and effects were seized by their murderers; and one in which long trains of wagons loaded with spoils were heading toward Kansas. Bingham had been present when several hundred Union supporters went to the military post at Harrisonville and asked for arms to defend themselves, only to be refused.[41]

When Schofield visited the area, he rescinded the portion of Orders No. 11 calling for the destruction of property, noting however, that much of this had already been done.[42] In an article published years later in the *St. Louis Republican*, Schofield asserted in defense of his action that there had existed only two ways in which to remedy the situation on the border during the time of his command—either by a large increase of military personnel, which was not possible, or by depopulation, which was. The execution of this order was carried out, according to Schofield, without the loss of a single life or any great discomfort to the participants.[43]

Two accounts varying as widely as those of Bingham and Schofield reflect the opposing viewpoints of the general public. Most histories, referring to the exodus, state a total of 20,000 residents were driven [from] or forced to evacuate their homes. Some of the people involved left vivid accounts of their experiences.

After the issuance of Orders No. 11, Richard C. Vaughn, prompted by what he had seen of the condition of the western counties of Missouri, obtained an audience with Schofield. Feeling little reassurance after this visitation, he wrote on August 28, 1863, to Edward Bates, attorney general of the United States:

Major General John M. Schofield

I cannot see the propriety of adopting a policy which is to involve the innocent and the guilty in common ruin. . . . It is a fact well known to me that hundreds of the people of Jackson and Cass Counties are true and loyal men; they have already been robbed of their property, insulted, and in many instances murdered by these troops from Kansas. . . . The great mistake was annexing a part of our State to the Military District of Kansas, and the next great error was in placing a Kansas politician in command of it.[44]

Vaughn included in his letter a "memorial" to be given to the president in which he asked for "Your Excellency's interposition in behalf of a suffering people."[45]

Martin Rice, Jackson County farmer and dairyman, was one of the "true and loyal men." For several weeks during the summer of 1863, he had heard rumors in the county that a depopulation order was being considered. Rice and his neighbors took little notice of the tales told them by Union scouting parties, but Union men who had taken refuge in Kansas City and Independence notified their friends in the county to be ready for such an order. On August 15, residents of Van Buren Township met to discuss the rumors; those attending decided to send resolutions to Ewing, using Rice as their emissary. Since Ewing was in Leavenworth, Rice talked with Major Preston B. Plumb and ultimately believed that his mission was a failure. Determined to prepare for the worst, he purchased material for making a wagon bed. When he arrived at his home, his family informed him that around three hundred bushwhackers had eaten supper the night before at the home of his neighbor, Benjamin Potter. Rice's own family had been "asked" for a half-bushel of bread to feed the men, and several of their neighbors had received similar requests.[46]

Making preparations to leave, Rice was not aware of Orders No. 11 until he saw it in the *St. Louis Missouri Republican* on August 30. It was senseless to appeal to neighbors for aid for they were all in the same predicament. On August 31 he and others went to Pleasant Hill to prove their loyalty and to obtain certificates or permits to remove to the military post or to other parts of the district. After waiting all day for John Ballinger of the First Regiment of the State Militia in order to receive instructions upon how to secure certification, Rice determined to run the risk of getting a permit later.

During the next few days, Rice and his neighbors hauled their possessions into Lafayette County. He had intended to rent a house in Pleasant Hill but changed his mind when his brother told him that this location would not be safe from bushwhackers. After Rice received his certificate of loyalty on September 5, he decided to move his family over the line into Johnson County near Basin Knob, only five or six miles from his home. He had one wagon and one yoke of oxen with which to move the bedding and clothing of his family and that of his son-in-law, William C. Tate. As they were leaving on September 6, a squad of the Kansas Ninth Regiment arrested him, his son Isaac, and his son-in-law. His neighbor David Hunter, Hunter's grandson Andrew Ousley, John S. Cave, William Hunter, and Benjamin Potter were also arrested.[47] Rice was the only one of the party with a certificate. After a short period, Captain Charles F. Coleman, the arresting officer, returned to him and told him to take his son and "travel." Rice left immediately and had gone only a short distance when he heard shots. He returned and found his six neighbors dead. The reason for this murderous act, Rice believed, was that Quantrill and his men had eaten supper at the Potter farm.

In addition to deceased friends, Rice left behind on his farm cattle, sheep, hogs, growing corn, corn in the crib, wheat in the granary, and orchards of peaches and apples. His original plan had changed, and he now proposed to move either to Ray or Clay counties across the river. In their exodus, his family saw long, moving trains of exiles, vehicles of every description drawn by teams of every variety except "good ones." They crossed the ferry at Lexington where "a substantial steamer" was exceptionally busy and making quite a profit.

It was difficult for the fugitives to get permission to stop in places of their own choosing. Since loyal citizens were permitted to go into Kansas and to the military post, none of the residents in the areas through which they were traveling were anxious to have "disloyal" people. Those with certificates, however, or those who could establish a "good reputation" were granted permits to stop. Some took chances and stopped without permission. Of Rice's original party, some stayed in the eastern part of Lafayette County; one family went to Indiana, and another to Wisconsin.

Notices and proclamations were posted by the roadsides north of the Missouri telling the travelers that they could not stop without permission of the military authorities of the county and counties farther north. On September 8, Rice joined the company of Cass Countians William C. Estes, Moses Bailey, and E. N. Rice, who obtained permits in Richmond to stop anywhere in Ray or Clay counties. Shelter was obtained from Reuben Holman, and although three families lived in a two-room house, they were quite grateful.

Rice, accompanied by his son and daughter, returned once to their home during November to collect the cattle and hogs which had proven too unruly to drive earlier. During this visit, they observed guerrillas in groups of twos and threes and Federals in larger groups, none of whom bothered them. The dogs, Rice noted, had become like wolves, preying on untended livestock.

Rice returned to his home with his family in April 1864. The month before, General Egbert Brown of the District of Central Missouri had issued a general order allowing those who made proof of loyalty to obtain permits for returning to their homes. Ironically, this order also was "Orders Number Eleven." Many did not immediately return for they believed that it would be unsafe. Rice noticed that enough corn and wheat remained to live on until a crop could be planted, a few hogs were left, and his farm had been little damaged. He attributed his good fortune to the fact that he lived in the eastern portion of the county. Most of his neighbors returned, but not until after the war.

George Miller, a Presbyterian minister in Kansas City, was another of those who went to plead with Ewing against the order.[48] The area, he argued, was not that important to Quantrill. Furthermore, there were no able-bodied men in the area, no crops to speak of raised in two years, and not one family in five with any means of transportation. He believed that the people would suffer undue hardship by relocating during the winter weather. The minister repeated the personal account of an elder in the Presbyterian church, Henry Cordell of Pleasant Hill, who was compelled to take his family on foot to Jefferson City. Their clothing was hauled by two yearling calves yoked to an old railroad cart. This gentleman, Miller emphasized, was a "highly cultured gentleman," and his wife was a "lovely Christian lady."[49] He related another incident about an old man, John Poyntz, who had been confined in a military prison for his sympathetic expressions on behalf of Southern friends.[50] He

was released into the custody of Miller, who kept him in his home until Poyntz was finally banished from Missouri. Miller believed that he had stirred Ewing with these comments but concluded that the general was too weak to withstand the local pressure.

Among the accounts of hardships suffered during the removal was that of the Twyman family. Mrs. Frances Fristoe Twyman, of Independence, was forced to travel the crowded roads with her aged mother, her doctor husband, and six children.[51] For conveyance they had one two-horse wagon and a buggy. The Twymans stayed for a time with friends in Howard County and then moved on to Missouri City north of the river. Mrs. Twyman was very pro-Southern in her sympathies, and it was humiliating to her to have people along the way cry out, "There come the refugees, take in your clothes," as they saw "the motley crowd" approaching. The Twyman family traveled through inclement weather and found it difficult to obtain shelter for the night. It was not possible to rent a room or even an outhouse. One night in desperation, the Twymans attempted to spend the night in a schoolhouse, but the neighboring farmer, a trustee of the school, refused to give them permission. After Mrs. Twyman's pleading, the farmer relented and invited her family into his home.

Mrs. Twyman indicated that she was arrested several times and nearly shot twice. Her mother owned slaves, and for this and being accused of sending "a ham of meat" to Quantrill's camp, the mother's home had been burned. Mrs. Twyman's only daughter became ill during the family exodus and died. The mother's accounts were related in a passionately bitter tone.

Some of the refugees buried their valuables before they left home. Amanda Fields returned to the family home in Jackson County, after a temporary stay in Cooper County, to find her family home, barn, and all of the outbuildings and the rail fence burned. Some of the fruit trees had even been cut down. The family valuables which they had hidden before leaving, however, were still safe.[52]

During this same period, young William H. Wallace was often chosen to run errands for his neighbors who were reluctant to venture into town for fear of arrest or detention.[53] He remembered two "fine Union men," Jack Winn and Jeremiah Massie, who were constantly pleading with the Federal soldiers for the Southern people in his section in Jackson County. William frequently was sent to spend the night with women in the area whose husbands were called away. He recalled that on one trip with a lady to visit her husband in southwest Missouri, they found their way by following the solitary chimneys of burned homes. These "Jennison's monuments" were landmarks for many years. Serving as an errand boy, William frequently found himself in both camps, feeding the horses of the Union soldiers in the morning at his home and the mounts of the guerrillas in the afternoon.

The Wallace family assisted as many neighbors as possible to reach Independence. The Wallaces had an old surrey, a "rockaway," four yoke of oxen, and two horses, each of which could draw sizeable loads. The buggy harness had been stolen, and their old sorrel was harnessed with a plow blind-bridle, a work backband, big wide breeching (commonly used on the wheelers in a six-horse team), and ordinary iron trace-chains. As they made their own plans to leave, they filled their wagons with household goods, mainly furniture and bedding. The route they chose led through Lafayette County. The Wallaces crossed the river at Lexington and proceeded to Columbia where friends and relatives of Mrs. Wallace received them affectionately. Later, William's father was granted a professorship at Westminster College, Fulton, and they lived on a farm near the town. It was often below zero that winter, and William had no overcoat and nothing to wear but a fall suit and a cotton shirt given to him in Columbia. The Baptist church in St. Louis, hearing of the family's condition, sent a box of second-hand clothing. This was refused and returned by his mother, who felt that the family had some pride left. Food, William recalled, was about as scarce that winter as the clothing. When his family returned to their home after the war, practically nothing remained but the house.

When the family of Clark Wix returned from Jefferson County, Kansas, to their home in Deepwater Township in Bates County in April 1866, they found their old home and the well intact.[54] Another Bates County resident, Theodrick C. Boulware, was the leader of the medical profession in his county. He moved to Butler in 1869 and noticed on his trips through the country that one could ride for a distance of ten miles on the prairie without seeing a single house, for they had all been burned.[55] Wilbur J. Park was a Bates County man of pronounced Union sympathies and could not abide the proslavery views and actions of his neighbors, so he moved to Linn County, Kansas. He was a very outspoken man and lost much property, but returned in the fall of 1865 and proceeded to repair the damages that his farm had suffered.[56] Located in the same county, the Lewis C. Eichler family, Southern in sympathy, left for Lafayette County. They lost all of their possessions, and even their fruit trees were destroyed.[57] John Robert Walters, who had served in the Union army during the war, returned to his home in Bates County to find the Walterses' home destroyed.[58] J. B. Newberry of Bates County later recalled that at the time his county was virtually barren of residents, with not a single family left. Most had moved away, leaving behind valuable property which was either stolen or destroyed. Newberry cited the 1,200 votes cast in Bates County in the 1860 general election as proof of the population before the war.[59] The devastation in the border counties seemed to increase in proportion to the distance south of Kansas City and the proximity to the Kansas border. Bates County was the only county for which total depopulation was ordered, since it contained no military posts.[60]

As a result of Ewing's order, Bates County became a tenantless wilderness. Fires raged unchecked through the prairie, woods, and overgrown fields. The territory became the haunt of wolves, dogs, and an occasional outlaw seeking refuge.[61] The history of the county until the close of the war remains a blank. Germantown, just over the Henry County line, had been made temporary headquarters for the county records; there were a few of the Bates County officials and citizens who attempted to keep up some semblance of government in the adjoining county. By the fall of 1864, a few Bates County residents under the protection of troops stationed at Germantown, returned to their county and met at Johnstown. There they went through the form of electing county officials. The county court tried to preserve its organization but could transact no business. There were no court sessions, no real estate transfers, no records, no taxes assessed or collected. As far as records or legal proceedings were concerned, Bates County had ceased to exist from September 1863 to the close of the war. At the war's end, three badly dilapidated schoolhouses and some homes were left standing along the eastern border—these and occasional "Jennison's monuments" were the only signs of past habitation in a large portion of the county.[62]

Cass County was almost completely depopulated. Only some six hundred inhabitants were allowed to remain, and they were crowded into military stations at Harrisonville and Pleasant Hill; the 1860 United States census had tallied 9,794 residents, including three free Negroes and 1,010 slaves.[63]

The year 1863 was the most chaotic in Vernon County's war history. The record of that year was one of murders, robberies, arson, and outrages of every kind. There was no peace, no security for life and property, and no immunity except under the protection of the military. The few families who tried living on their farms suffered greatly from both bands of outlaws. Many citizens had left earlier in the war when General Sterling Price was pushing southward. By 1863 the county population had already been greatly depleted.[64] Only the northern part of the county was included in the District of the Border.

Jackson County, largest in population, was most severely affected by Orders No. 11. Although the devastation was probably greater in proportion in the counties south of Jackson, much of it was occasioned by the general destruction created in those heavily concentrated pro-Southern counties by the forays of Kansans and by the guerrillas in the earlier days of the war. The greatest exodus, however, was made by the residents of Jackson County.

On August 26, 1863, the *Kansas City Journal of Commerce* informed its readers that the order could not work much hardship on "truly loyal men" for there were few such outside the towns in the counties of the border, and those who were loyal were at the mercy constantly of predators in the area. At worst, the *Journal* indicated, it would not make things any worse than they were at present or had been for the past two years. The editor concluded his defense of the order with the following comment, "It cannot permanently injure these counties for with the return of peace they will be resettled by an intelligent and loyal people." Five months after the order was issued, Colonel Theodore S. Case, chief quartermaster of the border under Ewing—now in his new position as postmaster of Kansas City, wrote a letter to the *St. Louis Missouri Democrat* referring to Orders No. 11 as the only plan which had succeeded in giving any semblance of peace to the area. The bushwhackers and Red Legs were gone from the border; stagecoaches, solitary footmen, and horsemen could travel unmolested from Kansas City to Lexington, Warrensburg, Harrisonville, or Fort Scott.[65]

The guerrillas, who had been the major reason for the order, seemed least affected by it. They were at least as strong in 1864 as they were in 1863. The order did, however, change their center of operation. Afterward, the Baxter Springs encounter and the Centralia massacre indicated that they had changed their theater of action. A semblance of peace was brought to the unoccupied area.[66] Nevertheless, many decades passed before the evidences of devastation disappeared, particularly in Cass and Bates counties, which were called the "Burnt District."

After the war, the Kansas City editor's prediction about resettlement proved correct. People began to return to Bates County in 1866, and the civil authorities began to assume control. They had no courthouse, no office buildings, and no money. Of the towns flourishing before the war, only Butler, the county seat, regained its prestige. Much of the land, never reclaimed by the original owners, was returned to the government and sold for taxes. Some claims were filed by loyal Unionists within the area, but few of these were ever settled.[67] By 1869 the county had almost fully recovered from the effects of the war. A Bates County historian said in retrospect: "It used to be popular to refer to this only as 'Ewing's infamous order.' History has approved it as wise and proper and salutary as a war measure. The necessity was urgent and the results beneficient [*sic*]."[68]

In February of 1864, the District of the Border was abolished.[69] Although Lincoln had not interfered with the depopulation order, having left it to the discretion of Schofield, he had determined to divide the old Department of Missouri into three departments and to assign each a commander suited to its peculiarities.[70]

Schofield had perhaps even outdistanced Ewing in bearing the censure for Orders No. 11. A Radical delegation had appeared in Washington the last of September seeking an audience with the president with the primary purpose of removing Schofield from command.[71] Over one hundred citizens from Kansas and Missouri, headed by Lane, presented their petition to the president. Lincoln listened patiently to their demands, but ended by backing his general and telling the delegation that he was unconvinced that their demand was valid. Schofield himself appeared in Washington and was personally vindicated by his commander in chief. No general, Lincoln assured him, could have satisfied the Union people of both Kansas and Missouri. For in Missouri, the conservative faction was friendly to Schofield and supported the president; the radicals opposed them both; in Kansas, the Lane and Carney factions, both radicals, supported the president but were hostile to Schofield; and this latter group was further divided in that Lane supported the president but was hostile to Schofield, while Carney was sympathetic toward Schofield but opposed to Lincoln.[72]

The opportunity for transfer, which had been much on the mind of Schofield, presented itself while he was visiting in Washington. Grant had indicated to the president his preference for either General James McPherson or Schofield to take command of the Department of the Army of Ohio. Grant, meanwhile, had been elevated to command of all the armies, and McPherson stepped into the harness of the Army of the Tennessee. The way was open for Schofield to accept the command offered, and he returned to St. Louis to relinquish his own post to General William Rosecrans.[73]

With the abolishment of the District of the Border and the attachment of the Kansas City Military Department to the Federal headquarters at Leavenworth, Ewing was transferred to St. Louis in March 1864. He remained in his command there only a few months and was then placed in command of the District of Rolla, returning again to the command of the District of St. Louis in December 1864; he served there until April 1865.[74] Ewing's Missouri ties were to prove far stronger than Schofield's, primarily because of the dedication of George Caleb Bingham to immortalize Ewing's "infamous" Orders No. 11. As a result of Bingham's hatred of Ewing and his policy, he painted Ewing into a strategic position in his artistic conception of *Order No. 11*. With this painting, Bingham toured Missouri. Two identical pictures of the order had been painted. One Bingham used on his tours, and the other was sent for engraving in order that low-priced prints might be reproduced.[75] This crusade of personal hatred of Ewing and of his policy was carried on by Bingham for sixteen years and, upon his death, was continued by his family. Bingham had been enraged that under Ewing's order no aid or protection was given the banished inhabitants. The citizens of the affected area, disarmed by federal edict, were placed in an indefensible position, Bingham believed. Moreover, his own personal observations of the area did not conform to those of Ewing and Schofield. Bingham had a crusade, and he proved an apt crusader. His two paintings of *Order No. 11* had personified this edict as he claimed to have seen it personally administered. Until his death in 1879, Bingham took every opportunity to unveil the role he felt Ewing had played in the issuance of Orders No. 11.

Ewing practiced law for a time in Washington, DC, after the war and then returned to his home state, Ohio, to pursue a political career. In 1880 he was the Democratic candidate for governor of his state. The opposition, with the help of Bingham's son Rollins, used an unpublished attack of Bingham's against Ewing emphasizing some particulars which were new to the argument. The pamphlets were entitled "The Voice from the Tomb," and whether or not they were the decisive factor, Ewing lost the election to Charles Foster by only 17,129 votes. A switch of 1.5 percent of the votes cast would have given

George Caleb Bingham [Missouri Valley Special Collections, Kansas City (MO) Public Library]

Ewing his victory.[76] After this defeat, Ewing departed from the political scene. Ewing's papers were released by his son over a period of years between 1909 and 1939. With the exception of a few telegrams, there is little else in the collection to shed any light upon Ewing's years as commander of the District of the Border.[77]

The Confederacy had justified accepting the aid of the guerrillas in their desperation to win the war. The same justification had been given Ewing in resorting to Orders No. 11. Much criticism was leveled at him, however, in the manner in which he carried out the order. His use of Kansas troops in depopulating the area caused great concern. Halleck had been of the opinion that all Missouri and Kansas troops should have been removed from the border and troops from other states put in their places.[78] Schofield had issued an order forbidding militia troops of both states not in the service of the United States from passing from one state into the other without orders from their district commander.[79] However, not only did Ewing use Kansas troops in enforcing the edict, but he also gave permission for certain Kansas units to cross into Missouri at the discretion of their commanders.[80] The actions of the Missouri officers and men, though not publicly lauded as those of Kansas, were at times just as outrageous.[81]

Richard C. Vaughn in his directive to Schofield seemed to hit the heart of the dilemma when he said that "the great mistake was annexing a part of our

State to the Military District of Kansas, and the next great error was in placing a Kansas politician in command of it."[82]

George Caleb Bingham believed that he had presented the facts of history on his canvas, "They teach a lesson which previous history had taught our fathers, but which our children of future generations should understand—that the tendencies of military power are anti-republican and despotic and that to preserve liberty and secure its blessings the supremacy of civil authority should be carefully maintained."[83]

In Eugene Morrow Violette's 1918 *History of Missouri* it is stated, "No greater act of imbecility was committed in Missouri during the whole Civil War."[84] The application of such measures, however, had been considered almost simultaneously by Schofield and Ewing. The issuance of the order was not a hasty repressive move but one that had already been under consideration by both commanders. It is difficult to escape the conclusion, however, that Ewing was unwise in his methods of carrying out the order. Pressure from Kansas political figures, especially Lane, undoubtedly led to his unwise decision to use Kansas troops. The results of this decision made a difficult situation a cauldron of confusion and earned for Ewing the undying hatred of many of Missouri's citizens.

NOTES

1. John Schofield, *Forty-six Years in the Army* (New York: Century Co., 1897), 95. An article concerning this same topic is Charles R. Mink, "General Orders, No. 11: The Forced Evacuation of Civilians During the Civil War," *Military Affairs* 34 (December 1970): 132-136.

2. Schofield, *Forty-six Years*, 87.

3. Ibid.

4. Edwin C. McReynolds, *Missouri, A History of the Crossroads State* (Norman: University of Oklahoma Press, 1962), 246.

5. *History of Vernon County, Missouri* (St. Louis: Brown, 1887), 269.

6. W. H. Woodson, *History of Clay County, Missouri* (Topeka: Historical Publishing Co., 1920), 319.

7. S. L. Tathwell and H. O. Maxey, comps., *The Old Settlers' History of Bates County, Missouri* (Amsterdam, MO: Tathwell & Maxey, 1897), 38.

8. *History of Clay and Platte Counties, Missouri* (St. Louis: National Historical

Co., 1885), 709.

9. May Simonds, "Missouri History as Illustrated by George C. Bingham," *Missouri Historical Review* 1 (April 1907): 183. Compare reception of speech by the *Leavenworth (KS) Daily Conservative*, the *Olathe (KS) Mirror*, and the *Leavenworth (KS) Daily Times* quoted in the *Kansas City Journal of Commerce*, 4 July 1863.

10. From a review of Ewing's Olathe speech in the *Leavenworth (KS) Daily Conservative*, 23, 26 August 1863.

11. Albert Castel, *A Frontier State at War: Kansas 1861-1865* (Ithaca, NY: Cornell University Press, 1958), 137. Compare *Kansas City Journal of Commerce*, 25 July 1863: "An honest man engaged in some honest business could do well in Fort Scott for he'd have no competition."

12. *Kansas City Journal of Commerce*, 20, 25 July 1863.

13. *History of Clay and Platte Counties*, 709.

14. Eugene Morrow Violette, *The History of Missouri* (Boston: Heath, 1918), 381.

15. *The War of the Rebellion: A Compilation of the Official Records of the Union and Confederate Armies* (Washington, DC: Government Printing Office, 1880-1901), ser. 1, vol. 22, pt. 2: 460-461 (hereinafter cited as *OR*; all references are to series 1). See also *Kansas City Journal of Commerce*, 13 August 1863; compare reception of the order in Kansas in the *Oskaloosa (KS) Independent*, 22 August 1863.

16. Castel, *Frontier State*, 122.

17. Ibid., 123.

18. *OR*, vol. 22, pt. 2: 503-505; compare the *Leavenworth (KS) Daily Times*, 22 August 1863.

19. Ibid. For imprisonment of guerrilla family members, see Richard S. Brownlee, *Gray Ghosts of the Confederacy: Guerrilla Warfare in the West, 1861-1865* (Baton Rouge: Louisiana State University Press, 1958), 118-119.

20. *Leavenworth (KS) Daily Conservative*, 22 August 1863. See also quotations of national reaction in ibid., 30 August 1863.

21. Ibid., 23 August 1863.

22. As quoted in ibid., 27 August 1863.

23. National press coverage as quoted in the *Leavenworth (KS) Daily Conservative*, 30 August 1863.

24. *Kansas City Journal of Commerce*, 26 August 1863; see also *Oskaloosa (KS) Independent*, 5 September 1863.

25. *Oskaloosa (KS) Independent*, 5 September 1863.

26. *OR*, vol. 22, pt. 2: 474. For reference to "Skowfield," see Jay Monaghan, *Civil War on the Western Border, 1854-1865* (Boston: Little, Brown, 1955), 289; editorial

on Schofield's order in *Leavenworth (KS) Daily Conservative*, 30 August 1863.

27. Schofield, *Forty-six Years*, 97.

28. *Leavenworth (KS) Daily Times*, 22 August 1863. See also *OR*, vol. 22, pt. 2: 472.

29. *OR*, vol. 22, pt. 2: 473.

30. Ibid.

31. *Oskaloosa (KS) Independent*, 5 September 1863. For Lane's speech, see also *Leavenworth (KS) Daily Conservative*, 28 August 1863.

32. *OR*, vol. 22, pt. 2: 472.

33. Ibid.

34. Castel, *Frontier State*, 143.

35. Ibid., 144; *Leavenworth (KS) Daily Conservative*, 1 September 1863.

36. *OR*, vol. 22, pt. 2: 471.

37. Ibid., 531.

38. Ibid.; *Leavenworth (KS) Daily Times*, 28 August 1863.

39. Lew Larkin, *Bingham, Fighting Artist: The Story of Missouri's Immortal Painter, Patriot, Soldier, and Statesman* (Kansas City: Burton, 1954), 194.

40. Ibid., 221.

41. Ibid., 222.

42. *OR*, vol. 22, pt. 2: 84.

43. Howard L. Conard, ed., *Encyclopedia of the History of Missouri* (New York: Southern History Co., 1901), 5: 19.

44. *OR*, vol. 22, pt. 2: 484-485.

45. Ibid., 485-486.

46. Martin Rice, *Rural Rhymes, and Talks and Tales of Olden Times*, 3rd ed. (Kansas City: Hudson-Kimberly, 1893), 105-119. The account of Martin Rice is pursued fully here because of its thoroughness of coverage and because it (with exception of the murders) was representative of many read by the author.

47. *Kansas City Star*, 6 March 1939. In this issue of the *Star* appeared the obituary of Cave's daughter, Mrs. Matilda Reid. The manner of his death was reiterated. Of interest was the mention that a concrete wall was built around the grave of the men killed, a monument erected, and the burial site deeded to the relatives of the deceased.

48. George Miller, *Missouri's Memorable Decade, 1860-1870* (Columbia, MO: E. W. Stephens, 1898), 100-107.

49. Ibid.

50. Photocopies of Order No. 11 [technically General Orders No. 11] by General Thomas Ewing, 25 August 1863, from National Archives and Records Administration, and transcription. Also is a photocopy of Special Orders No. 64, issued to A. O. Runyan and family of Independence, MO, announcing on 29 August 1863 their ordered removal from Jackson County, Document L44F23, Jackson County Historical Society, Independence.

51. United Daughters of the Confederacy, Missouri Division, comp., *Reminiscences of the Women of Missouri During the Sixties* (Jefferson City, MO: Hugh Stephens Printing Co., n.d.), 263-266.

52. "Story Hour Manuscripts, or, True Stories of Jackson County," Independence, Missouri, Young Matrons Records, 1964, including: "Uprooting of Families of Order No. 11," by Mary Mildred Zick DeWitt, and "Order No. 11: Missouri's Guerrillas," by Mary Fitzgerald Green, Documents 66F39 and 66F40, Jackson County Historical Society.

53. William H. Wallace, *Speeches and Writings of Wm. H. Wallace: With Autobiography* (Kansas City: Western Baptist Publishing Co., 1914), 251-258.

54. W. O. Atkeson, ed., *History of Bates County, Missouri* (Topeka, KS: Historical Publishing Co., 1918), 329.

55. Ibid., 334.

56. Ibid., 353.

57. Ibid., 365.

58. Ibid., 340.

59. Ibid., 318.

60. Ibid., 42.

61. Ibid., 43.

62. Ibid., 45.

63. Missouri Historical Records Survey, Work Projects Administration, comp., *Inventory of the County Archives, No. 19, Cass County, Missouri* (St. Louis: Missouri Historical Records Survey, 1941), 23.

64. *History of Vernon County*, 291.

65. *The History of Jackson County, Missouri* (Cape Girardeau, MO: Ramfre Press, 1966), 290.

66. Darrell Garwood, *Crossroads of America: The Story of Kansas City* (New York: Norton, 1948), 60.

67. Ibid. See also Daniel A. DeWitt, "List of losses to Federal troops, 1861-1863, or, Damage Claim to Federal Government," Document 69F5, Jackson County Historical Society. Damages were not paid.

68. Atkeson, *History of Bates County*, 136.

69. *History of Jackson County*, 475.

70. Schofield, *Forty-six Years*, 109.

71. Ibid., 91.

72. Ibid., 108.

73. Ibid., 109.

74. Frederick H. Dyer, comp., *A Compendium of the War of the Rebellion* (New York: T. Yoseloff, 1959), 1: 547.

75. Larkin, *Bingham, Fighting Artist*, 296.

76. Ibid., 333.

77. Microfilm copies of the Thomas Ewing, Jr., Papers are in the Kansas State Historical Society, Topeka.

78. *OR*, vol. 22, pt. 2: 521.

79. Ibid., 511.

80. Ibid., 514.

81. Ibid., 542. This page contains a dispatch from Colonel J. B. Rogers to General Clinton B. Fisk reporting "outrageous excesses" (murder and stealing) of the 6th Missouri Cavalry near Sikeston, Missouri. See also page 591. A dispatch is found here from General Brown to General Schofield indicating the robbing of citizens near Lexington by troops under Federal officers Colonel William Weer and Major Preston B. Plumb.

82. Ibid., 485.

83. Larkin, *Bingham, Fighting Artist*, 242.

84. Violette, *History of Missouri*, 384.

Beginning of the Park and Boulevard Movement in Frontier Kansas City, 1872-1882

WILLIAM H. WILSON

In April 1876 an editorial writer for the *Kansas City Times* reminded his readers that a citizen of New York City recently had chosen Central Park as the place to commit suicide. "A park is no place for that kind of foolishness," he warned. "Don't let the custom come in vogue in Kansas City."[1]

The editorial writer need not have worried about Kansas City's residents committing acts of self-destruction in public parks, for Kansas City in 1876 had no public parks. It was also innocent of many other improvements. Although for nine years the city had enjoyed the first railroad bridge across the Missouri River and a consequent commercial and industrial boom, its unpaved streets were alternately gritty dust or gluey mud. Municipal action was slow to improve sewers, drain ponds, and show genuine concern for matters of public health. Improvements were primitive. Careful construction was the virtue of a few major business buildings and opulent homes of the rich, while humbler callings and citizens were housed in a collection of frame structures scattered over the city's rough topography without order or beauty.

A visitor to Kansas City in the 1870s would see little indication of public concern with parks as beauty spots and recreational areas. Yet there were many editorials in Kansas City newspapers directed to the practical problem of obtaining city parks and not, like the example cited above, to moralizing over how people should behave in nonexistent ones. Those editorials formed part of a growing effort, begun in 1872, to secure municipal parks and, later, a park and boulevard system. They appeared in the three largest Kansas City newspapers of the decade to 1882, the *Times*, the *Journal*, and, from

its founding on September 18, 1880, the *Star*. The *Times* and *Journal* were morning papers and political rivals; the *Times* was Democratic and the *Journal* Republican. The *Star*, an evening sheet, called itself independent.[2] Besides the editorials, the newspapers recorded various attempts to secure parks and boulevards during the decade, another indication that Kansas City was at least partly alive to the recreational and aesthetic needs of its citizens.

The first attempt to provide Kansas City with a public park in 1872 is significant because historians who have traced the origins of the beautification movement in Kansas City uniformly have dated the beginnings of this movement nine years later, with the publication in the *Kansas City Star* of an editorial advocating parks. The tacit assumption that the *Star* and its great editor, William Rockhill Nelson, evoked interest in parks and boulevards in 1881 has obscured at least six separate efforts to beautify Kansas City prior to that time. It also has hidden those many editorials in other newspapers which together developed a rationale for city beautification, a rationale well advanced before the *Star* was founded. This editorial drive for parks and boulevards is especially noteworthy because it presented developed thinking about a beautiful city in the midst of a rough frontier river town whose corporate age was less than thirty years. Examination of these early ideas and efforts will provide a setting for judging the importance of William Rockhill Nelson's first editorial demand for a park.[3]

Writers trying to generate interest in something more than perfecting municipal services realized how little aesthetic considerations affected postbellum, business-oriented citizens with their eyes on a goal of riches and hands grasping for the main chance to attain it. Not that pure beauty was ignored. On the contrary, the relatively unrestrained writers of that era waxed purple and prolix as they gushed forth descriptions of the lush loveliness of parks, but they were careful to include a few direct and unadorned references to a park's supposed economic utility as well. Parks are beautiful, yes, but they are also a refuge for the laboring poor, who become more productive workers through their contacts in parks with healthful, renewing nature. Parks also "pay" because their salubrity decreases doctor bills and morticians' fees and because their existence raises the value of adjacent land. Parks draw people who decide among urban areas on the basis of pleasant surroundings. There was possibly a contradiction that passed unnoticed between this last argument and the newspapers' supreme confidence in a sharp rise in the population of the city no matter what aesthetic level it might attain. Tens of thousands of people will jam into Kansas City, and they will require parks. Though they may not be needed yet, parks will come more cheaply if provided now while open spaces are available in the city and land values relatively low. Finally, other cities have parks, and boulevards, too; they are the adjuncts to genuine metropolitanism.

Some of this seems a bit forced, yet the partisans of parks often were challenged on economic grounds and had to reply in kind. Their ideas did not develop in a vacuum; they matured over a decade of struggle to make Kansas City beautiful.

The struggle began when James W. Cook, a local landowner, offered to sell forty acres of unimproved land for park purposes at $2,000 per acre in what was then the southwest section of the city. When Cook appeared before the city council in February 1872 to advance his proposition, the *Times* reported that "a lively debate ensued." One councilman "dwelt at some length upon the folly of the measure . . . had something to say about sewers, street improvements, water-works, and other things needed by the city before parks." Another advised his fellows to "retrench expenditures" and spoke against issuing bonds. Although Cook claimed he was making the offer at the request of "many citizens" and that he could receive double the amount he was asking from the city by cutting up his property into town lots, the council rejected his offer, five votes to seven.[4]

For five years the matter rested. Then Cook, who had not cut his pasture up into lots after all, repeated his park offer in June 1877. "I will take 8 [percent] City Bonds, payable in 20 years," ran Cook's written proposal to the council. Regular tax assessments on the increased value of land adjacent to the pasture, he was sure, would easily pay interest on the bonds, "thereby getting the

City a fine native Grove park—with at least 1,000 Beautiful shade Trees to commence with as an orniment [*sic*] to our Growing City."[5]

Six days after Cook's second proposal, the *Times* gave it editorial support. "Parks," said the *Times*, drawing a figure of which it was very fond, "are as indispensable to a large city as lungs to an animal. They are breathing places," it continued, "where the laboring poor can go from their crowded tenement houses to rest and refresh themselves under the shade of trees, and see their too much imprisoned children draw new health and spirits from the flowers, the foliage, and the music of fountains."

If they are denied parks, "the poor fall sick at the public expense, and the mortality, especially among children, soon compels the city to provide parks of easy access to all." Kansas City was urged to buy park land while undeveloped tracts remained cheap and accessible, or it might "become a seminary of pestilence . . . like some of the cities of Asia." Another reason for providing parks immediately, the *Times'* scribe asserted, was because Kansas City some day would be a teeming town. "Kansas City may get on very well without a park for a while," he wrote, but unimproved ground "that can be secured for a few thousand now, will cost as many hundred thousands when the population is doubled."[6]

The *Times'* warning was followed by a letter to the *Journal* in which Cook publicly stated his offer and renewed his threat to sell off the pasture for residential development.[7] "A city without a park is like a body without lungs," the *Journal* said editorially. Though it asserted that parks "are essential to man morally and physically," the newspaper stressed the natural advantages of the site and the wisdom of buying the rolling, forested ground to save future costs of landscaping a less desirable tract.[8]

The council's committee on public buildings and grounds reported in July that Cook had named a sale figure of about $62,000, "for which there is no provision in our Charter authorizing us to lay out for Parks."[9] The council, apparently unimpressed by an $18,000 reduction from the price of four years before, took no action.

Lack of a charter provision did not prevent the *Journal* from commenting on "the liberal terms proposed" and the need for a park to benefit "people of moderate means, who never rest but once a week." The Republican *Journal* professed no concern for "citizens of wealth, who keep their own carriages and can ride out at will" to discover "pure air, fine prospects, and all the variety and beauty that nature and art have given to rural resorts and private estates."[10] Later the same month, the *Journal* warned that "Mr. Cook has made arrangements to survey and lay off his forty acres for sale. This will be done within a week." Quick action to purchase the land was necessary, or it

Kansas City in 1871

would be lost forever. Despite the alarm, the citizenry did not act to buy the land, nor did Cook carry through any plans to develop the tract.[11]

In September the *Times* played upon new themes. It discovered that people are drawn to a city not only by its factories and stores, but also by its parks. "Hundreds of people go to Paris every year mainly for the enjoyment afforded by its parks," the *Times* disclosed. It found that the same reason impelled people to journey to New York, Philadelphia, and St. Louis. There was no suggestion that sophisticated, worldly Paris and the mature cities of its own continent might have other, more compelling attractions for visitors than the rough little river town of Kansas City. The *Times* also dwelt upon the benefits to workmen and their families who flocked to Chicago's Lincoln Park, where healthful and moral influences prevailed, in contrast to the "feverish excitement of the streets, the temptations to drink and riot found at the gin mills, and the hardening influences of the more depraved of their own class." In the midst of this naïveté, one cogent passage stands out. It speaks with the same realization of the need for comprehensive plans that is found some fifteen years later in the report of a trained, experienced landscape architect who surveyed the Kansas City scene. The newspaper said:

Now if we go about it let us have a park in the full sense of the word—one that has something to recommend it besides mere grass and trees. By this it is not meant that the whole work should be begun and the whole expense incurred at once, but the scope and plan of the enterprise should be grasped in its entirety, with an eye to the future, and the business of laying out, advancing, &c., entered upon, so that the foundation of the work may be laid broad and deep, on a scale commensurate with our future needs.[12]

Unfortunately for its reputation, and perhaps for the aesthetic qualities of the city it served, the *Times* chose not to hammer home this theme in subsequent editorials. Yet it is a little surprising to find that the idea of a comprehensive plan combined with prudent building as funds allowed existed at all in the Kansas City of the 1870s. This editorial is a milestone in the development of park and boulevard thinking even though it was written long before the city had a permanent public park.

The idea of a boulevard system designed to link several parks came later. It grew from a plan to broaden and surface two existing roads from Kansas City to the neighboring towns of Independence, Missouri, and Rosedale, Kansas. Although these roads were called boulevards, there is little indication their promotors thought of them primarily as scenic drives; they were more concerned with easing the flow of commercial traffic in the Kansas City area and capitalizing upon the rise in land values along the rights-of-way. Even for some time after the movement began in 1879, the *Times* regarded the noncommercial advantages of boulevards solely as "driving parks" where gentlemen could display their horses and horsemanship. Only later did the concept of boulevards as playgrounds of the rich and the notion of parks as playgrounds of the poor merge into the idea of a park and boulevard system for all to enjoy. Although the *Journal* made brief references to the beauty of the proposed boulevards or the beautiful suburban areas through which they would pass, neither it nor the *Star*, founded during the boulevard movement, pressed for expanding the boulevard idea into a park and boulevard system. That task was left to the *Times*.[13]

Turning again to the French capital for an example, the *Times* remarked that "It has been said of Louis Napoleon that he almost compensated for the evil of his corrupt reign by the splendid boulevard he gave to Paris," and that boulevards "have done more to commend the reign of the Third Napoleon to his people than all his other acts." The French ruler had recognized that "to do business, buy and sell and build houses is not all of the mission of cities."[14] Coupled with this bow to Napoleon's enlightened despotism was the first editorial linking of parks and boulevards. "Parks," the editorial's writer penned with modest anonymity, "have been called the lungs of the city: broad cool inviting streets are then the external organs of respiration, as necessary to the life of the civic body as the lunings [*sic*] themselves." Through the medium of this unsophisticated biological analogy the writer's anthropomorphic city now required, presumably, a nose. What was more important, the link between parks and boulevards had been made in the public prints.[15]

"Kansas City is strong limbed and level headed, and now . . . the imperative want is lungs for our proud young giant metropolis," said Thomas B. Bullene, a wealthy dry goods merchant, as he assumed the presidency of the Rosedale Boulevard Association, the business group formed to build a southwest boulevard. Whether or not Bullene was as concerned with the city's respiration as he was with its commercial growth, the *Times* gleefully announced that "the era of boulevard and park building has been fairly inaugurated." The people, it said, would realize economy in boulevard construction if the work were undertaken immediately. Applying anew an argument already developed in reference to parks, the newspaper declared that:

> Never was a generous public spirit more opportunely awakened among a people, because the want is here, and boulevards, parks and public drives can be created now at a cost our people will not feel, and the

marvelous growth and increase of real estate is such that, if not secured now, it will soon require thousands of dollars where hundreds will effect the same beneficent purposes.

The article introduced the further idea that parks and boulevards are necessary to a metropolitan area:

A boulevard is a good thing for all, it supplies a want felt alike by the poorest and richest—a benefaction that grows with the lapse of time. And when you add to this great and inviting parks—resting, as well as breathing places for tired, cribbed, begrimed mankind—you will have built a city to properly welcome the half million people that are coming to your town.[16]

The private boulevard projects languished for lack of money despite the *Times'* careful, elaborate efforts to convince citizens of their worth.[17] These private efforts might fail, but in June 1877, a few days after Cook's second offer to sell his forty acres and two years before the ill-fated boulevard movement, the first partially successful public move to secure a park was made when the city council adopted a resolution "to have the Old Grave yard graded By the work house force, with a view to a Public Park."[18]

The graveyard was very old by Kansas City's standards. A plat drawn in 1847 showed it as an irregularly shaped block dedicated to burial purposes in the southeastern corner of the original town, but interments had been made even before then. In 1857 the council forbade further burials and ordered existing graves removed. It became evident that all graves had not been exhumed when, in the late 1870s, grading of streets around the square and improving the block itself for park purposes revealed a number of coffins. Some of these were reburied in the park so the city could claim the land ostensibly for a graveyard, a claim the heirs of the original town company opposed in a long court battle the city was to lose, along with the park, some years later.[19] In 1877, however, it enjoyed uncontested possession of the ground and set the workhouse inmates to the task of improving the square. Mayor George Shelley was interested in the project and began in 1878 to raise money for embellishment. "An attractive central park," said the *Times* in support of Shelley's efforts, "would be esteemed a substantial blessing as a place of frequent pleasant resort during the sultry summer season; and Cemetery Park . . . is, by location, the most favorable."[20] By November 1878, Shelley had perfected a fund-raising organization which reached into all wards, and he was planning to visit local artisans to urge them to donate their labor and skills to the community beautification and recreation project.[21] Some aldermen were so impressed with this work they proposed to name the block "Shelley Place," but Shelley himself forestalled a formal resolution to that effect. Not everyone was so smitten by the mayor's civic mindedness. Grumblers pointed out how the proposed park was located in the First Ward and hinted that political considerations, rather than availability of the ground, provided the motive for Shelley's dogged efforts.[22]

In December the *Times* reported that projected improvements included a central fountain, shaded walks, and a bandstand. "The topography and small extent of the ground will not permit of any striking arrangements of landscape," it admitted, but the object was only to provide an attractive area within "easy reach of the busy streets."[23]

The council revealed it was not entirely satisfied with its legal position when, in response to an inquiry from State Senator George F. Ballingal about the city's legislative needs, it requested him to present a bill empowering Kansas City to condemn the block for use as a public park.[24] Legal doubts did not arrest improvement, for in March 1879 the council resolved to purchase a fence for "Cemetery Park."[25] Though there is no record that the most ambitiously planned embellishment, the fountain, ever became reality, the square was improved with grass, trees, walks, and night lighting.[26] These refinements were made with a mixture of private and public funds, but the proportion of each, or whether the improvements were executed badly or well, is difficult to determine after the lapse of almost a century.

Whatever its limitations, the park was near workingmen's neighborhoods, and though it was spare of beauty, it should have encouraged the newspapermen who demanded a beginning. Besides its nearness to workers and their families, it was close to the city hall and only a few blocks from retail districts. The cost of acquisition was nothing, and improvement expenses were low. Its existence demonstrated that the city government was awakening, however slowly, to aesthetic needs.

Yet newspaper comment was unfriendly. The scribes wanted something more extensive. "We have a park of one block," the *Times* sarcastically remarked, "sacredly dedicated to the welfare and happiness of the people. . . . It will afford a recreation for the tired mothers and puny babies. . . . Who would think of saying that this 'oat patch' bears any comparison to what a real genuine park for the city should be? Instead of a patch for a park, a hundred acres should be secured in close proximity to the city without delay."[27]

In July 1880 the *Journal* berated the local aldermen who, it claimed, had failed to provide "lungs for the city," in contrast to municipal officials elsewhere. "In Kansas City people cannot enjoy even the smallest kind of a park" except the "little dornick on the East Side." "Shelley square," the *Journal* asserted, was "without grass, with no shade, no fountain or anything to render it attractive." The only local refuge from the heat the writer could recommend was the fairgrounds, at that time in the southeastern section of the city. The only hope for improvement lay, not with the city council, but with "some rich and philanthropic citizen" who might, "in a fit of frenzy, superinduced by 110 degrees in the shade, dedicate his front yard for park purposes and invite the public in."[28]

The *Journal* could print its whimsical hopes for successful private efforts to obtain a park, but the only concerted private attempt to secure a public park during the period did not gain even the limited and temporary success of the council's action on the old graveyard. This private effort was made by residents of McGee's Addition, a self-conscious residential neighborhood in the south-central section of the city.

Councilmen representing McGee's Addition attempted to discover some municipal claim to a square lying within the addition commonly known as McGee Park, which had stood vacant and was used as a recreational area and also as a circus grounds. A check of deeds revealed the city had no claim to the ground, as the land was reserved in the names of the investors who had platted the addition.[29] Undaunted, the citizens of McGee's Addition held a mass meeting the night of October 10, 1879, about the time the old graveyard to the north of them was being transformed into a park. The citizens determined to

Kansas City's West Terrace Before Improvement

take the only course open to them under the law: to assess property owners near the square for purchase of the land, then deed it to the city as a public park.[30]

Four months later, the city formally declined to take the initiative, when the council's finance committee reported there were no funds in the city treasury to spend on a park.[31] In June 1880 the finance committee again considered an ordinance to establish the area as a public square, and in August it recommended passage of an ordinance to convert the tract to a park, but with an amendment limiting the city's liability to one dollar. This cut the ground from under any dwellers in McGee's Addition who had hoped for substantial aid from the city. The council solemnly passed the ordinance with the crucial amendment.[32] In the face of this piece of metropolitan realpolitik, the drive for a public square in McGee's Addition subsided for a year. The only indication it revived even fitfully is a story in the *Times* reporting, in contradiction to previous accounts, that the tract in controversy had been set aside for public use on the original plat, but that the city had compromised its rights by taxing the land and was therefore beginning a condemnation suit to recover McGee Park. Nothing indicates a suit ever was brought.[33]

The exposition grounds were also the subject of editorial urges to positive park action. Editorials on the exposition grounds are not important for the support they lent to a purchase movement—such a movement did not exist in 1880—but they are noteworthy because of the growing space given to assertions that Kansas City had achieved metropolitanism and the strident insistence that parks and boulevards were the *sine qua non* of metropolitan areas. Drinking deep of its own boosterism, the *Journal* declared in May:

> In the next twenty years Kansas City will have a population of 250,000. . . . It is no longer a badge of dishonor for a man in this community to have his hair cut short, black his boots, and put on a clean collar not less than once a week. These evidences of modern civilization, in fact, have grown by degrees into favor. . . . The town, like a great big, awkward country boy, is loosely put together—yet growing rapidly—literally spreading in all directions. . . . Every city of any size has a public park, to which all classes of citizens go for pleasure and recreation. Before many years this city must have a park of five hundred or a thousand acres. . . . Let the park be on the boulevard that leads to Independence.

If Kansas City's citizens found current legislation for park condemnation inadequate, "we would suggest," continued the *Journal*, "that there will be

West Terrace as Improved in 1910 [Greater Kansas City Chamber of Commerce]

a session of the legislature next winter when an enabling act may be passed without an effort hardly."[34] Six months later, on November 16, 1880, the *Journal* reminded its readers that "Kansas City should begin to look up the legislation needed this winter. We have the street question, the park question, the boulevard question."[35]

These remarks prompted the first comment on parks from the city's new evening paper. "The *Journal* enumerates the street question, the boulevard question, the park question and many other subjects," the *Star* informed its readers that same evening. Possibly because of this reference to the *Journal*, those who gave the *Star* virtually exclusive credit for beginning the park and boulevard movement prefer to place the first park editorial in the following year.[36]

The original biography of the *Star*'s founder, William Rockhill Nelson, was the first book to date the *Star*'s maiden call for a park, and, indiscriminately, the beginning of the park and boulevard movement on May 19, 1881. This volume was written by the *Star* staff during 1915, the year of Nelson's death. Writing in the shadow of the man they so greatly respected, the biographers sought, perhaps unconsciously, to lengthen that shadow with the statement that Nelson "was probably the only man in Kansas City who saw that the bluffs and hills and ravines had elements of real beauty." They also wrote of Nelson that "when The Star was only eight months old, he began the long,

long struggle for public parks, which finally, after many reverses and delays, triumphed splendidly."[37]

The May 19, 1881, *Star* editorial obviously did not begin the "long, long struggle for public parks," but it could have been important in other ways. It could have taken sister newspapers to task for their relatively infrequent mention of park and boulevard matters, because they often let months pass with no attention to the city's aesthetic and recreational needs. It could have shown how invoking the plight of the overworked poor or examples of more progressive cities had failed to stir Kansas Citians to action. Though the *Journal* once remarked that "'don't let up on the Park question' is the frequent injunction of readers and correspondents" and printed a letter commenting favorably on one of its park editorials, the *Times* was more sensible and realistic when it grumbled, "If the citizens were only in earnest about the matter [of a park] and would hold the council up to the mark, it would not be long until such an improvement would be an accomplished fact."[38] The editorial could have urged a park committee for the city council, which had no administrative machinery for park matters and shunted them to the committee on public buildings and grounds, or the finance committee, or to individual councilmen. It could have focused on the one small park Kansas City did have, beginning a campaign for its improvement or for a system of similar small parks. It could have discussed the need for comprehensive park planning or for park amendments to the city charter, subjects which had received almost no attention in the press. It did none of these things.

Instead, that famous editorial began with a canard. Ignoring the converted cemetery, it asserted that "Kansas City has no public parks" and went on to mention the impending loss of the exposition grounds, the necessity for quick action by the city before rising property values placed all possible park sites beyond reach, and the need for special state legislation to simplify problems of park acquisition. There was nothing about a park and boulevard system, nothing about comprehensive planning, no indication of fresh thinking about park and boulevard needs.[39] These objections would be of little importance had the editorial been the first in a series of regular park articles. No newspaper had yet planned a campaign consisting of regularly appearing editorials extending over a long time span. Something like that, coming from the *Star*, might have awakened citizens to Kansas City's needs.

Nelson's biographers suggest that this is exactly what happened. "That was the beginning of a campaign that continued for fifteen years," wrote the *Star* staff, "before Kansas City, with soul uplifted, sat in joy upon its first park bench. The people of Kansas City who read The Star . . . had parks and boulevards for dinner every night."[40] Twenty years later, another biography, by

Icie F. Johnson, told how "the readers of the *Star* . . . had parks and boulevards every night for supper."[41] Writing still later in a general history of Kansas City, two *Star* editors, Henry C. Haskell Jr. and Richard B. Fowler, claimed that the fight for parks and boulevards "began as early as 1881, when the Star pointed out that . . . Kansas City still had made no provision for public recreation."[42] The *Star* staff and Johnson further claimed that Nelson's "campaign" was careful and systematic. "Mr. Nelson entered upon the campaign for parks in no haphazard way," commented the *Star* staff.[43] "He obtained all available details on park development and planned his campaign carefully," Icie F. Johnson wrote, "There was nothing haphazard about anything Nelson did."[44]

The test for these assertions is an examination of newspaper commentary on James W. Cook's last offer to sell his still undeveloped forty acres to the city for a park, an offer he made less than a month after the *Star*'s highly touted park editorial appeared. The *Star* began well, with a story on May 28 informing readers that Cook was to propose a twenty-five-year lease of the pasture, with a yearly rental of ten cents for each Kansas City resident.[45] True to the *Star*'s advance information, Cook made the proposal to the council on June 6, "I understand that the city cannot purchase a park under the present City Charter," he wrote. "I therefore propose to lease for 25 years my 40 acres of Ground . . . for the Sum of 10 cts a year for Each inhabitant for the use of Sedd Grounds, the Sensis to be taken every five years."[46] Cook's business sense was better than his spelling. The *Journal* reported Alderman [J. M.] Ford of the First Ward had estimated the cost to the city for rental alone "would amount to $7,500, and keep increasing yearly." The alderman charged that Cook would be the only financial beneficiary of the plan, which showed how little attention Ford had given to editorial proof that parks paid everyone. The matter was referred to the Fourth Ward aldermen.[47]

"Kansas City is at the present time in absolute want of a public park," the *Times* asserted editorially three days after Cook made his third offer. "The Romans had parks," said the *Times*, and "If there were half a dozen parks in this city it would be none too many." Kansas City needed to emulate Rome's public baths too, the rambling editorial continued, pointing out how, instead of such improvements, "nearly every line of street cars has a beer garden for its terminus. There is a painful aridity about a city which has neither parks or drinking fountains. . . . It is to be hoped that these blunders will soon be corrected."[48]

The *Journal* noted its rival's editorial with amusement. "Our neighbor, the *Times*, has a peculiar article on parks. . . . But it don't get down to practical things." The *Journal* got down to practical things. It praised the natural advantages of Cook's pasture, then critically examined the council's reaction to the proffered rental. "But the proposition met with that prompt opposition and denunciation which everything but dirt and pipestem sewers meets in that remarkable body. There was not a word said," it went on, "about the necessity of a park, its sanitary or aesthetic uses. Not a word, but Mr. Cook was pounced upon as if he had been a public enemy. . . . We are tired of this mere opposition statesmanship. . . . If a man is to be denounced and drummed out of town for offering grounds for a park, people will be slow to make such tenders."[49]

The council's Fourth Ward aldermen never reported, and this time Cook sold his property. The land was apparently so well known and desirable that its developers contrasted the blatant half- and full-page real estate announcements of the day with this chaste advertisement: "We have just closed the purchase for Chas. Merriam, of Boston, for $125,000, of that tract of land known as Cook's Pasture. We will at once place this property on the market. Its magnificent forest trees, commanding view, and accessibility, is so well known that no extended description is essential."[50] This advertisement closed the unsuccessful fight to convert Cook's pasture into a public park. What was the *Star*'s role in the fight?

Except for the announcement that the offer was to be made, the *Star* said nothing about Cook's proposal. It was silent while other newspapers spoke. Considering this neutralism and inaction, it is easy to accept Haskell's and Fowler's lament, in their *City of the Future*, that public response to the opening of the *Star*'s fight for parks was less than spirited. "At first," they wrote, "the city's apathy was monumental." No doubt it was.[51]

The most compelling reason to question the legend of the *Star*'s initial importance in the park and boulevard fight is the yearlong gap between editorials in that newspaper devoted to the park idea. During the year from May 19, 1881, to May 16, 1882, the date of the second editorial, the *Times* again came out in favor of parks, and the local Greenback Party stood upon a plank demanding parks.[52] In that second editorial, the *Star* urged the city to purchase the old exposition grounds, but only after an earlier editorial gave the impression the *Star* was resigned to residential building on the grounds and hoped only for a beautiful "Residence Park" there.[53] Further, the idea of parks and the idea of a boulevard system did not meld in the *Star*'s columns until 1885, long after its competitors had urged Kansas City to follow the example of Paris in park and boulevard construction.[54]

Thus the claims for Nelson's early, carefully planned campaign for parks and boulevards, begun by the *Star* staff's tender memorial and perpetuated by some subsequent writing, do not stand up under analysis. Other works such as Carrie Westlake Whitney's *Kansas City Missouri*, published in 1908, or *Crossroads of America* by Darrell Garwood, which appeared forty years later, give Nelson and the *Star* heavy credit for the ultimate realization of the park and boulevard system while they avoid a search for origins of the city beautiful idea. Such analyses may be more superficial, but they are safer than assertions or implications that Nelson initiated the park and boulevard movement. Nelson's genius lay, not in beginning it, but in ably adding impetus to a movement already under way.[55]

Many causes might explain the meager success of the park and boulevard movement in the decade 1872-1882. Kansas City was as yet a raw city, and problems of street grading and paving, sewers and water supply, educational buildings, and police protection probably loomed larger to its citizens than beautification matters. No prominent citizen devoted his energies to acquiring parks. No newspaper took up the editorial cudgels in a sustained campaign for a beautiful city. Some Kansas City residents doubtless viewed the city as an economic organism in which parks would serve no useful purpose and were therefore superfluous. Had its citizens considered parks and boulevards necessary, the booming city surely could have supplied the means to finance them. The reason they did not, and the greatest single reason for the failure of attempts to secure public parks, is that attractive open spaces lay within the city limits and within easy reach of much of the city's population.

These open spaces finally were built over, but for most of the decade, they were available to the public. Cook's pasture was not sold until 1881, and the exposition grounds remained undeveloped until the following year. McGee Park was in use throughout the decade. Then too, there was the forlorn "little dornick," Shelley Park, which the newspapers discounted so heavily. Finally, there were private parks. The most important of these was Merriam Park, owned by the Kansas City, Fort Scott and Gulf Railroad, lying southwest of the city in Kansas. It was to reach a high state of landscape development in later years. Former President Ulysses S. Grant spoke there in 1880, and his appearance was followed by an extended revival meeting.[56] Other parks were Garth's and Gaston's. But even the *Times*, very partial to the Gaston establishment on "Reservoir Hill," admitted it was "not . . . precisely what Kansas City wants."[57]

By 1882, however, most of these open places in Kansas City became residential developments, and the problem of catching a glimpse of nature in the burgeoning town became acute. The next ten years were to see a greater and more successful effort to meet that problem.

NOTES

1. *Kansas City Times*, 26 April 1876.

2. All these newspapers experienced minor variations in their masthead titles, but each title included the basic names given above.

3. Three books which credit Nelson and the *Star* with beginning the park and boulevard movement are Members of the Staff of the Kansas City Star, *William Rockhill Nelson* (Cambridge, MA: Riverside Press, 1915); Icie F. Johnson, *William Rockhill Nelson and the Kansas City Star* (Kansas City: Burton Publishing Co., [c. 1935]); and Henry C. Haskell Jr. and Richard B. Fowler, *City of the Future* (Kansas City: Frank Glen Publishing Co., [c. 1950]).

4. *Kansas City Times*, 13 February 1872.

5. Kansas City Council Document No. 15086, 2nd ser., 4 June 1877; Kansas City Council Proceedings, binder 8, reg. sess., 4 June 1877, 101. See also *Kansas City Times*, 7 June 1877.

6. *Kansas City Times*, 10 June 1877.

7. *Kansas City Journal*, 24 June 1877.

8. Ibid., 4 June 1877.

9. Document No. 15275, 2nd ser., 12 July 1877; Kansas City Council Proceedings, binder 8, special sess., 12 July 1877, 115.

10. *Kansas City Journal*, 22 July 1877.

11. Ibid., 27 July 1877.

12. *Kansas City Times*, 8 September 1877.

13. Ibid., 16 August 1877; 20 April, 17 September 1879; *Kansas City Journal*, 14, 18 September 1879; 23 December 1880.

14. *Kansas City Times*, 21, 25 April 1880.

15. Ibid., 25 April 1880. Fortunately for the sensibilities of his readers, the writer did not extend the analogy to the city's sewers.

16. Ibid., 12 May 1880.

17. Ibid., 26 March 1881.

18. Kansas City Council Proceedings, binder 8, spec. sess., 16 June 1877, 107.

19. *Campbell et al. v. The City of Kansas*, 102 Brown 338, 350-355 (1891).

20. *Kansas City Times*, 17 October 1878.

21. *Kansas City Journal*, 19 November 1878.

22. *Kansas City Times*, 26 November 1878.

23. Ibid., 7 December 1878.

24. Kansas City Council Proceedings, binder 8, spec. sess., 12 December 1878, 264.

25. Ibid., 24 March 1879, 288-289.

26. *Campbell*, 102 Brown, 338, 353. See also W. J. Ward, *In the Supreme Court of Missouri* (Kansas City, 1890), in Cemeteries/Charities/Churches Scrapbook [15.1], Native Sons of Kansas City Scrapbook [NSA], Western Historical Manuscript Collection–Kansas City, and *Kansas City Journal*, 20 April 1884.

27. *Kansas City Times*, 5 May 1880.

28. *Kansas City Journal*, 21 July 1880.

29. Ibid., 10 October 1879.

30. Ibid., 11 October 1879; 21 July 1880.

31. *Kansas City Times*, 6 February 1880.

32. Kansas City Council Proceedings, binder 8, spec. sess., 11 June 1880, 473, and 18 August 1880, 495; *Kansas City Journal*, 12 June, 19 August 1880.

33. *Kansas City Times*, 1 September 1881.

34. *Kansas City Journal*, 9 May 1880.

35. Ibid., 16 November 1880.

36. *Kansas City Star,* 16 November 1880.

37. *William Rockhill Nelson*, 35.

38. *Kansas City Journal*, 22 July 1877; 1 October 1880; *Kansas City Times*, 22 June 1881.

39. *Kansas City Star*, 19 May 1881. The census of 1880 reported that Kansas City had "one small park or block of ground, containing 2.11 acres, used originally for a cemetery, of which it retains possession from the fact of its still containing the remains of persons buried therein. There is no attempt at maintenance except mowing

the grass." U.S. Census Office, *Tenth Census of the United States 1880, Report on the Social Statistics of Cities* (Washington, DC: Government Printing Office, 1887), vol. 19, pt. 2: 556.

40. *William Rockhill Nelson*, 35.

41. Johnson, *William Rockhill Nelson and the Kansas City Star*, 85.

42. Haskell and Fowler, *City of the Future*, 71.

43. *William Rockhill Nelson*, 36.

44. Johnson, *William Rockhill Nelson and the Kansas City Star*, 59-60.

45. *Kansas City Star*, 28 May 1881.

46. Kansas City Council Document No. 21025, 2nd ser., J. W. Cook to "Hon Common Council of Kansas City," 30 May 1881.

47. *Kansas City Journal*, 7 June 1881; Kansas City Council Proceedings, binder 8, reg. sess., 6 June 1881, 561.

48. *Kansas City Times*, 9 June 1881.

49. *Kansas City Journal*, 9 June 1881.

50. *Kansas City Times*, 12 September 1881.

51. Haskell and Fowler, *City of the Future*, 72. The *Star* editorial received some attention from the *Journal*, which praised the "commendable" park editorial. "The Journal," it said, "has urged the park question until it has about become discouraged, and if our evening contemporary can move public feeling to undertake the enterprise we shall be glad and do all we can to help it along." *Kansas City Journal*, 22 May 1881.

52. *Kansas City Times*, 28 August 1881; 3 March 1882.

53. *Kansas City Star*, 9 March, 16 May 1882.

54. Ibid., 9 May 1885.

55. Carrie Westlake Whitney, *Kansas City, Missouri: Its History and Its People, 1808-1908* (Chicago: S. J. Clarke, 1908), 1: 386; Darrell Garwood, *Crossroads of America: The Story of Kansas City* (New York: W. W. Norton, 1948), 157-160, 174, 202-207.

56. *Kansas City Times*, 3 July, 2, 4, 9 August 1880.

57. Ibid., 4 June 1876.

The Kansas City Meat Packing Industry Before 1900

G. K. RENNER

Perhaps nothing was so important to Kansas City's industrial growth before 1900 as meat packing. In a sense it was only a part of the growing livestock industry which centered around Kansas City, but more than any other aspect of the livestock business, it made Kansas City a metropolitan center. Packing determined that the city would become a manufacturing town with its attendant heavy capital investment in plants, its marketing and financial connections, and above all, its large force of laborers who would make the city their home. But since packing lacks the drama attached to the raising and marketing of livestock, its story has been obscured by tales of the cattlemen and of the development of Kansas City's livestock market.

The Kansas City meat-packing industry arose between the Civil War and 1900, although some commercial packing had existed even earlier. In 1858, M. Diveley and a few others began packing hogs, and in 1859, J. L. Mitchener opened the most extensive of the antebellum packing establishments, but the Civil War brought these operations to an end.[1] They were never more than local operations, even though Kansas City by the late 1850s was the most important livestock market on the western frontier.[2]

The city's development of a meat-packing industry of national importance depended on factors that became operative during the Civil War and postwar periods. Clearly, the most important factor was development of adequate transportation facilities to connect Kansas City with both the markets in the East and the burgeoning cattle herds on the grasslands of the West. Primarily, this need was met by railroads, though Kansas City's excellent water connections via the Missouri River were also important to its early packing industry.[3]

The Civil War virtually ruined Kansas City's thriving economy and brought about a precipitate decline in its population from approximately 10,000 to 5,000, but already the railroad building that enabled Kansas City to dominate the Missouri River valley was beginning.[4] On July 25, 1860, ground was broken on a connection to link Kansas City with the Missouri Pacific Railroad then building westward across Missouri from St. Louis. In September 1865 the first passenger train from St. Louis arrived in Kansas City.[5] In 1862 the Kansas Pacific Railroad (now the Union Pacific) began building westward from Wyandotte (now Kansas City, Kansas).[6] By December 1866 a bridge had been completed across the Kaw River between Kansas City, Missouri, and Wyandotte, giving the Kansas Pacific direct connections with the Missouri Pacific, St. Louis, and points east.[7] The key event in Kansas City's growth as a railroad center came in 1869 when the Hannibal and St. Joseph Railroad completed at Kansas City the first bridge across the Missouri River, giving direct connections with Chicago and the eastern railways.[8] Other railroads rushed to build or merge their way into Kansas City in order to take advantage of its bridges and rail connections. By 1877 seven railroads were operating out of Kansas City, and its future as the rail hub of the Missouri River valley was assured.[9]

Hannibal and St. Joseph Railroad Bridge, Kansas City, in 1869

During the Civil War, cattle on the Texas plains multiplied enormously, and equally important, the growing industrial population in the East created a lucrative market for beef. Attempts to tap this market led to the famous cattle drives in which massive herds of wild Texas longhorns were driven to the nearest railroad and shipped eastward. In 1867, Joseph G. McCoy, who is often called the father of Kansas City's livestock industry, saw the possibility of directing these drives to a railhead on the new Kansas Pacific Railroad and shipping the cattle to Kansas City, where excellent rail connections with the East were becoming available. By 1868 he succeeded in establishing such a railhead at Abilene, and in the fall of that year, the first shipments of Texas cattle came into Kansas City. There were no stockyards, and the railroads were forced to build pens where the stock could be unloaded for rest and food before moving on to the East.[10]

Observers quickly noted the possibilities offered by this development. They saw that Texas stock could be bought and slaughtered in Kansas City, avoiding the expenses of shrinkage on the long trip east and of shipping the waste poundage of a live animal.

The *Kansas City Daily Journal of Commerce* had noted in 1866 that "the dozen railroads that will center here the next five years, will afford transportation facilities in every direction, and the result will be that a number of packing houses will be built at this point."[11] In 1867, Edward W. Pattison and J. W. L. Slavens started the first extensive beef-packing operation in Kansas City. During the first year, they packed 4,209 head of cattle. In the same year, an Irishman, Thomas J. Bigger, rented an old hide house and slaughtered hogs for the Irish and English markets. In 1869, Slavens sold his interest to Dr. F. B. Nofsinger and formed a new partnership of Ferguson, Slavens, and Company.[12]

A number of additional companies were organized, reorganized, and abandoned in the next few years, but these were small operations carried on at the edge of the frontier, far from the rich market centers of the East. They were engaged in by men with limited capital and little experience in the managerial techniques of operating an interstate business. Yet any substantial packing plant founded in Kansas City at that time would have needed connections with eastern markets, for Kansas City with a population in 1870 of 32,260, in the midst of a semideveloped territory, could not support a large packing plant with its local demand.[13]

At this time, a man with the necessary entrepreneurial prerequisites moved onto the Kansas City scene. He was Philip Danforth Armour of Chicago, whose Armour and Company was rapidly gaining a national reputation as a meat packer. As a young man, Armour made a journey across the western plains and apparently envisioned its vast possibilities as a livestock-producing region.[14] This may have influenced him to locate in Kansas City, but the immediate reason was that he saw that Kansas City provided an ideal location for packing Texas beef near its source.[15] To carry out this venture, he formed a partnership consisting of himself; his two brothers, H. O. and S. B. Armour; and his original business partner in Milwaukee, John Plankinton.[16]

S. B. Armour and a nucleus of trained manpower moved to Kansas City in 1870 to begin operating a new firm known as Plankinton and Armour.[17] Their first season was a successful one; 13,000 cattle and 15,000 hogs were slaughtered.[18] In 1869 only 4,420 cattle and 23,000 hogs were slaughtered in Kansas City, while in 1870, with Plankinton and Armour in operation, total slaughter rose to 21,000 cattle and 36,000 hogs.[19] The Armours were so pleased that during the summer of 1871 they built a new plant near the confluence of the Kaw and Missouri rivers. During the summer of 1871, Plankinton and Armour had 15,000 cattle, which they were holding for the beginning of the packing season, grazing in Kansas.[20] At this time their buyers were forced to go into the country because Kansas City lacked an organized stock market where packers could buy their animals.[21] Though Kansas City was later to be famed for its livestock market, it actually had a thriving packing business before the first stockyards company was chartered on September 14, 1871.[22] Packing operations undoubtedly stimulated the development of this market, the first centralized livestock market organized west of Chicago.[23]

An account written in 1874 describes Plankinton and Armour's plant as one of the finest in the United States. It was striking because of its neatness, cleanliness, and the advanced steam machinery used for handling the meat.[24] Yet meat packing at this time was still primitive by today's standards. It was a seasonal operation; beef was packed in the fall and early winter after the weather turned cool enough to preserve the meat but while the grass-fattened cattle were still at their prime. Grain-fattened hogs could be packed on through the winter and spring until warm weather ended all operations for the season.[25] Not until 1877 did Plankinton and Armour have a chill room that enabled them to pack hogs the year around.[26]

In any account of the early years of Kansas City meat packing, it is difficult to overemphasize the contributions of the Armour family, which moved to Kansas City when the town offered little more than opportunity and capitalized on that opportunity to lay the real foundations for the future growth of meat packing in Kansas City. Not only were the Armours first to bring to Kansas City the necessary capital, skills, and market connections for carrying on large scale meat packing, but they were also first to demonstrate that such

Dressing Beeves at Plankinton and Armour, Kansas City

an operation could be carried on successfully. They alone of the early packers were to survive the difficult years of the 1870s and the early 1880s.

This lone survival demonstrates the difficulty encountered in developing Kansas City's full potential as a meat-packing center. The decade from 1870 to 1880 proved to be a critical one for the budding young industry. The panic of 1873 struck before packing could be firmly established. Following this, the grasshopper plague of 1874-1875 laid waste to large sections of the surrounding country.[27] In addition, railroad rate discriminations over a long period of time tended to favor Chicago and other eastern cities as livestock centers.[28] However, the biggest obstacle faced by Kansas City packers during these early years came from the transition going on within the industry itself. Formerly meat packing was confined almost exclusively to pork, but the growing industrial population of the East demanded beef. Unlike pork, which had always been preferred in the cured variety, this demand was for fresh beef. In those days before refrigeration, it was necessary to ship the animals alive to the locality in which the beef would be consumed.[29]

Kansas City packers could not benefit from this development because of their location far from the principal market centers, but they did continue to pack and cure salt beef, which could be shipped anywhere in the world. And there remained a considerable demand for packed beef from the British and French navies, whaling vessels, lumbering and mining districts, in fact, any location where it was difficult or impossible to supply fresh beef.[30] Kansas

City soon dominated this limited market; by 1874 it had become the principal source of supply for packed beef.[31] This domination was due only in part to Kansas City's proximity to a supply of cattle. Of equal importance was the peculiar nature of the grass-fattened Texas longhorns available to the Kansas City packers. These ferocious-looking creatures produced a particularly tough and stringy meat that was ill suited for eating fresh but became a superior type of packed beef. "It was stated that a fat Texas steer was better for packing purposes than a native, that its meat was better 'marbeled,' i.e., the fat was distributed in alternate layers with the lean fiber, and the meat when cut presented the appearance of variegated marble."[32] The Kansas City packers relied almost exclusively on Texas longhorns for many years. As late as 1879, all the cattle slaughtered by Plankinton and Armour were Texas stock.[33] Not until well into the 1880s did local cattle become available in sizeable quantities to the Kansas City packing industry.[34]

However, even before the demise of the Texas longhorn, packed beef was on its way out. Of the 29,149 head of cattle slaughtered in 1879, only one-half went into packed beef, with most of the remainder being canned, and by 1880, American canned beef had replaced packed salt beef on ships.[35] Large quantities were sold in Europe, and unlike packed salt beef, it was also popular in the East.[36]

Kansas City Stockyards in the Early 1870s

Few companies succeeded at this canning operation. The Kansas City firm of Slavens and Oburn started canning beef in 1878.[37] Shortly afterward, Plankinton and Armour also began to can, and after Slavens and Oburn suspended operations in 1884, they continued as the only beef-canning firm in Kansas City at that time.[38] But the operation grew enormously. In 1880, 778,720 tins were canned; by 1885 production had risen to 1,095,410 tins.[39]

In retrospect we can see that during the 1870s and early 1880s Kansas City developed into a very important production center for specialty products such as packed salt beef and canned beef. However, this was a limited operation; the demand for these products could never develop on a large scale like cured pork or fresh dressed beef. In fact, pork packing was virtually a necessity to supplement this limited market, as it would have been difficult to make a profit from the packing of beef alone.[40] All this is reflected in the statistics for the period. During these years, the slaughter of cattle showed a relatively slow growth while the slaughter of hogs increased greatly. In 1870 the slaughter of hogs was less than twice that of cattle, yet by 1880 the ratio had increased to approximately 17 to 1.[41] In fact, the growth of pork packing paralleled the development of farming in the Kansas City area. As the supply of hogs from the farms increased, pork packing expanded. For many years, the Kansas City packers purchased nearly all the hogs shipped to the local stockyards.[42]

However, the rapid growth of pork packing should not minimize the importance of beef packing in Kansas City. Kansas City's peculiar advantages as a packing center for Texas beef had brought in Armour even before there was a stockyards company. Domination of the specialty beef market helped to establish nationwide and international markets for the Kansas City packers far more effectively than could have been done with the more generally available pork products. Perhaps most important of all, though, was that Kansas City, firmly established as a beef slaughtering center, was able to capitalize on new developments in the processing of beef ahead of other growing livestock centers west of Chicago.

Though the sweeping increase in demand for fresh dressed beef in the 1870s had not been favorable to Kansas City's packers, technological developments turned this demand to their advantage during the next decade. Refrigeration revolutionized the processing and handling of meat, and the refrigerator car enabled Kansas City packers to capture a sizeable portion of this market.

Packing men saw at an early date that savings could be made by shipping fresh dressed beef to the eastern markets rather than transporting the live animals, but mobile refrigeration posed so many problems that its development was slow. G. F. Swift, founder of Swift and Company, is generally given credit for making the refrigerator car a practical success, but one of the early experimenters was Nofsinger and Company, a Kansas City packer,[43] which shipped dressed beef to eastern cities from 1875 to 1879.[44] It was a crude but successful operation that could only be carried on during cold weather.[45] The railroads, trying to protect their investments in cattle cars and eastern stockyards, finally raised rates so high that Nofsinger was forced to quit.[46] However, it was only a temporary setback, for by 1884 all the packers in Kansas City were shipping dressed beef; but continued railroad discrimination limited their growth. It remained for the big packing companies to overcome railroad opposition before shipping dressed beef by refrigerator car could be commercially practicable on a large scale.[47]

The Kansas City packing industry grew spectacularly after 1880. Slaughter of hogs rose from 539,097 in 1880 to 1,805,114 in 1892, an increase of 235 percent. Slaughter of cattle increased even more impressively, from 30,922 head in 1880 to 676,725 in 1892, an increase of nearly 2,100 percent.[48] This explosive expansion resulted largely from perfection of the refrigerator car. Other factors promoting the overall growth were an increase in the supplies of livestock, the general expansion in population, and the opening of new markets as additional railroads branched out from Kansas City. Chicago continued to dominate the eastern market, but Kansas City found a growing trade territory in the north, south, west, and overseas.[49]

With this rapid increase in business after 1880, other large eastern firms were attracted to Kansas City, where eventually all the nation's large packers were to join Armour. In fact, with Kansas City becoming the second largest livestock market in the world and supplying a rich trade territory, they had to consider whether they could afford to remain out of this area.[50] In 1880 and 1881 the Anglo-American and Jacob Dold plants located in Kansas City; in 1885, Morris and Butt started a plant that was, after a series of changes, to become Wilson and Company; and in 1887, Kingan and Company built a plant that eventually became the site of a Cudahy Packing Company establishment.[51] Besides these, there were other smaller packers.

However, the most significant developments involved Swift and Armour. In 1887, Swift and Company built at a cost of $500,000 the first large dressed beef plant in Kansas City.[52] Swift's influence, coupled with that of Armour, was such that railroad opposition to refrigerator cars could be overcome, and Kansas City's future as a dressed beef processing center was assured. The slaughter of cattle jumped from 79,000 in 1885 to 511,000 in 1890 under the stimulus of this new operation.[53] Armour's dressed beef operations in Kansas City had been increasing, and in 1892, P. D. Armour and his brothers built a $1,000,000 dressed beef plant.[54] At that time their plant was the largest business in Kansas City, and by 1901 they employed 4,000 people and produced more than $50,000,000 worth of meat products annually.[55]

A considerable factor in the rapid growth of packing in Kansas City during the 1880s and 1890s was the Kansas City Stock Yard Company's dynamic leadership. This organization, anxious to make its yards the nation's greatest cattle market, looked upon promotion of the local packing industry as the surest way to develop this livestock trade. To further this plan, they paid handsome bonuses to important packers who would locate in Kansas City. The largest payment, consisting of $500,000 in Stock Yards Company stock, went to the Armour family in 1892 for locating its new plant in Kansas City. Other payments made during this period were:

Fowler and Company	$80,567.18 in land and cash
Hollis and Company	2,752.00 in land
Kingan and Company	30,000.00 in land
Schwarzschild and Sulzberger	100,000.00 in cash
Swift and Company	62,175.00 in land[56]

Important though these payments were, they were less basic to the Kansas City packing industry's surging growth than the transition brought on by refrigerator cars. By the time the Armours completed their new dressed beef plant in 1892, the fight to introduce refrigerated dressed beef into the nation's markets had been won. Not only did the public accept refrigerated

Kansas City Livestock Exchange and Stockyards About 1900

beef, but it found that the aging process improved its flavor. The railroads ceased to struggle against this movement, and the big yellow refrigerator cars of the packers became a common sight on the nation's railways. Local slaughtering houses and butchers were on their way to extinction. Packing was being consolidated into the hands of a few big companies. In reality, the meat packing industry had taken on the essential outlines of its modern form, in which packing plants economically located near the supplies of live animals are able to produce dressed products for a national and international market.[57]

By 1900 the Kansas City meat packing industry had reached maturity. It was clearly the largest industry in town. As early as 1893, the *Kansas City Daily Journal* estimated that packing furnished a livelihood for 35,000 people.[58] In fact, Kansas City had become the second-largest meat packing center in the nation as total slaughter of hogs, sheep, and cattle rose from 588,171 in 1880 to 4,555,950 in 1900.[59]

Optimists freely predicted that Kansas City would overtake Chicago and establish itself as the livestock capital of the world, but forces were already at work that blocked any such hegemony. The growth of railroads that had given Kansas City its initial advantage as a livestock center in time favored other cities as well. The transfer of packing plants from the East to Kansas City to be nearer the source of supply was but the beginning of a process of decentralization of meat packing. Other cities in the rich grain-growing regions of the Midwest proved to have advantages rivaling those of Kansas City, especially as the demand for grain-fattened beef increased. Kansas City was to remain one of the great meat packing centers, but its relative importance has declined since 1900.

NOTES

1. Theodore S. Case, ed., *History of Kansas City, Missouri* (Syracuse, NY: D. Mason, 1888), 217.

2. Joseph G. McCoy, *Historic Sketches of the Cattle Trade of the West and Southwest*, ed. Ralph P. Bieber (Glendale, CA: Arthur H. Clark, 1940), 349n.

3. Rudolf A. Clemen, *The American Livestock and Meat Industry* (New York: Ronald Press, 1923), 452-453.

4. McEwen and Dillenback, *Kansas City in 1879* (Kansas City: Ramsey, Millet, and Hudson, 1879), 30.

5. *Kansas City Journal*, 5 March 1922.

6. "History of Kansas City Stockyards," *Hereford Swine Journal* 3 (May-June 1943): 12. This article is bound into a booklet available at the State Historical Society of Missouri.

7. *Kansas City Journal*, 5 March 1922.

8. *Kansas City Star*, 4 June 1950.

9. "History of Kansas City Stockyards," 16.

10. Joseph G. McCoy, *Historic Sketches of the Cattle Trade of the West and Southwest* (Kansas City: Ramsey, Millet, and Hudson, 1874), 38ff.

11. *Kansas City Daily Journal of Commerce*, 20 January 1866.

12. Case, *History of Kansas City*, 217.

13. U.S. Bureau of the Census, *Census of Population: 1950* (Washington, DC: Government Printing Office, 1952), 1: 25-10.

14. Clemen, *American Livestock*, 150.

15. W. H. Miller, *The History of Kansas City* (Kansas City: Birdsall and Miller, 1881), 170.

16. Clemen, *American Livestock*, 154.

17. *Kansas City Star*, 29 March 1899.

18. *Kansas City Daily Journal of Commerce*, 22 July 1871.

19. Case, *History of Kansas City*, 219.

20. *Kansas City Daily Journal of Commerce*, 22 July 1871.

21. Miller, *History of Kansas City*, 170.

22. *Kansas City Daily Journal of Commerce*, 4 October 1871.

23. Clemen, *American Livestock*, 203-204.

24. McCoy, *Historic Sketches* (1874), 302ff.

25. Ibid., 309-310.

26. *Kansas City Daily Journal of Commerce*, 14 January 1877.

27. Cuthbert Powell, *Twenty Years of Kansas City's Live Stock Trade and Traders* (Kansas City: Pearl, 1893), 90.

28. Clemen, *American Livestock*, 200-203.

29. Ibid., 173ff.

30. *Kansas City Daily Journal of Commerce*, 26 October 1879.

31. Miller, *History of Kansas City*, 170.

32. Clemen, *American Livestock*, 452-453.

33. *Kansas City Daily Journal of Commerce*, 26 October 1879.

34. U.S. Department of Agriculture, *First Annual Report of the Bureau of Animal Industry for the Year 1884* (Washington, DC: Government Printing Ofiice, 1885), 247.

35. Clemen, *American Livestock*, 464-466.

36. *Kansas City Daily Journal*, 1 January 1887.

37. McEwen and Dillenback, *Kansas City in 1879*, 35.

38. *Seventy-Five Years of Kansas City Livestock Market History 1871-1946* (Kansas City: Kansas City Stockyards Co., 1946), 36; Clemen, *American Livestock*, 466.

39. Commercial Club of Kansas City, *Twelfth Annual Report of the Trade and Commerce of Kansas City, For Year Ending June 30, 1891*, 61.

40. McCoy, *Historic Sketches* (1874), 348.

41. Case, *History of Kansas City*, 220.

42. *Kansas City Daily Journal*, 1 January 1886; Richard L. Douglas, "A History of Manufacturing in the Kansas District," *Collections of the Kansas State Historical Society, 1909-1910* (Topeka: State Printing Office, 1910), 11: 125.

43. Clemen, *American Livestock*, 221, 231-232.

44. *First Annual Report of Bureau of Animal Industry*, 266.

45. *Kansas City Daily Journal of Commerce*, 4 January 1877.

46. *First Annual Report of Bureau of Animal Industry*, 266.

47. Clemen, *American Livestock*, 238.

48. Case, *History of Kansas City*, 220; Powell, *Twenty Years*, 134.

49. *Kansas City Daily Journal*, 31 December 1882; 1 January 1888.

50. Clemen, *American Livestock*, 453.

51. *Seventy-Five Years*, 36-37.

52. Powell, *Twenty Years*, 93-94.

53. *Twelfth Annual Report of the Trade and Commerce of Kansas City*, 56.

54. *Kansas City Star*, 26 May 1892.

55. Ibid., 28 September 1901.

56. Ibid., 25 May 1897.

57. Clemen, *American Livestock*, 231ff.

58. *Kansas City Daily Journal*, 1 January 1893.

59. U.S. Department of Commerce, *Report of the Commissioner of Corporations on the Beef Industry, March 3, 1905* (Washington, DC: Government Printing Office, 1905), 7.

Kansas City Free Speech Fight of 1911

TOM N. McINNIS

City officials in many American communities found themselves involved in a free speech fight with the Industrial Workers of the World (IWW) in the ten years between 1907 and 1917.[1] At stake was the right of the IWW to agitate on street corners in order to promote the goals of the union, which included industrial unionism and worker control of the means of production. Use of street corners in many communities represented the only meaningful organizational tool available to the IWW. Loss of the right to promote the union and its goals by open street meetings would have meant the death of the union in many communities throughout the United States because of the transitory nature of the workers. Philip S. Foner wrote about the usual pattern of the major free speech fights: "Speak; be arrested; crowd the jails; demand a separate trial—a trial by jury—for each and every Wobbly in jail clog the administrative machinery of the courts, indeed the machinery of the entire municipal administration; become a burden on the taxpayers."[2]

Historians have drawn these conclusions from the major free speech fights which took place in Spokane, Washington; Missoula, Montana; and Fresno, California. They have done little work with the minor free speech fights, such as the one that happened in Kansas City, Missouri, during October and November of 1911.

The Kansas City free speech fight erupted in full force in October 1911. The symptoms of discontent, however, had existed long before the IWW actually declared war in Kansas City. The harassment of the IWW began almost immediately after the creation of Local No. 61 in March 1911. After

City Hall, Kansas City, Mo.

This three-story, Romanesque building, designed by architect A. B. Cross, served as Kansas City's city hall from 1891 to 1936.

a couple of weeks, its members began to agitate parts of the local work force, hoping to organize an industry in Kansas City. This activity occurred both on the job and from the soap box at street meetings beginning in mid-March and continuing throughout the year.

The local grew in size, and its agitation continued to confront the law. In the spring, the local clashed with the law, resulting in the arrest of two members for singing revolutionary songs on a street corner after a policeman had asked them to stop. A local leader of the IWW, A. B. Carson, was arrested in June and charged with disturbing the peace. He had cursed the American flag and the police department during a speech at the corner of Missouri Avenue and Main Street. After Carson's arrest, another local Wobbly, Ed Darner, went to the police department with bail for Carson. The authorities informed Darner the organization had to eliminate antipatriotism in the speeches given on the streets of Kansas City. Local No. 61, at this time, decided on a wait-and-see attitude for any other possible limitations the police might make eventually. Late August and early September brought a new series of interferences for street meetings from the Kansas City police. So disturbed by the actions of the police, the local formed a committee to contact the police department and see about guidelines for street speaking in Kansas City. They were informed their members would benefit from not using radical language in their speeches. After hearing this, the local feared the possible loss of rights to agitate on the streets. A warning appeared in both papers published by the IWW, the *Industrial Worker* and *Solidarity*:

> Now fellow workers, we have done everything possible to avoid a free speech fight, but it seems inevitable.
> We'll not make a call for fighters until we have several fellow workers arrested and tried. So fellow workers, don't come unless you are coming this way, until we force the police authorities to take a stand one way or the other.[3]

Trouble began again on October 6, when the police would not allow a night meeting on the corner of Sixth and Main streets. While the police tried to disperse the crowd, Albert Roe, a veteran of the Spokane and Fresno free speech fights, stepped up on a box and began speaking. The police immediately arrested Roe and charged him with disturbing the peace and obstructing traffic. He later was fined $50 and released on appeal.[4]

The next set of arrests of IWW members and the real start of the Kansas City free speech fight occurred on October 14. The local was holding a meeting at the corner of Sixth and Main streets when the police arrived and arrested the speaker, Frank Little. Then law officers walked through the crowd and asked other members if they were leaders in the organization. Informed the organization had no leaders in the crowd, the police decided that being a member of the IWW was sufficient cause for arrest and began seizing all who admitted membership in the organization. They arrested five members along with Little, all of whom they booked on charges of obstructing sidewalks.

The police and the IWW disagreed about the real reasons for the arraignments during the free speech fight. The department believed it was enforcing the law and not discriminating against the IWW in any way. Complaints from various members of the business community in the neighborhood accused the IWW with disturbing the peace at the street meetings. Responding to these complaints, which they believed to be legitimate, the police stopped the street meetings.

Members of the IWW believed the complaints represented stronger feelings. Hugh Scott, an active member of Local No. 61, believed the IWW disturbed the peace of the business interests in the area through efforts to organize the workers. He said, "Getting beef steak instead of liver for the working man always disturbs the peace of the capitalist." Scott blamed the arrests of members on "capitalists, who are just beginning to realize that we may organize one great union and put them to work."[5]

The arrest of Frank Little ignited the Kansas City free speech fight of 1911, and again in 1914. A proven leader in the IWW, Little commanded considerable respect from members of the organization. Although he spent the entire period of the fight in jail, he, "more than any other individual, personified the IWW's rebelliousness and its strange compound of violent rhetoric, pride in physical courage, and its seemingly contradictory resort to nonviolent resistance."[6] Little certainly appeared no stranger to free speech fights when he was arrested in Kansas City. Both the Missoula and Fresno episodes started with the seizure of Little. He had been arrested numerous times for everything from reading the Declaration of Independence to trying to organize police strikes for the eight-hour day. His arrest led the Kansas City local to ask what other locals in the organization thought should be done. Members sent the following telegram on October 14, published in *Industrial Worker* and *Solidarity*: "Seven members arrested here for speaking on the street tonight. Frank Little was arrested when speaking. Others were arrested for being members of the IWW. We want immediate opinion of all locals on starting free speech fight here. Publish answer at once."[7]

The men arrested on the night of the fourteenth were sent to the Northside Municipal Court to appear before Judge Clarence A. Burney. They asked for

A Kansas City street scene looks east on Tenth from Main, circa early 1900s.

a jury trial. The judge replied, "I know what you men want and I don't want to be bothered with you this winter, and I am not going to stand for any stump speeches." After rejecting the request for a jury trial, Judge Burney conducted an informal hearing. The IWW presented twenty witnesses, but none were allowed to speak. The judge considered only as evidence a copy of [E. S.] Nelson's pamphlet "Appeal to Wage Workers." He then questioned the IWW members about the contents of it. After the judge heard the members admit they believed in doing only as much work in a day as they were paid for rather than working a full day for low wages, the judge sentenced them. He fined Frank Little $25 and all the others $10. All refused to pay the fines so they were sentenced to Leeds Farm, a municipal farm in Jackson County, to work off their fines at the rate of 50 cents a day.[8]

While the men were held over in jail before going to the municipal farm, members of the local conferred with Judge Burney. The local warned that if their fellow workers went to jail, the city would have a free speech fight on its hands. The judge reconsidered the sentences and paroled all of the men except Little. He believed keeping the leader in jail would allow the controversy to blow over.

The arrest and imprisonment of Little attracted the attention of the national IWW headquarters. Vincent St. John, general secretary of the national, sent a telegram to all locals and to several of the leading radical journals on October 17, 1911. The telegram told of the Kansas City local's troubles conducting street meetings and the recent arrests of Little and others. St. John demanded the harassment in Kansas City stop and the matter be quickly settled: "Therefore, all local unions are requested to enlist volunteers who will report at Kansas City ready to fill the jails until the authorities at that point are forced to cease their interference with the organization."[9]

The imprisonment of Little led Local No. 61 to call an emergency meeting on October 16. They purposed to make plans for the battle that had to be fought. The strategy decided upon appeared very similar to the procedures used by the IWW in previous free speech fights. The battle plan would be as "fast as members of us are arrested, others will take their places. We will fill the city jails to overflowing, and we will stay there until the city grows tired of the expense of caring for us."[10]

Hearing reports that a telegram had been sent to every IWW local asking them to send volunteers to be jailed in Kansas City, the police department seemed unsure how to handle the threat. Policemen chose to wait until after a meeting of city officials to pursue the arrests of more IWW members for street speaking. This allowed a meeting conducted by one of the members earlier arrested to go on uninterrupted on the night of October 17. Led by H. G. Perry, the meeting continued for a full hour and ten minutes.

The police received orders to continue the fight against the IWW after a meeting of the Kansas City Board of Police Commissioners on October 18. The police commissioners in a general hearing allowed both sides in the dispute to air their positions about the imprisonment of Little and the overall situation. The first witness, Dr. E. A. Burkhart, a local Kansas City resident, appeared in defense of the IWW and made several charges against the police. He believed discriminatory actions had caused members of the IWW to call the police "the hired servants of the oppressive class who would stoop to anything."[11]

The second witness, Albert Roe, already had been arrested twice in October, but remained free on appeal. Roe complained to the commission that he belonged behind bars if Little was guilty of a crime, as did members of the Salvation Army and anyone else who obstructed the sidewalks. Roe also related that $9.60 worth of literature unjustly had been taken away from him and another man after Roe had been clubbed on the head by a policeman. Roe asked to have the literature back, but Police Chief W. E. Griffen told him it was "incendiary and shall not be sold or distributed on the streets of Kansas City."[12]

Commissioner Solon T. Gilmore asked Roe about the meaning of an article he signed that had appeared in the October 14 issue of *Solidarity*. Roe had said the IWW should give the city a dose of direct action. Roe explained:

> That means to give this city a dose just like we gave Spokane, Wash. There they pinched us for gathering on the streets and we sent out the call and gathered men there in great numbers and actually filled the jails. Not until then did they get hep that it would be cheaper to give us the right of free speech than to board and room the jails full of our men the year around. That is giving the town a dose of direct action.[13]

Chief Griffen then presented a history of the IWW, informing the commissioners the organization opposed capital, labor, law, order, the church, the Bible and the dove of peace. He predicted terrible consequences if the IWW continued action. Members of the commission then spoke about the situation. Commissioner Theodore Remley told Roe he had attended some of the street meetings and believed the IWW was looking for a fight and would get one if it blocked sidewalks or broke laws. Mayor Darius A. Brown added, "If these men came here to speak on the streets and obey the law I have no objections, but if they are here for the purpose of defying the police power and

Solon T. Gilmore, born in 1862, served as a member of the Board of Police Commissioners from 1910 to 1913.

try to override all law they are going to be arrested whenever they offend." Commissioner Gilmore agreed with the mayor and suggested the board leave the entire situation in the hands of Chief Griffen.[14]

The Board of Police Commissioners meeting caused the *Kansas City Journal* to ask the next day, "Who is going to run Kansas City, Mayor Brown and the Board of Police Commissioners or the organization known as the IWW's." The police quickly set out to show the IWW they controlled the city. On the night of October 19, they broke up a street meeting of the IWW, resulting in the arrest and imprisonment of four members. The following day, police disrupted another street meeting, arresting Albert Roe and three others. A busy day for Roe, prior to his arrest in the evening, his third arrest in the month, he lost the appeal to his first conviction. Roe reported that on the way to the station the men sang "The Red Flag" until the police slugged them and made them stop. The next morning before court, the men again sang "The Red Flag," but this time they sang so loudly that Judge Burney temporarily had to stop the proceedings of the court. When the men were finally brought before the judge, he fined all four $100 and sent them to the municipal farm. Roe told the judge that as long as members remained in jail the city would continue to have trouble with the IWW.[15]

On October 23 activities centered around 211 East Missouri Avenue, location of the Kansas City local. A group of men at the headquarters worked to develop further strategies to continue the free speech fight. To win a victory, members of the local sought to recruit more free speech fighters with a telegram to *Industrial Worker*. "They are arresting every member in sight. Send men in at once. They claim they have lots of room here for the IWW. We must fight to finish."[16] According to the IWW headquarters, Kansas City would soon become a storm center as had Missoula, Spokane, and Fresno. Reportedly, hundreds of other members were on their way to Kansas City, to go to jail and die if necessary. When asked if he was afraid of getting arrested, one of the men answered: "Afraid of getting arrested? Hardly! We want to get arrested. We'll flood the jail and the county farm and any other place they want to send us."[17]

The police department also became busy on October 23. Chief Griffen received information from the Spokane, Washington, police department concerning its free speech fight against the IWW. Chief W. J. Doust of Spokane encouraged the Kansas City department to arrest the leaders of the IWW and stop the fight from becoming a major battle. Doust also said the fight in Spokane had cost the city $3,000.

The three members arrested two days earlier appeared before Judge Burney on October 23 on charges of blockading the street and disturbing the peace. They were fined $100 each and sent to the municipal farm. Chief Griffen and Assistant City Counselor John Mathias thought the process of individual prosecution proved too slow to rid the city of an IWW influence. They developed an alternative method. Chief Griffen and Mathias planned to contact the owner of the headquarters building and have the IWW evicted. Mathias stated, "As fast as the so-called workers find other places to meet I shall have the premises vacated by other owners." To which Chief Griffen added, "And if Mr. Mathias does not succeed in having the headquarters of the organization vacated I will find a way."[18]

On the night of October 23, the police again practiced their first line of attack with further arrests. The IWW held a street meeting attended by 200 people, some holding banners in red and white saying their brothers had been kidnapped and eventually murdered. The speakers did not raise their voices more than necessary to speak to the crowd. One reporter noted none were as loud as the religious speakers. Several workers spoke, and all wore red badges with the slogan "Free Speech for Kansas City." All gave remarks similar to the speaker who said: "Brothers we are meeting here to protest against the stand taken by the Kansas City police department in denying us the right of free speech. But, as doubtless all of you have been told, our protest will be one of passive resistance. If policemen break our heads with their clubs we won't resist."[19]

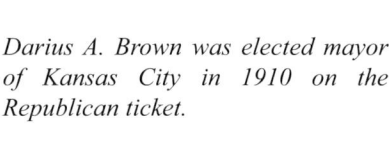
Darius A. Brown was elected mayor of Kansas City in 1910 on the Republican ticket.

This emphasis on passive resistance remained a common strategy of all the free speech fights. Joseph Conlin noted, "The IWW was not interested in lawbreaking as such but in demonstrating the injustice of the law through the disruption caused by its enforcement."[20] Before the meeting ended on the twenty-third, passive resistance again triumphed with three more members arrested. All were sent to the municipal farm after being fined $100 by Judge Burney. Activities continued on October 24 for both sides in the dispute. The Kansas City reporters believed the invasion promised by the IWW to be just around the corner. The *Journal* reported, "Words of 'Tyranny' of Kansas City's police is said to have been wired to distant points and 5,000 'loyal' members of the society are now claimed to be on the way." The local IWW headquarters also reported that reinforcements had started to arrive and would continue to do so with every passing day. They claimed: "We're not putting all our available men on the street, however. We're going to have a systematic fight, and what's more we're going to win it."[21]

Reportedly, James Howe, the millionaire tramp from St. Louis, planned to send five or six thousand men as reinforcements in the winter. Howe, the son of a wealthy St. Louis contractor, like the IWW, had a similar history trying to organize transitory workers and hobos. In discussing Howe's reinforcements, the union men commented, "He'll have plenty on his hands when the cold weather sets in. We don't think that Kansas City'll stand a siege like that, do you?"[22]

City officials seemed to take the news of a coming invasion to mean that they had to harden the city's resolve to win the battle. In an interview with the *Kansas City Star*, Chief Griffen stated, "As long as there are objections against them from the men conducting business there, we shall make the arrests." Charles Mill, the president of the Public Welfare Board which controlled the IWW inmates, also wished to show the city's resolve to win the battle. He spoke of several measures taken with the IWW prisoners. Mill stated that the city believed it "absolutely necessary to segregate these men from the regular men at Leeds farm." Mill worried that members of the IWW would refuse to work and spread that idea to other prisoners. To force the men to work, he favored the Spokane method of putting them on a bread and water diet. All of these fears proved to be well founded. The men did not refuse to work, but practiced passive resistance in the form of a work slowdown. They also took advantage of every opportunity to agitate the other prisoners and show them what solidarity could achieve. The guards believed their discipline among the prisoners was slipping. As a result, jailers isolated five IWW prisoners into solitary confinement. The inmates declared a general strike, which lasted for

This early twentieth-century photograph depicts the Jackson County Courthouse in Kansas City.

half an hour, until the five men gained their release. After the strike, the IWW prisoners were isolated from other prisoners at the farm. This action caused Chief Griffen to plan a special rock pile for the IWW to further isolate them from others.[23]

On the night of October 24, another street meeting by the IWW drew a crowd estimated to be from 360 to 500 people. The meeting started at 7:30 at the corner of Sixth and Main streets and ended at 8:00 with the arrests of several speakers. A speech by Don Scott enticed the police to break up the meeting. Scott told the crowd about the IWW's goal to organize all workers into one big union, and because of this, the police opposed them. Scott added that attendance at the meetings had grown since the police started arresting members for street speaking. He emphasized the willingness of the workers to be arrested, adding, "I quit my job yesterday to take the place of one of the men who has been sent to the municipal farm." Granting his wish, the police arrested him. As the officers began making arrests, a small man wearing glasses shouted: "Wait a minute, fellow working men, this meeting isn't over. There are more of us willing to go to jail. We, the workingmen, built the jails and we, the workingmen, will live in the jails." A policeman interrupted, saying, "All right, come on. Your room is ready."[24]

A total of six men were arrested for meeting on October 24. They appeared before acting judge Charles Clark, a justice of the peace, the following morning. Clark denied their request for a jury trial. All refused to take the oath during the hearing. Judge Clark fined the six men $500, declaring: "I'm for honest unionism and honest strikes. But it's my impression that you and your kind are the cause of much of the sentiment against organized labor. You are the cause of strife and riots in labor strikes, because you work in strikes not for the benefit of labor, but against the federation of labor." Clark was "sorry he was not able to fine them $5,000 or send them to the penitentiary." When told they would have to spend a year at the municipal farm if they did not pay the fine, "each smiled and thanked the judge as all of them have done."[25]

Meeting the following day, Board of Public Welfare President Charles Mill believed the city could handle any situation resulting from the free speech fight. If the jails became overcrowded as they had in Spokane, Mill declared, "I have a list of a number of buildings in the city where these men can be kept if the police arrest them and send them to us." Another option for the city was the building of large stockades at the rock piles. The stockades would be useful in keeping the IWW prisoners isolated from others, and requiring them to work longer hours would enable the city to make a profit from their labor. The board recognized a problem with stockade imprisonment. The stockades would not have any buildings. As a result, the IWW prisoners "will have to work out in the cold. . . . This means they will work there from the morning to dinner and from the time they eat their dinner until night."[26]

As the city tried to toughen its stance, the IWW also developed some new ideas on how to fight the battle and win. The union changed its way of recruiting new volunteers to go to jail. Recruitment began to focus on the favorable conditions Kansas City had to offer. One article in *Solidarity* told volunteers to come to Kansas City because the farm at Leeds fed its prisoners well and the winters were mild. Both of these conditions led the writer to declare, "We think the city will put up a rather poor fight."[27]

As another change in tactics, the IWW tried staggering the time of its nightly meetings. On October 25 the union announced the meeting to be held at the corner of Twelfth and Oak, but it actually occurred at Sixth and Main at 9:15, two hours later than the usual starting time. The tactic must have caught the police off guard because they made no arrests at the meeting.

Walker Smith, a national organizer from the Chicago headquarters and a veteran of the Denver free speech fight, also suggested other changes. He had ten thousand proclamations printed for distribution throughout the city. Meant to be educational, the proclamations informed Kansas Citians what the fight against the IWW would cost the city in tax dollars. The union also announced it had rented a hall at 1226 Grand Avenue for October 28 and Walker Smith would be speaking on the topic "Industrial Unionism Is the Way Out of Wage Slavery."[28]

A lawyer by training, Wentworth Edwin Griffen served as Kansas City chief of police from 1908 to 1913.

A final activity of the IWW on October 25 created a special coordinating committee to make policy for the rest of the free speech fight. The committee would stay away from the local headquarters so that, in case of a raid, it would not lose any of its members. In this way, all those developing strategies would be able to decide the direction of the fight.

On October 27 the national IWW made its first direct contact with the city officials. Vincent St. John sent the following telegram to the police commissioners: "Our advices . . . established that the police under your control . . . are arresting and jailing members of this organization for attempting to exercise their rights supposedly guaranteed by the constitution of Missouri and the United States. Members there have the backing of the entire organization."[29] The police responded that they would not arrest any members who did not break the law.

That evening the IWW started a meeting on the corner of Sixth and Main. Five minutes later, the speakers encouraged the crowd to follow them to the next corner. They continued this pattern, singing songs from the Wobbly *Little Red Song Book* until they reached the final destination at Twelfth and Grand. This procedure showed the crowd where the lecture would be held the next night. The large crowd blocked the street at the final destination, but the police did not interrupt Walker Smith when he started to speak and arrested no one that evening.

The next day, October 28, marked the turning point in the free speech fight in Kansas City. That morning a committee representing the IWW attended a meeting of the welfare board but accomplished little. Walker Smith and Tom Halcro then went to the police department to get permission to visit members at the municipal farm. They were asked to return at 3:00 p.m. when Chief Griffen would be there. When they did so, not only Chief Griffen but also other members of the Public Welfare Board waited to see them. They asked Smith and Halcro if they would hold an impromptu meeting to discuss the situation. The conference lasted for three hours. The fact that the city would meet the IWW caused Smith to write, "It conclusively demonstrated the tremendous power of organized might and clearly showed that we are building the new society within the shell of the old."[30]

During the meeting, both Smith and Halcro talked about the IWW and its objectives. One board member asked Halcro if the organization stood for revolution in any form. Halcro answered that "free speech was the safety valve of discontent and if that were denied the workers could not be educated and organized. This stops all possible chance of a peaceable solution and the result would be a bloody revolution and the destruction of that which had required centuries to build."[31]

After listening to Smith and Halcro, Charles Mill proposed to parole the men in jail. The two sides then negotiated a settlement agreeable to both. As a result of the settlement, according to Smith: "The IWW can speak on any corner in Kansas City, without securing a permit of any kind, where such meetings will not endanger the life and limb of passersby and where no valid objections are raised by abutting property owners."[32]

On the night of October 28, the IWW held a large meeting at 1226 Grand Avenue. The leaders of the organization did not tell the rank and file about the agreement negotiated earlier in the day. They wished to keep their members' spirits in a militant mood and insure the city would carry forth its part of the deal and release the prisoners. Walker Smith, the first speaker, limited his address to traditional themes in IWW ideology, including a history of the organization, the meaning of direct action, and the union goals, including an eight-hour workday.

Hugh Scott, a member of Local No. 61, spoke about the local situation. He summed up the issues of the free speech fight in Kansas City and elsewhere: "The fight we are having here is going to be settled by the men now in jail. The terms will be that we be allowed to talk industrial unionism on the streets of Kansas City—unmasked by anyone. We do not fight for free speech because it is in the Constitution of the United States; not on your life. We fight because we need it in our business."[33]

The following day, the Board of Public Welfare sent a letter to Chief Griffen, Judge Burney, and Assistant City Counselor Mathias verifying the agreement with Smith and Halcro for the release of the IWW prisoners. If the board heard no objections within twenty-four hours, the prisoners would be paroled if they signed a statement specifying conditions of future good behavior. Reaction to the offer was not positive, and all three officials opposed parole. They would agree only if the prisoners left town upon release. The Board of Public Welfare took the recommendation to the IWW prisoners who were not Kansas City residents. The eleven out-of-town members agreed to sign the special paper to leave town, and all the IWW prisoners signed the general agreement about future good behavior.

All of the IWW members received their paroles on November 2, 1911. Upon release, the prisoners went directly to the local union hall for a banquet. Members of the local had prepared it for them in its appreciation for their part in winning the right of free speech in Kansas City.

With the release of all IWW prisoners, each side believed it had won at least a partial victory. The IWW received the right to speak on the streets and the release of all its prisoners. The city claimed victory because it made no

Clarence A. Burney, a graduate of the University of Kansas Law School, was elected judge of Municipal Court District No. 1 in 1910.

apology for the IWW arrests, and it forced the nonresident prisoners from the city.

The tactics used by the IWW in the Kansas City free speech fight of 1911 proved similar to those in earlier battles. It primarily intended to have so many members arrested and imprisoned they would become a financial burden on the city's resources. At the same time, the IWW hoped to gain the sympathies of the populace to pressure the city officials to allow street meetings.

The city officials of Kansas City reacted similarly to others experiencing free speech fights. Most cities in similar circumstances tried to arrest the leadership of the IWW and create an unpleasant environment to discourage other IWW prisoners.

The main differences between the Kansas City free speech fight and others can be traced to influences of earlier confrontations upon the Kansas City situation. The impact that Spokane, Missoula, and Fresno had upon the country's attitude towards the IWW reached Kansas City. The image of an unbeatable militant labor organization had resulted from the ability of the IWW to win victories. In other cities the battles lasted for months, and hundreds of members had been imprisoned.

Kansas Citians realized other cities had lost after a long and bitter battle. As a result, Kansas City put up a determined front. The Kansas City episode represented a battle of perceptions to determine which side was willing to suffer more hardships. It became a game of bluff played out only in the opening moves. The IWW effectively gave the impression that armies were ready to fill jails. Charles Mill's statement illustrates the perception: "It began to look like there wouldn't be enough hammers in Kansas City to equip all the IWW members for stone breaking and the prospect of finding a building big enough to hold them appeared to be hopeless."[34] This belief in the organization's resolve to win the battle and its past record caused the city to give in to the IWW demands to speak undisturbed for industrial unionism on the streets of the city.

NOTES

1. The actual number of free speech fights has been disputed. Two authors have found the number of fights to be twenty-six: Paul Brissenden in *The IWW: A Study of American Syndicalism* (New York: Columbia University, 1919), 367, and Joseph Conlin in *Bread and Roses Too: A Study of the Wobblies* (Westport, CT: Greenwood, 1969), 71. Two authors have found the total number of fights to be about thirty: Patrick Renshaw, *The Wobblies: The Story of Syndicalism in the United States* (Garden City, NY: Doubleday, 1967), 129, and Joyce Kornbluh, ed., *Rebel Voices: An I.W.W. Anthology* (Ann Arbor: University of Michigan Press, 1964), 94.

2. Philip S. Foner, *History of the Labor Movement in the United States. Volume IV: The Industrial Workers of the World, 1905-1917* (New York: International Publishers, 1965), 174-175. Patrick Renshaw in *The Wobblies*, 20, attributes the first printing of "Wobbly" as a synonym for the Industrial Workers of the World to Harrison Gray Otis, editor of the *Los Angeles Times*, in 1911.

3. *Industrial Worker*, 7 September 1911; *Solidarity*, 2 September 1911.

4. In the reports of Roe's activities in the Kansas City papers, his name was spelled in a variety of ways, including Row, Rowe, and Roe.

5. *Kansas City Journal*, 2 October 1911.

6. Melvin Dubofsky, *We Shall Be All: A History of the Industrial Workers of the World* (Chicago: Quadrangle Books, 1969), 186.

7. *Industrial Worker*, 19 October 1911.

8. Ibid., 26 October 1911.

9. *Solidarity*, 28 October 1911; *The Agitator*, 1 November 1911.

10. *Industrial Worker*, 26 October 1911.

11. *Kansas City Journal*, 19 October 1911.

12. *Industrial Worker*, 2 November 1911.

13. *Kansas City Journal*, 19 October 1911.

14. Ibid.

15. *Kansas City Journal*, 19, 22 October 1911.

16. *Industrial Worker*, 2 November 1911.

17. *Kansas City Times*, 24 October 1911.

18. *Kansas City Star*, 24 October 1911.

19. Ibid.

20. Conlin, *Bread and Roses Too*, 75.

21. *Kansas City Journal*, 25 October 1911.

22. Ibid.

23. *Kansas City Star*, 25 October 1911.

24. *Kansas City Journal*, 25 October 1911; *Kansas City Times*, 25 October 1911.

25. *Kansas City Star*, 25 October 1911; *Kansas City Journal*, 26 October 1911.

26. *Kansas City Journal*, 26 October 1911.

27. *Solidarity*, 28 October 1911.

28. *Kansas City Journal*, 26 October 1911.

29. *Kansas City Star*, 27 October 1911.

30. *Industrial Worker*, 9 November 1911.

31. Ibid.

32. Ibid.

33. *Kansas City Journal*, 29 October 1911.

34. *Kansas City Star*, 19 October 1911.

The 1918 Kansas City Influenza Epidemic

KEVIN C. McSHANE

"I believe the epidemic had its start in Kansas City by girls kissing soldiers in the army schools and from the cantonments who had become carriers of the disease. They carried to their homes, kissed others and in their turn these others have aided in communicating the disease. There is a great deal of kissing . . . and if a ban should be placed on it there would be less influenza."[1] This statement by Dr. A. J. Gannon, head of the contagious disease division, reflected his opinion of the origin of the influenza epidemic of 1918.

First reports of the disease in Kansas City came from the army-sponsored Sweeney Motoring School for mechanics. Within twenty-four hours, 170 cases developed, followed by 500 in the next forty-eight hours, and 800 in the next week. Soon 2,300 of the 3,000 students contracted the disease. Between September 29 and October 4, fifteen of the motor mechanics died. In an attempt to check the spread of influenza, Major F. H. McGregor, commandant of all the army mechanic schools, ordered a quarantine—a measure that proved to be the most successful in combating the disease. Army officials described the quarantine as a "reverse quarantine" because it was designed to protect the army men from civilians instead of the opposite.[2]

Few pestilences have spread so quickly and left such a pattern of desperate attempts to thwart it. The dread "flu" of 1918 killed more than five hundred thousand Americans, and twenty million suffered a temporary attack. No effective cure for the viral influenza was developed during the worldwide pandemic.[3] New York City and other eastern ports received the initial impact that began in the battlefields in Europe. Medical research tried but failed

From a Drawing Titled "We've got that durned influenzy agin," by A. B. Frost, published in the Kansas City Star, *November 27, 1918.*

to combat the influenza until 1931, when Dr. R. E. Shope, author of *Swine Influenza*, isolated the virus.

The speed and ferocity of the epidemic overwhelmed the authorities in the early stage. Within a few days, three girls who had visited the motoring school began sneezing and coughing.[4] Civilian officials, led by Dr. Gannon and Dr. E. H. Bullock, health director and head of the General Hospital, believed in a quarantine, but opposition to this health measure came from business and political interests.[5]

Although few people gave the cooperation that Dr. Gannon needed, no detail escaped him. His office made suggestions, offered advice, and finally dictated many directives. Rules about public gatherings were published October 17, 1918, in the *Kansas City Star*:

> All theaters and motion picture shows, all schools and all churches must close. Public gatherings of twenty or more persons [interpreted by the health board to include dances, parties, weddings, and funerals] are forbidden. Stores employing twenty-five or more persons may not open until 9 o'clock and must close at 4 o'clock. Crowding in any store is forbidden. Not more than twenty persons standing may be carried on street cars. Music and amusement in hotels, restaurants, and cabarets is forbidden.[6]

Any public gathering place either complied with these directives or Dr. Gannon's office placarded it with yellow signs marked "Unfit for human habitation."[7]

Health inspectors served notices on two principal offenders, restaurants and streetcars. Many cafes and restaurants served meat scraps in soup stock pots. These were used a second or third time when the customer did not eat the meat. Dr. Gannon denounced it as a "dangerous practice." The streetcar situation also bothered the health department. Inspectors insured the cleaning of streetcars. By the second week of the epidemic, it became necessary to fumigate thirty-two cars before they could return to duty.[8] On October 8, Earnest B. Atchley, publicity man for the Kansas City Railways Company, said, "This company employs a force of 100 men, whose duty it is to clean, sweep and disinfect the cars every day, and since the influenza has come to Kansas City, the cars are cleaned, instead of every day, twice a day."[9] On the same day in the *Kansas City Times,* an article reported that conductors rejected inspectors from many streetcars and would not recognize the inspectors' authority. Mayor James Cowgill's proclamation on October 8 gave inspectors the necessary power to regulate the streetcars according to section 9, article 14 of the city charter, which gave the hospital and health board "the power to take all steps necessary to avoid, suppress or mitigate such a disease."[10]

A majority of the upper house of the city council agreed that all places of public gatherings be kept closed. But one alderman declared the resolution "Hun propaganda," intended to frighten Kansas Citians.[11] Theater operators toiled under the first ban of eight days which began on October 7. When a second ban began on October 17, they became incensed. Mayor Cowgill and William P. Motley, president of the hospital and health board, listened to their complaints at a mass meeting, actually forbidden by law since 150 attended. Motley told the film distributors, operators, and owners that he had signed the ban because he felt that his office required it. He quickly added that theater owners had a legitimate complaint. Heated discussions followed this statement, with the result that motion picture men volunteered to check the public places allowed to stay open.[12]

Signs of a rift between Motley and Dr. Gannon developed in early October when Motley, with the efforts of business interests behind him, urged a lifting of the first ban. After an analysis of the ten-day period showed that the highest death rate occurred on the exact day the ban was lifted, Motley claimed that he was not informed of the number of cases in the city. He then staged open warfare against advisers of the health board and Dr. Gannon in particular. Motley and Cowgill were attacked for neglecting to do more constructive work. An editorial in the *Kansas City Journal* criticized, "Those

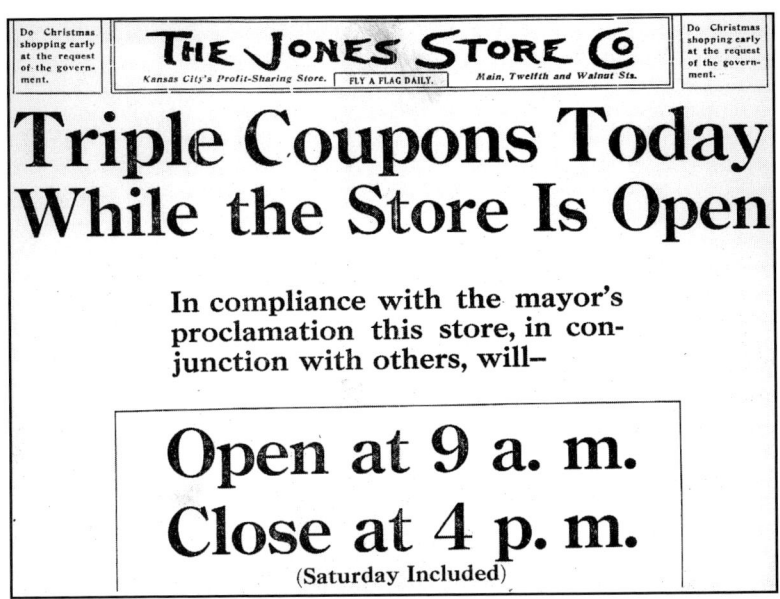

This advertisement appeared in the Kansas City Times *two days after Mayor Cowgill's October 17 directive.*

selfish interests that have been besieging the municipal authorities in order that they may continue to make money, will now find that their selfishness will cost them far more dearly than if they had actively and willingly co-operated in protecting the public health."[13]

As Kansas City attempted to "shadow box" the disease, profiteering appeared. One physician informed a girl she had influenza, and he requested that an ambulance take her to a hospital. He collected nine dollars, a notable sum in 1918, and she went to a hospital where doctors diagnosed her to be suffering from "revelry" the night before.[14] Druggists profiteered by exacting tribute for simple nose and throat washes. Dr. Gannon condemned their actions when he stated, "I could make a tub full of antiseptic wash for the price some druggists are charging for a few ounces of salty water."[15] North-Mehornay Furniture Company advertised, "The best preventive for Influenza is to keep your rooms warm and dry. Buy one of our excellent heaters and be safe and comfortable."[16] Saloon owners joined in the profiteering by placing large signs behind the bars recommending the use of quinine and whiskey as a precautionary measure.[17]

James P. Cowgill

Other businessmen disregarded the seriousness of the epidemic. Hotels neglected to report cases, feeling that their establishments might suffer.[18] Many landlords failed to maintain a temperature of seventy degrees in their flats and rooming houses. One city alderman commented, "Hundreds of citizens have complained of lack of heat, and the hospital and health board had declared that the landlords are prolonging the epidemic of influenza and pneumonia by not furnishing enough heat."[19] An inspector for the contagious disease division found one man with discontinued gas service who "probably lived through the night through the kindness of neighbors who heated bricks to keep the sick man warm."[20] Debate over the question, business first or health first, continued throughout the epidemic.

Some landlords feared condemnation of their apartments and other buildings. Fire wardens examined and condemned forty-two structures. One warden explained, "In the building at 1009 St. Louis Avenue we found tenants dumping slops and sewage out of the window into the alley. One of the women tenants told us that eight families lived in this building and there was no plumbing in the place."[21]

This spotlighted a major health problem in Kansas City. In 1912, 15,000 privies existed within the city. One housing report stated: "In the Penn Valley district, inhabited by working men and their families—substantial, everyday, you-and-I-kind of people—there are 1,179 dwellings. The toilet facilities are comprehended in the following: Modern, 200; dry sewer connected, 439; vaults, 530."[22]

McClure Flats, an area between 19th and 20th streets with Central Alley in the middle, also caused the health department concern. Condemnation efforts met with resistance. It was reported in the *Kansas City Journal*:

> About two hundred persons, white, Mexican and colored live and die,—'mostly die' doctors say . . . the place was raided by the health squad and twenty-three cases of influenza found. Garbage cans had been provided but the residents of McClure Flats do not believe in garbage cans. . . . Children played in the garbage in the rear of a flat where an influenza patient was dying. On this garbage pile was poured the slops from the sick room.[23]

On November 27 the health board pronounced McClure Flats unfit for habitation. Henry Benjamin, health board member, asked if the flats could not be cleaned up. Dr. Bullock answered this by saying, "The brick walls are crumbling, underneath the floors which are built directly upon the ground—there are no cellars—large numbers of rats have nests. As you know, rats are one of the greatest carriers of disease. A number of large holes in the

A Congested District of Kansas City

floors of the rooms afford rodents entry into the living quarters of hundreds of persons."[24] Benjamin's question illustrated the apathy of the health board.

Conditions such as these warranted more direct action. But politics interfered. An editorial declared:

> Practically every member of the health and sanitary departments hold their jobs by the grace of the bosses, and the same is true of members of the police department who are charged with enforcement of the multitude of health ordinances. . . . Sanitary and police officers long ago learned that it is of little avail to cite offenders into court or order them to clean up. In either instance there is a scurrying for "Tom," for "Mike," or for "Johnny" or some other ward boss with sufficient power to ward off punishment.[25]

Kansas City suffered from a fifty-fifty arrangement for jobs in the health department between Joe Shannon's "rabbits" and Tom Pendergast's "goats."[26]

Politics dominated the history of the General Hospital and the hospital and health board. In 1909 doctors faced charges of inhuman treatment for throwing pneumonia patients into tubs of ice water and making convalescent patients work on a patient's ulcerated leg as a punishment, and patients were fighting in terror against having operations the doctors were trying to press upon them. Finally, an investigating committee for the city found the charges "purely a political move to embarrass the Democratic administration."[27]

The same situation prevailed in 1918. Nothing missed Motley's surveillance. Early in October, Motley insisted that the city hospitals stop purchasing cauliflower and shelled pecans. He said, "These are war times. I want patients and employees to get plenty to eat but we're not going to put out non-essentials."[28] His attack upon petty problems never ceased, while larger problems faced the health board.

Dr. Gannon tried to ignore the political squabble. With the powers of a "health czar," he cajoled, threatened, and harassed the citizenry. His efforts included fumigating schools, barber colleges, and factories; ordering stores to provide disinfectant finger bowls for cashiers; complaining about undertakers who allowed inexperienced employees who normally served as chauffeurs to practice on influenza victims; and requesting insurance agents and house-to-house peddlers to stay away from quarantined homes. Health inspectors needed motorcars to help in the cleanliness campaign. Instead of the health board obtaining the use of the city's vehicles for the doctors and inspectors, the health department relied on the courtesy of the public welfare board, who loaned the cars.[29]

The shortage of motorcars troubled the health department almost as much as the shortage of nurses and doctors. Many Kansas City doctors and nurses had enlisted in the armed services. The demands of the war coupled with the influenza epidemic impeded nurses' training in all the hospitals.

St. Joseph's Hospital, erected in 1917, had barely established any routines before the epidemic struck the city. "The new structure where every room had sunlight a part of the day . . . saw ambulances wheeled to the back doors day and night, chaplains and nuns were on constant vigil as time was so short for some of the victims that no hospital stay could help them and the same ambulance delivered the silent ones elsewhere."[30] One young nurse recalled the treatment of "silent ones." She cleaned patients with bichloride baths to kill the germs before the undertakers arrived.[31]

Pitiful cases occurred as the invading influenza swept through the area. Inspectors discovered one woman who had been dead for twelve hours and had died without medical assistance. Two small children, hungry and grief-stricken, both too young to understand, had vainly tried to waken their mother.[32] The hardships of a family in Kansas City, Kansas, were reported in the *Kansas City Kansan* on December 3. "Leo L. Jones of 837 Sandusky died at St. Margaret's hospital. The same day all three of the children and a brother of Mr. Jones who was visiting him from Memphis, Tenn. were taken to the

hospital with the dread disease. This morning, one of the girls, Essie Thelma, aged 5, died. A little boy, Jenidous, is very low and at noon his recovery was said by hospital officials to be doubtful, although the best is hoped for."[33]

The populace was partially responsible for the spread of influenza. People ignored the signs of coughing or dizziness that preceded the illness. The suddenness of the disease surprised healthy young men in particular. One employee at the Armour packing plant said, "I picked up one box off a truck and I thought someone had stabbed me in the back."[34] As one reporter commented, "Men in prime physical condition and those of strongest physique have been the easiest victims while the more frail have almost invariably recovered."[35] Influenza respected no class, no geographic area, and no age group. Many victims relied on remedies. Whiskey and rock candy remained remedies for some, although many doubted their help. Skunk oil hung around the neck of Orville Dalton, a Kansas Citian. This, he thought, helped him to ward off the disease.[36] One woman "with the fear of death and 'flu' in her heart, and with a trusting disposition had been taking the advice of her neighbors and eating a cake of yeast each day." It was reported on December 5, 1918, "Now she is sick in bed with severe pains in her stomach. She is belching gas and is afraid she is bloating. Scoffing friends intimate that the yeast has begun to work and she is 'rising.' She fears that she will have to have an operation but continues to eat the yeast."[37]

Earnest Crain, a nonsmoker, heeded the suggestion of a neighbor and smoked cigarettes to stave off the disease.[38]

Dr. Gannon offered one remedy by telling people they should eat onions and garlic. One woman sliced onions and put them on windowsills, behind pictures, and on the mantle of her home. A nurse in charge of the contagious disease ward at General Hospital said she had used soda through smallpox, fever, and other epidemics and had never had an ill day.[39] Eye, ear, nose, and throat specialists proposed gauze masks to prevent influenza.

So with "Ku Klux seriousness," Kansas Citians donned white masks. Barbers, hotel and restaurant waiters, factory employees, elevator operators, cashiers, bankers, streetcar conductors, and conductorettes placed their confidence in masks since "the wearing of masks as a preventive against influenza is said to be the only truly trustworthy safeguard against contraction of the disease."[40] However, wearing a mask provided a cover for certain activities. "Everybody should wear an influenza mask," said a soft-voiced gentleman to J. F. Elsworth, a grocer at 6427 East Thirteenth Street. "A freezing temperature also prevents influenza," the man declared, "and a grocery man should take all precautions against it. Try the ice box and see if it won't cure your cold." Mr. Elsworth did not take kindly to the suggestion,

Dr. Eugene H. Bullock

but when a revolver was produced, he did not hesitate. When he was released, he found twenty-five dollars had been taken from the cash register.[41]

On November 11, 1918, a frightened populace emerged from a hermit-like existence. Nearly one hundred thousand Kansas Citians joined in the armistice celebrations. As Mayor Cowgill said later, "Every man, woman, and child able to be out of bed was on the streets."[42] On November 17, one report stated that influenza as an epidemic no longer existed in Kansas City, as was evident from the sparse and sporadic cases reported.[43] While optimism persisted, however, Kansas Citians died.

The health board became concerned over the second phase of the epidemic and sought a scapegoat. They dismissed Dr. Gannon in a secret meeting. Motley objected to the doctor "doing too many things on his own initiative."[44] The volatile meeting rang with insults. "'You're a --- ---' shouted W. P. Motley. 'No man can call me a --- --- and get away with it,' answered Dr. Gannon. 'Give me that badge, you're fired.' 'I'll keep my badge you can't fire me,' came the reply."[45]

Henry Benjamin, health board member, resigned from the health board after Dr. Gannon's dismissal. Dr. Bullock resigned his job as superintendant of the General Hospital but decided to remain as health director. Miss Geraldine Borland, superintendent of nurses at General Hospital, resigned in late January. Her resignation, never explained in the newspapers, remained a mystery. An editorial explained the resignations of Gannon, Bullock, and Benjamin in this manner:

> The unfortunate feature of bossism in the conduct of municipal affairs is that it invariably leads to driving out the good men rather than the political henchmen who are often the victims of factional wrangles. Personal wrangles between the president and almost anybody who differs with him have characterized the situation, even during the epidemic which has cost so many lives in the community.[46]

Regardless of the political difficulties, influenza cases multiplied. With Dr. Gannon dismissed, Dr. Bullock tried to carry on a campaign against the pestilence. Finally, Dr. Bullock, a flu victim himself, admitted the futility of resistance. He summoned help from the United States Public Health Service in a telegram in which he said, "Assistance is needed at once from your department to help control influenza epidemic in Kansas City, Mo. May we hope for your immediate help?"[47] Two United States Public Health officers arrived. These men enacted no special legislation. Rather, the tornado-like pattern of the disease continued, and the epidemic touched down in areas west of Kansas City.

"Life's Darkest Moment"

In contrast, St. Louis exerted every effort to stop the epidemic. St. Louis enforced a harsh quarantine that aroused the business population. Health Commissioner Charles Starkloff of St. Louis met with Mayor Henry W. Kiel; Dr. B. C. Wilkes; Assistant Health Commissioner Henry Jordan; Dr. James Woodrugg of the Health Department; Dr. A. S. Barnes of the Chamber of Commerce; Dr. Canby Robinson, dean of the Washington University Medical School; Dr. Ellsworth Smith, president of the St. Louis Medical Society; Major L. C. H. Bahrenberg, Missouri representative of the United States Public [Health] Service; and John Schmoll, director of public welfare, to discuss the epidemic. The business interests asked the obvious question, "But why should St. Louis be made the example of a nation?" Dr. Starkloff retorted, "Because St. Louis has to date the best influenza record of the nation and we mean to keep it the best."[48] This city, larger than Kansas City, fought the epidemic without political involvement.

Instead of a spirit of cooperation in Kansas City, apathy greeted the health department's efforts to correct unsanitary conditions. The new year, 1919, saw the end of the epidemic. Kansas City emerged with an alarming death rate. The 1918 death rate from all forms of influenza and pneumonia soared to 718.1 per 100,000 population as compared to a death rate of 205.0 in 1917 and 301.1 in 1919. During the last four months of 1918, 1,865 Kansas Citians died from influenza and pneumonia.[49]

Kansas City's high death rate was caused by the refusal of merchants, restaurant owners, and motion picture operators to comply with orders, by the use of home remedies, and finally and fatally, by the political feud between Motley and Dr. Gannon. Dr. Gannon refused to accept the political situation and apathy. He attempted to assert the power of a medical dictator, necessary in an epidemic. But hampered by the fifty-fifty political arrangement and the feud with Motley, he was unsuccessful as Kansas Citians tolerated the worst epidemic in the history of the city.

NOTES

1. *Kansas City Times*, 18 October 1918. St. Mary's Hospital at 2900 Main, the only hospital with 1918 medical records, refused permission to look into the personal records. All other Kansas City hospitals had disposed of their medical records of 1918 and 1919.

2. *Kansas City Star*, 27 September 1918; *Kansas City Post*, 6 October 1918.

3. Frank L. Horsfall Jr. and Igor Tamm, eds., *Viral and Rickettsial Infections of Man* (Philadelphia: Lippincott, 1965), 717.

4. *Kansas City Star*, 27 September 1918.

5. *Kansas City Times*, 18 October 1918.

6. *Kansas City Star*, 17 October 1918. Also under section 729 of the *Charter and Revised Ordinances of Kansas City* (1909), 738: "Whenever any residence, or portion of the city to the extent of one residence or one or more blocks or squares of ground shall in the opinion of the Health Commissioner, be infected with any malignant or infectious or contagious disease, he shall have the power, by and with the approval of the board to cause the said residence, block or blocks or squares of ground to be vacated by the residents or inhabitants thereof for the purpose of disinfecting or fumigating the same or if this not be deemed expedient or judicious by the Health Commissioner, he shall have the power and authority to close up the street."

7. *Kansas City Journal*, 6 October 1918.

8. *Kansas City Star*, 7 October 1918; *Kansas City Times*, 9 October 1918; *Kansas City Journal*, 10 October 1918. Streetcars brought complaints to the Health Department as early as 1915. Trash, banana peels, peanut hulls, and papers left on the seats and not removed caused the Health Department concern in the *Monthly Report of the Hospital and Health Board* 3, No. 3.

9. *Kansas City Journal*, 8 October 1918.

10. Ibid.

11. Ibid., 15 October 1918. Mr. George Hook, a Kansas Citian, revealed the same sentiment in an interview on March 6, 1966. He felt the Huns used germ warfare against the United States to spread influenza.

12. *Kansas City Times*, 18 October 1918.

13. *Kansas City Journal*, 18 October 1918; *Kansas City Times*, 18 October 1918; *Kansas City Star*, 8 November 1918. During the epidemic, doctors neglected to report pneumonia and influenza cases even though they violated section 737 of the *Revised Ordinances* that required the "sex, age, and residence of the party" having pneumonia. In the *Monthly Report of the Hospital and Health Board* of January 1912, physicians received a stiff warning from the Department of Health for failure to report pneumonia cases.

14. *Kansas City Star*, 27 October 1918.

15. *Kansas City Journal*, 14 October 1918. In the *Kansas City Post*, October 10, 1918, an article explained that a salt nose and throat spray manufactured for 25 cents a gallon sold for 75 and 85 cents an ounce.

16. *Kansas City Star*, 27 October 1918.

17. *Kansas City Times*, 25 October 1918.

18. Ibid., 19 October 1918. Sections 733 and 739 of the *Charter and Revised*

Ordinances of Kansas City forbade any "physician, hotel clerk, boarding house keeper or householder who shall secrete any smallpox patient or mislead the Health Commissioner so as to prevent the control of the same, any person who shall prescribe for or treat any case of scarlet fever, measles, typhoid fever, diptheria, smallpox or any disease of a pestilential or epidemic nature and shall not immediately on receiving knowledge that the person or persons afflicted with any of the said diseases, report the same to the Hospital and Health Board shall be deemed guilty of a misdemeanor."

19. *Kansas City Journal*, 14 January 1919.

20. *Kansas City Times*, 26 October 1918. The gas company continually received criticism during the epidemic for stopping gas service to homes.

21. *Kansas City Post*, 21 October 1918. Fire officials condemned the buildings for violation of fire and health ordinances.

22. Kansas City Board of Public Welfare, *Report on Housing Conditions in Kansas City, Missouri* (Kansas City: Fratcher, 1912), 18.

23. *Kansas City Journal*, 21 October 1918.

24. Ibid., 27 November 1918.

25. *Kansas City Times*, 24 October 1918.

26. William M. Reddig, *Tom's Town: Kansas City and the Pendergast Legend* (Philadelphia: Lippincott, 1947), 82-83.

27. *Jackson County Medical Journal* 26 (1 October 1932): 19. No health records other than county reports exist within this journal.

28. *Kansas City Post*, 2 October 1918.

29. Ibid., 9 October 1918; *Kansas City Star*, 9 October 1918; *Kansas City Journal*, 20 October 1918.

30. *Jackson County Medical Society Commemorative Issue* 50 (30 June 1956): 1560.

31. Mrs. Ester Dunn, in interview with the author, 3 March 1966.

32. *Kansas City Journal*, 20 October 1918.

33. *Kansas City (KS) Kansan*, 3 December 1918.

34. Mr. William Taylor, in interview with the author, 13 March 1966.

35. *Kansas City Times*, 8 October 1918. Mr. George Hook, a Kansas Citian stationed at Camp Dodge, Iowa, substantiated this account in practically the same words. A. A. Hoehling in *The Great Epidemic* (Boston: Little, Brown, 1961), mentioned this same phenomenon on page 40. Unfortunately, Hoehling's book sketched the influenza epidemic poorly.

36. Mr. James Silverman, in interview with the author, 3 March 1966; Mr. Orville Dalton, in interview with the author, 6 March 1966.

37. *Kansas City (KS) Kansan*, 5 December 1918.

38. Mrs. Edris Crain (daughter of Mr. Earnest Crain), in interview with the author, 4 April 1966. Mr. Crain, interested in athletics, never smoked until the epidemic. Dr. Gannon contradicted this remedy in the *Kansas City Journal* on October 20, 1918, when he stated that many deaths occurred among "inveterate inhalers of cigarette smoke."

39. *Kansas City Times*, 18, 19 October 1918; Dunn, interview.

40. *Kansas City Star*, 21 October 1918.

41. Ibid., 27 October 1918.

42. *Kansas City Journal*, 12 November 1918; *Kansas City Post*, 9 December 1918; *Jackson County Medical Journal* 26 (1 October 1932): 22.

43. *Kansas City Post*, 17 November 1918.

44. *Kansas City Star*, 27 November 1918.

45. *Kansas City Journal*, 28 November 1918.

46. Ibid., 3 December 1918; 28 January 1919.

47. *Kansas City Post*, 5 December 1918. Dr. Bullock gave a daily record of the influenza in the telegram:

Date	Cases	Deaths
November 23	58	6
November 24	46	3
November 25	157	7
November 26	204	14
November 27	318	7
November 28	170	8
November 29	414	12
November 30	345	6
December 1	185	12
December 2	401	16
December 3	397	20
December 4	343	16

48. *St. Louis Globe-Democrat*, 9 November 1918.

49. U.S. Bureau of the Census, *Mortality Statistics, 1920* (Washington, DC: Government Printing Office, 1922), 30.

"Nearest by Air to Everywhere": Aviation Promotion in Kansas City: 1925-1931

JAMES W. LEYERZAPF

Between 1925 and 1931, the Kansas City Chamber of Commerce sponsored a major campaign to promote both commercial aviation and the aircraft industry in Kansas City. The chamber's aviation promoters, led by Louis E. Holland, believed that the city's proximity to the geographical center of the country and its central location in the great plains made it an ideal site for the hub of air transport systems and the center of the aviation industry. Armed with a strong faith in the city's natural advantages, Holland and his fellow aviation enthusiasts directed an intensive effort to make Kansas City the aviation center of the United States.

Aviation promotion in twentieth-century Kansas City fits within a broad pattern of transportation development in American history. The objective of Kansas City's aviation promoters—economic growth through the development of transportation—was identical to the goal of nineteenth-century canal and railroad promoters. Furthermore, the promotional method of the city's aviation enthusiasts—combining private and public resources to attract transportation companies—was similar to the procedure employed by the proponents of canals and railroads. The development of canals and railroads had been heavily dependent upon public assistance from all levels of government. Railroads, because of their large capital requirements, especially had been dependent upon public aid in the form of land grants, investment of public funds in private railroad companies, and outright cash bonuses.[1] Nineteenth-century Kansas City followed this pattern of public and private cooperation on behalf of railroad development. The local chamber of commerce had

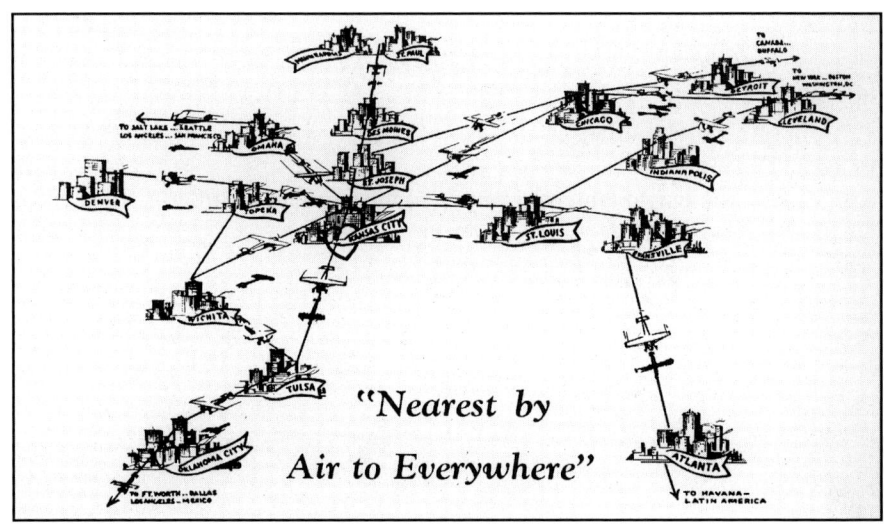

"Nearest by Air to Everywhere"

[Greater Kansas City Chamber of Commerce]

organized a vigorous campaign to attract railroads and had persuaded the community to invest public funds in private projects.[2] The twentieth-century chamber of commerce followed in this tradition of combining private and public enterprise to stimulate transportation development.

Before 1925 little effort had been exerted to promote aviation in the city. In March 1920 the chamber of commerce appointed an aerial promotion committee, but the committee was relatively inactive during the first five years of its existence. The major effort to stimulate aviation in the early 1920s had been the construction of Richards Airfield in 1922 by the Air Terminal Association, an organization of air-minded local businessmen. The field was leased to the War Department, which supervised flying at the field and operated a flying school. In addition, the Air Terminal Association built a hangar for private use, but no commercial development occurred at the field until 1926.[3]

The year 1925 was crucial to Kansas City's development as an aviation center. First, Louis E. Holland, an enthusiastic supporter of aviation, acquired substantial influence within the Kansas City Chamber of Commerce. In March he was appointed first vice president of the chamber, and in September he was elected president.[4] Second, commercial aviation was stimulated throughout the country by the passage of the Kelly Air Mail Act, which transferred the air mail from government operation to private carriers.[5]

From 1922 to 1925, Holland served as president of the Associated Advertising Clubs of the World (AACW). While president of that organization, he had done considerable traveling by air. In 1924 the AACW held its annual convention in London, and after the convention, Holland flew from London to Paris. While on the continent, he was deeply impressed by the successful operation of the Royal Dutch Airlines and the German Lufthansa. Because of his early exposure to air travel, Holland became convinced long before most Americans that commercial aviation was feasible.[6]

For several years prior to 1925, considerable opposition to government operation of the air mail had been building. The railroad industry led the opposition, largely because most mail was carried by rail and the industry consequently resented government competition. The railroads and other business interests wished the government to transfer air mail operations to private carriers. The opponents of government operation achieved their objective in the Kelly Act, which President Calvin Coolidge signed into law on February 2, 1925. Although the act provided for the eventual transfer of all air mail operations to private carriers, the transcontinental route was not transferred immediately to private operation. Spur air mail routes connecting

Louis Holland was already a successful businessman in the early 1920s, owning his own engraving company and inventor of a commercial-grade lawn sprinkler. [Lou Holland Collection, Union Station/Kansas City Museum, Kansas City, MO]

with the transcontinental service were opened first, so that the commercial lines could gain experience before bidding was opened on the transcontinental route.[7]

Holland immediately saw the commercial possibilities inherent in the spur routes. He believed that if Kansas City were located on one of the spurs, the city's trade territory would expand considerably as a result of the faster communication between the city's businessmen and their regional customers. He also shrewdly perceived that the initiation of privately operated air mail was the first step toward the establishment of commercial aviation. He had little doubt that express and passenger service would soon be successful economic enterprises. He was convinced that Kansas City had a large stake in acquiring air mail service because he believed that those cities establishing an early foothold in aviation would reap the largest benefits.[8] To insure the city's future in aviation, Holland launched an effort to establish Kansas City on one of the spur routes.

While serving as president of the Associated Advertising Clubs of the World, Holland acquired considerable influence within the Post Office Department. The AACW sponsored the Truth-in-Advertising Movement and attempted to enforce truth in advertising through a National Vigilance Committee, of which Holland was a director. Because the vigilance committee often cooperated with postal inspectors in those cases where fraudulent advertisers used the mails, Holland became acquainted with high-ranking Post Office Department officials, including Postmaster General Harry S. New. Holland ably exploited his influence within the department in his efforts to obtain air mail service for Kansas City.

In March and April 1925, Holland met several times with New and Paul Henderson, assistant postmaster general in charge of air mail. Holland was primarily interested in what requirements the department intended to set for the establishment of air mail service. Informed by Henderson that potential mail volume would be the primary consideration, Holland returned to Kansas City and instructed the chamber of commerce to conduct a survey of the potential mail volume of the city's large business establishments. In late April the Post Office Department published the requirements for establishing air mail service. Within twenty-four hours, Kansas City Postmaster William E. Morton had mailed the chamber survey and a formal petition for air mail service to the postmaster general. On May 16, 1925, the Post Office Department approved the Chicago to Kansas City air mail route.[9]

The approval of the route did not guarantee air mail service, however. The Post Office Department only authorized such service; private airlines had to bid for the right to carry the air mail over the route. If the bids were too high, the department had the right to cancel the projected route. The airline most interested in the Chicago to Kansas City service was National Air Transport (NAT) of Chicago. Organized by former Assistant Postmaster General Paul Henderson, who had resigned from the Post Office Department shortly after the Kelly Act was passed, the line was backed by such noted businessmen as Phillip Wrigley, Lester Armour, and William A. Rockefeller.[10] In order to assure that its bid would permit operating the air mail route at a profit, NAT requested the Kansas City Chamber of Commerce to make another air mail survey in August 1925. The chamber's industrial committee conducted the survey under Holland's direction and forwarded the data to the airline. On October 7, NAT bid successfully on the Chicago to Kansas City route, which by that time had been extended to Dallas.[11]

NAT required more of the cities on the route than mail volume surveys, however; an airfield and airplane hangar that met both NAT and Post Office Department requirements also had to be provided. To meet the physical requirements, the chamber began looking for suitable facilities in the late summer of 1925. When NAT representatives met with Holland on November 17, they chose Richards Field as the best of the available landing sites. Fortunately, the chamber was able to persuade the Air Terminal Association to offer free use of the Richards facilities for a year. Although no suitable hangar was available at the site, the chamber guaranteed NAT that a hangar would be constructed before air mail operations began in the spring. In return for the promise of a hangar, NAT pledged to locate its operating and executive headquarters in Kansas City.[12]

Because the estimated construction cost was $15,000, the erection of a hangar posed a substantial problem for the chamber. Holland and several chamber officials approached the city council for funds, but the council was unwilling to help.[13] Unable to raise funds from public sources, the chamber attempted to solicit the money from the business community. The chamber acted as trustee of all funds collected and was to hold title to the hangar, which would be rented to NAT. The city's businessmen were less than enthusiastic supporters of aviation, however. By March 1926 total subscriptions had fallen considerably short of the amount needed to build the hangar, and NAT officials had become concerned that it would not be completed before mail service was inaugurated. A last-minute drive succeeded in raising the necessary funds, however, and the hangar was finished two weeks before NAT began air mail operations on May 12, 1926.[14]

Holland was elected chamber president in 1925 largely because the organization's board of directors felt that he was best qualified to direct the chamber's industrial expansion program. When his term of office expired in

Paul Johnson Flying First Air Mail into Kansas City, May 12, 1926 [Lou Holland Collection, Union Station/Kansas City Museum]

1928, the directors created the position of executive manager so that he could continue to supervise the expansion effort.[15] The purpose of the program was to diversify the city's manufacturing, which at the time was based largely upon food processing. Holland's effort to promote aviation was an integral part of the industrial expansion plan. He believed that the aircraft industry offered the most fruitful possibilities for industrial growth because the city could meet all the requirements of aircraft production. First, the industry was based primarily upon assembly rather than heavy manufacturing, thus obviating the need for large fuel supplies. Second, the flat terrain surrounding Kansas City assured safety for experimental flying. Third, the city's inland location guaranteed relative invulnerability to the builders of military aircraft. Fourth and finally, the city's central location assured rapid delivery to any point in the country.[16]

Holland made his first attempt to attract the aircraft industry in the summer of 1925. In 1924, Anthony Fokker, the noted Dutch airplane designer and manufacturer, had created the American Aircraft Corporation to capitalize on the growing American market for airplanes.[17] Because he was highly conscious of the military vulnerability of a coastal manufacturing location, Fokker considered building his projected plant in the Midwest. In June 1925 he sent representatives to survey several midwestern cities, including Kansas

City. On June 15 the representatives discussed the aircraft plant proposition with Holland. After assuring Holland that Kansas City was one of the sites under consideration, they asked if the city's businessmen would be willing to subscribe half of the $2,000,000 capitalization. Unable to answer the question offhand, Holland called a meeting of the chamber's new industries committee to determine the availability of local capital for the proposition. Because the committee was also unable to answer the inquiry, a subcommittee was created to investigate the matter.[18]

On June 22, Fokker arrived in Kansas City and met with the subcommittee members, who assured him that the necessary capital could be raised in the city. Because he had not yet decided upon a location, Fokker asked the subcommittee whether the capital would be made available if he were to build the plant elsewhere in the Midwest. The subcommittee answered that the interested businessmen would only invest in the firm if it were a local project. Fokker agreed to build the plant in the city, and on July 15, 1925, three prominent Kansas City businessmen, Herbert Woolf, Conrad Mann, and Arthur Hardgrave, formed an underwriting syndicate which signed contracts with Fokker for the construction of a $2,000,000 aircraft factory.[19] Ground was never broken for the plant, however, because the syndicate was unable to raise the required capital. On November 27, 1925, Holland informed Fokker that the chamber's board of directors had abandoned the project.[20]

During his tenure with the chamber of commerce, Holland attempted to attract other large aircraft firms to the city, but none of his efforts proceeded as far as the Fokker project. Kansas City's achievements in the aviation industry between 1925 and 1931 were limited to the small private plane industry. By 1930 the city had three aircraft companies, representing a total investment of $300,000 and employing three hundred men.[21] The city's accomplishments in the light plane industry were modest, however, compared to the spectacular accomplishments of a rival city barely one-fourth the size of Kansas City— Wichita, Kansas. By 1930, Wichita was producing over a fourth of all private planes built in the United States, and the city's businessmen had invested $5,000,000 in sixteen aircraft companies employing over two thousand men. Wichita's success was partly entrepreneurial; a vigorous chamber of commerce and a business community willing to invest in aviation had attracted such aeronautical geniuses as E. M. Laird, Walter Beech, and Clyde Cessna in the early 1920s. Their early successes had created the foundation upon which the aircraft industry had grown.[22] By contrast, Kansas City's businessmen were less than enthusiastic supporters of aviation; the failure of the Fokker proposition and the difficulty in funding the NAT hangar testified to the business community's reluctance to back Holland's promotional efforts.

Kansas City's relative lack of success in the aircraft industry cannot be explained wholly in entrepreneurial terms, however. Aviation promotion was also dependent upon the cooperation of public authorities. Adequate airfields were necessary for the development of aviation-related industries because aircraft manufacturers required facilities for experimental flying and delivered most of their products by air. By 1930 most large American cities had either completed or had initiated construction of municipal airports. Wichita was no exception to this trend; the city's public officials willingly maintained and improved airport facilities.[23] By contrast, Kansas City's public authorities reluctantly assumed responsibility for the acquisition and development of a municipal airport.

Holland was acutely aware that both the industrial and commercial facets of aviation required adequate airport facilities. Consequently, from 1926 to 1929, the heart of his aviation program was his effort to persuade the city administration to build a municipal airport.

By the fall of 1926, it had become apparent that Richards Field could no longer serve as an adequate airfield. National Air Transport had expressed its dissatisfaction with field facilities, and the War Department had informed Holland that it intended to remove the air squadron from Kansas City unless better facilities were provided.[24] In response to the crisis, Holland requested the local Army Air Corps Reserve Officers' Association to make a survey of possible airport sites in the area and to recommend one of them for a municipal airport. The survey, released in January 1927, suggested a site in the industrial suburb of North Kansas City. The recommended location was a flat peninsula formed by a sharp bend in the Missouri River. The peninsula pointed south towards Kansas City's business district, only five minutes away by car or taxi. The owner of the property, a syndicate composed of the Burlington Railroad and the Armour and Swift meat packing interests, offered to lease the land to the city under an option-to-purchase arrangement.[25]

City Manager Henry F. McElroy, who represented the powerful Pendergast machine that governed the city, was skeptical of aviation and was therefore reluctant to invest in an airport. Because Pendergast's power was rooted in every social and economic group within the city, the chamber of commerce did not possess sufficient political leverage to force the city administration to build the airport.[26] It was therefore necessary for Holland to supplement pressure with persuasion; he had to convert McElroy into an aviation enthusiast. One technique Holland employed was to bring to McElroy's office every airline official, aircraft manufacturer, or noted aviator who visited the city. Holland and his air-minded guests would then attempt to sell the city manager on the commercial and industrial potential of aviation. Holland also used his great

The National Air Transport Office, Kansas City, Before 1927 Fire [Lou Holland Collection, Union Station/Kansas City Museum]

diplomatic skill upon McElroy, frequently taking him to lunch, where he informed the city manager of recent developments in the chamber's aviation program. On January 20, 1927, Holland finally persuaded McElroy to discuss with the city council the possibility of leasing the airport site.[27]

Holland's objective of building a municipal airport was aided in late February by a fire at Richards Field that destroyed the NAT hangar and three of the transport company's aircraft. Although Holland persuaded the army squadron to allow NAT temporary use of the government hangar, the destruction of facilities threatened Kansas City with the loss of air mail service. Holland skillfully exploited the crisis by advising McElroy that the fire made construction of a municipal airport imperative. McElroy agreed; in May 1927 the city leased the North Kansas City site, and in July the public works department began field improvements, including the construction of a hangar.[28]

Shortly after the city leased the site, McElroy informed Holland that the airport would be dedicated in August. The chamber of commerce president seized the opportunity presented by the dedication to impress upon the Kansas City public the importance of aviation. In May, Charles A. Lindbergh had made his heroic transatlantic flight. Holland believed that if he could persuade Lindbergh to dedicate the airport, the attendant publicity and public enthusiasm would benefit the chamber's aviation program immeasurably. Fortunately,

Charles A. Lindbergh Dedicating the Kansas City Airport [Lou Holland Collection, Union Station/Kansas City Museum]

Holland had several close friends within the rival St. Louis Chamber of Commerce who were willing to arrange a meeting with the flyer. The meeting was successful; on August 17, 1927, the *Spirit of St. Louis* landed at the Kansas City Municipal Airport. A gala parade and reception welcomed the hero, and in the afternoon, Lindbergh dedicated the new airport.[29]

The city administration proceeded with the airport improvements in the latter half of 1927. By the end of the year, two hangars, one for air mail planes and one for general commercial use, had been completed. Although both NAT and the army squadron were operating on the new field by January 1928, Holland was not satisfied. He urged McElroy to purchase the site so that a permanent municipal field would be assured. McElroy and the city council responded to his request by submitting a $1,000,000 airport bond issue to the electorate on May 8. The bonds failed to carry, however, barely missing the required two-thirds majority.[30]

Despite the improvements made in 1927, airport facilities were grossly inadequate. The cinder runways and taxi roads were so rutted and rough as to be unsafe, the hangars were unsatisfactory, and passenger facilities were nonexistent. NAT was so dissatisfied by June 1928 that it considered moving its operations from the city. Several manufacturers of aircraft and aircraft accessories also threatened to leave, and aviation interests in other parts of the country vetoed the erection of branch plants in Kansas City because of airport conditions.[31] Matters were brought to a head in June 1928 when two major air transport companies offered to service the city if the airport were improved.

Transcontinental Air Transport (TAT) had been created in May 1928 to operate a combination air and rail coast-to-coast passenger service. Known as the "Lindbergh Line" because the famous pilot had associated with the company, TAT had substantial Wall Street financial backing. Kansas City was a logical stop on the projected New York to Los Angeles route, but the airline threatened to bypass the city if the intolerable airport conditions were not remedied.[32]

The other airline, Scenic Airways, planned to establish air-rail service from Kansas City to Los Angeles. G. Hall Roosevelt, vice president of General Electric, was president of the company. Roosevelt suggested to Holland and McElroy that the creation of a private syndicate to lease and develop the field would be the wisest solution to the airport problem. After adequate facilities were developed, the lease would be returned to the city so that the airport could be purchased when funds became available. Roosevelt offered to subscribe up to 75 percent of the syndicate stock. Holland was amenable to the proposition, but McElroy refused to turn over the city's lease to a private developer.[33]

Faced with the prospect of losing both airlines, the chamber of commerce appointed an aeronautics subcommittee to formulate a solution to the problem. The subcommittee, headed by Holland, recommended that the chamber's board of directors insist that the city administration make the necessary airport improvements, including the erection of additional hangars and the construction of a passenger terminal. Meanwhile, in early June the city council had authorized a resubmittal of the airport bonds in August. The chamber's board of directors considered the council decision in formulating the resolution to be sent to McElroy. The resolution, delivered to the city manager on June 18, requested that the city make the improvements specified by the subcommittee. In return for the city's investment in airport facilities, the chamber promised vigorous support of the airport bond issue.[34]

In his response to the resolution, McElroy expressed a reluctance to invest in airport improvements before the city purchased the site. Nevertheless, because he believed that chamber support guaranteed passage of the bonds, he agreed to proceed with the improvements. On June 21, the city began construction of hangars to house TAT and Scenic.[35]

In order to assure passage of the airport bonds, Holland organized a massive campaign. The chamber appropriated several thousand dollars for publicity and set up a complex campaign organization. Four chamber representatives

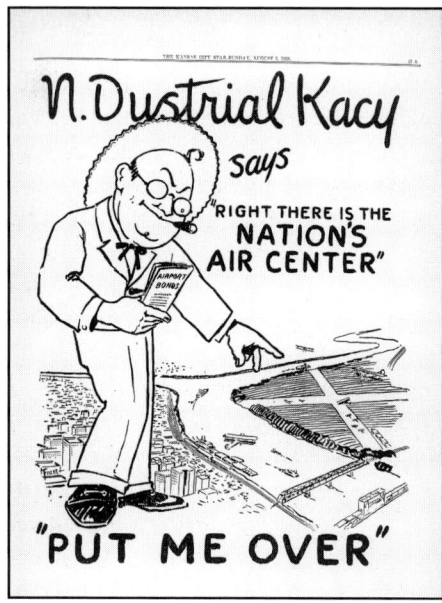

This political cartoon appeared in the Kansas City Star, August 5, 1928, two days before the $1,000,000 bond issue for the purchase and improvement of the municipal airport was passed.

were appointed to each precinct, and Boy Scouts were recruited to distribute literature to voters at the polls. All campaign literature bore the phrase, "Industrial expansion is dependent upon a municipally-owned air-port." On August 7, 1928, the voters of Kansas City approved the $1,000,000 bond issue for the purchase and improvement of the municipal airport.[36]

Improvements at the airfield, however, were delayed several months. In the fall of 1928, suits were filed in the state supreme court, contesting the constitutionality of not only the Kansas City airport bonds but also the airport bond issue recently passed in St. Louis. The court, citing the precedent of municipal aid to railroads in the nineteenth century, ruled that the expenditure of municipal revenue for airports was constitutional.[37] By the time the court had ruled favorably on the bonds, winter had set in, and improvements had to be delayed until spring.

Airport improvements, however, were not resumed when the winter ended. The Public Works Department did not break ground for the terminal until June 1929, and other improvements were similarly postponed. The worst problem was the deteriorating condition of the cinder runways, which were extremely dangerous in inclement weather.[38] Because of its poor facilities, the municipal airport was almost displaced as the major metropolitan airfield by the privately owned Fairfax Airport, directly across the Missouri River in Kansas City, Kansas.

In 1928 the Woods Brothers Corporation, developer of the Fairfax Industrial District, had purchased a private airfield adjoining the Fairfax property and had invested heavily in the field in an effort to attract commercial aviation and the aircraft industry. An impressive administration building was erected, asphalt runways were laid, and several hangars and maintenance shops were built.[39] The Fairfax developers fully intended to make their field the primary metropolitan airport. When the Fairfax Airport manager heard that NAT had become disaffected with the municipal field, he approached the operations manager of the airline and offered the use of the Fairfax facilities. NAT accepted the offer, and from December 3, 1928, until June 15, 1929, local air mail operations were based at Fairfax.[40]

The failure of the city administration to proceed with improvements in the face of the rival threat of Fairfax angered Holland. He wrote a strong letter to public works director Matthew Murray, asserting that it would be impossible to attract commercial airlines to the municipal field unless more rapid progress was made on improvements. In response to pressure from Holland and other chamber officials, Murray accelerated the pace of improvements at the airport. On December 8, 1929, the passenger terminal was dedicated, and its facilities were turned over to the transport companies. The completion of the terminal blocked the efforts of the Fairfax developers to attract to their field the commercial lines serving Kansas City. The inability of the Woods Brothers Corporation to make further improvements at Fairfax Airport during the depression insured the primary position of the municipal field.[41]

The completion of municipal airport facilities in 1929 had a decisive impact upon Kansas City's aviation development. At the beginning of 1929, only NAT conducted passenger service to and from Kansas City. By the spring of 1930, however, eight passenger lines served the city, including TAT and Western Air Express (WAE), both of which operated coast-to-coast services. The other six lines connected Kansas City with such cities as Denver, Dallas, Minneapolis, and Atlanta.[42]

The acquisition of TAT and WAE proved to be more valuable than Holland originally realized. In 1927, United Air Lines had been awarded the transcontinental air mail service. The United route traversed the northern third of the country, the principal stops being New York, Chicago, Cheyenne, and San Francisco. In 1930, Postmaster General Walter F. Brown decided to open two additional transcontinental routes, one to stretch from New York to Los Angeles by way of St. Louis and Kansas City, and the other to connect Atlanta with Los Angeles. Because TAT and WAE were experienced and financially secure companies, Brown wished to award them the central route, provided that they would merge. The two airlines had been competitive and consequently hesitated to combine, but the mail contract incentive eventually persuaded them to do so. The new company, Transcontinental and Western Air (T&WA), the predecessor of Trans World Airlines, was awarded the central air mail route on August 25, 1931.[43]

In January 1931, Holland had heard that T&WA wished to combine its scattered maintenance and operating headquarters and to locate the consolidated headquarters in the midcontinent. Immediately, he launched a personal effort to persuade the company to locate in Kansas City. Pittsburgh Aviation Industries Corporation, a creation of the Pennsylvania Railroad, had been a part of the T&WA merger. Although Pittsburgh Aviation Industries Corporation controlled only 5 percent of the T&WA stock, it held the balance of power between the mutually antagonistic TAT and WAE executives.[44] Shrewdly sensing where the balance of power lay in the airline's board of directors, Holland first contacted board member D. M. Sheaffer, traffic manager of the Pennsylvania Railroad. Holland asserted that since the Pennsylvania had recently acquired the Wabash, whose western terminus was Kansas City, it would be in the railroad's interest to locate the T&WA headquarters in the city. Less than a week after he wrote to Sheaffer, Holland arranged a lavish chamber of commerce luncheon for Pennsylvania Railroad president W. W. Atterbury, who was visiting the city. Holland also persuaded city manager McElroy to write to Sheaffer.[45]

T&WA was not initially receptive to Kansas City's bid for the headquarters. Holland had two highly placed friends within the T&WA organization who secretly informed him of the board of directors' decisions. On February 6 one of those friends, Ted Everett, wrote Holland that the directors favored Tulsa because the city had offered $300,000. The directors had deferred their final decision, however, until a recently appointed location committee had studied the problem and had issued a recommendation.[46]

Alarmed by the prospect that Tulsa might acquire the headquarters, Holland flew to New York in early February to confer with company executives. He discovered that Everett's report that Tulsa had offered $300,000 was essentially correct. However, the money had not been offered as a cash bonus: the city had offered to expend the sum on buildings to house the airline. The buildings were to be leased to the company at 5 percent of cost, with an option to buy. Holland immediately wired chamber of commerce president Conrad Mann, asking him to ascertain as quickly as possible Kansas City's willingness to match Tulsa's offer. Four days later, in long letters to Mann and McElroy, Holland elaborated upon the situation. He had discovered that many T&WA

executives would prefer Kansas City if it would provide the same facilities as Tulsa had offered. He had also discovered that additional competitors had entered the picture; St. Louis, Wichita, and Amarillo, Texas, were also making vigorous efforts to obtain the headquarters. Holland had met with the location committee, however, and had persuaded the committee to postpone its recommendation until Kansas City made a decision on the erection of a headquarters building.[47]

Holland returned to Kansas City and attempted to persuade McElroy to match Tulsa's offer, but the city manager would not commit himself to erecting facilities for the airline. Armed only with a prospectus containing basic economic data on Kansas City, Holland flew to Los Angeles in early March to try to persuade location committee members Jack Frye and Jack Maddux that Kansas City's general economic advantages outweighed the material offers of the other cities. Maddux and Frye were impressed by Holland's data but stated that the financially hard-pressed company had to have material help. They also told Holland that Tulsa was no longer the prime candidate for the headquarters; several other cities had not only offered to erect physical facilities but had also offered large cash bonuses. Unable to commit Kansas City to material aid, Holland persuaded Frye and Maddux to delay their decision further.[48]

A TAT Maddux Ford Tri-Motor at the Municipal Airport, Kansas City, in 1929 [Lou Holland Collection, Union Station/Kansas City Museum]

Holland returned to Kansas City and again attempted to persuade the city administration to construct facilities for the airline. Again he failed. In early May, T. B. Clement, one of Holland's friends within the company, wrote that the board of directors had become impatient and had asked Frye to give an interim report. Frye had informed the directors that although Kansas City was the most desirable location, the city was unwilling to offer tangible assistance. Frye also reported that Amarillo was first on the location committee's list because it had made the most substantial offer and also had the cheapest labor market. Clement suggested that Holland continue to work on Sheaffer and the location committee because a decision would be made in the near future.[49] Holland wrote again to Sheaffer, pointing out Kansas City's many advantages, but the T&WA director confirmed what Maddux and Frye had told Holland in Los Angeles: the company badly needed financial aid.[50]

On May 26, 1931, Kansas City's electorate endorsed a $30,000,000 ten-year public improvements program. One of the bond issues passed was an appropriation of $500,000 for municipal airport improvements. The Civic Improvement Committee that had formulated the bond program had recommended that three-fourths of the airport appropriation be expended on diking and grading.[51] The city council was under no legal obligation, however, to spend the airport bond money precisely as the citizens' committee recommended. Realizing that there was no legal impediment to utilizing part of the airport appropriation for T&WA facilities, Holland met with McElroy and persuaded him to discuss the matter with the city council.

On June 17, 1931, T&WA announced that its operating and maintenance headquarters would be moved to Kansas City. The company's ostensible reason for its decision was the city's central location, but undoubtedly the decisive factor was the city council's decision to appropriate $280,000 of the airport bond money to build facilities for the company. The city agreed to erect a 400-by-120-foot hangar with adjoining offices and maintenance shops. The structure was to be rented at 5 percent of cost, and the company was given a twenty-year option to purchase the building.[52]

Holland had played a decisive role in the acquisition of the T&WA headquarters. He had delayed the company's choice of a location until the city could make a material offer, he had convinced company officials of the general economic advantages of Kansas City, and he had persuaded the city administration to provide the company with facilities. His role did not end with the city's agreement to build the hangar, however. He also acted as liaison between the company and city hall during the erection of the building. T&WA executives, particularly board chairman Richard W. Robbins, were concerned that the Pendergast machine might try to take advantage of the

Municipal Airport [Greater Kansas City Chamber of Commerce]

company during the construction of the hangar. Holland assured Robbins, however, that he would act as mediator between the airline and the machine and would prevent any interference. Holland performed that role successfully; the T&WA facilities were erected on a wholly businesslike basis.[53]

The acquisition of T&WA was the capstone of Holland's aviation program. The transport company brought a large payroll to the city and was an important stimulant to the city's economy during the depression years. From 1931 to 1944, the company expended over $40,000,000 in the city on salaries and materials.[54] T&WA also lent prestige to Kansas City as an aviation center and helped to consolidate the city's position as a hub of air commerce.

Louis E. Holland, through his vigorous and imaginative leadership, played a decisive role in the effort to establish Kansas City as a center of commercial aviation. The city's successes in aviation were not wholly attributable, however, to the community's economic leadership. The city's political leaders also played a vital role. At several critical junctures, the city administration invested in airport improvements that were crucial to the success of the chamber's promotional efforts. The practice of combining private and public enterprise to promote economic growth was as essential to the city's aviation promoters as it had been to the community's railroad promoters.

NOTES

1. The literature on canal and railroad promotion is voluminous. Some of the more important studies are Carter Goodrich, *Government Promotion of American Canals and Railroads, 1800-1890* (New York: Columbia University Press, 1960); Frederick A. Cleveland and Fred Wilbur Powell, *Railroad Promotion and Capitalization in the United States* (New York: Longmans, Green, 1909); Edwin L. Lopata, *Local Aid to Railroads in Missouri* (New York: Parnassus Press, 1937).

2. Charles N. Glaab, *Kansas City and the Railroads: Community Policy in the Growth of a Regional Metropolis* (Madison: State Historical Society of Wisconsin, 1962); A. Theodore Brown, *Frontier Community: Kansas City to 1870* (Columbia: University of Missouri Press, 1963), chap. 4.

3. *Kansas Citian*, 9 March 1920, 255; 21 July 1925, 577; *Kansas City Journal*, 12 November 1922. Most citations to Kansas City newspapers are to clippings in the Chamber of Commerce Scrapbook, Louis E. Holland Papers, Western Historical Manuscript Collection, University of Missouri-Kansas City.

4. *Kansas Citian*, 17 March 1925, 235; 13 October 1925, 813-814.

5. *New York Times*, 3 February 1925; Henry Ladd Smith, *Airways: The History of Commercial Aviation in the United States* (New York: A. A. Knopf, 1944), 84, 94.

6. Holland to Harry Davis, 19 April 1954, Personal folder (A-G), box 133; Holland to William A. Ong, 12 October 1955, Personal folder (A-F), box 138, both in Holland Papers; *Kansas City Times*, 3 August 1959.

7. *New York Times*, 3 February 1925; Smith, *Airways*, 84, 94, 103-104; Roger Bilstein, "Technology and Commerce: Aviation in the Conduct of American Business, 1918-29," *Technology and Culture* 10 (July 1969): 398; John B. Rae, *Climb to Greatness: The American Aircraft Industry, 1920-1960* (Cambridge: MIT Press, 1968), 22-23.

8. *Kansas City Star*, 24 January, 7 June 1926; *Kansas Citian*, 2 February 1926, 108; *Kansas City Times*, 20 October 1926.

9. *Kansas Citian*, 17 March 1925, 237; 7 April 1925, 287; 21 April 1925, 323; 24 November 1925, 914; *Kansas City Star*, 17 May 1925.

10. Smith, *Airways*, 107-108.

11. *Kansas Citian*, 25 August 1925, 665; Report of the Industrial Department of the Kansas City Chamber of Commerce for the year ending Sept. 20, 1925, folder 54C, box 191, Holland Papers; Smith, *Airways*, 104.

12. *Kansas Citian*, 24 November 1925, 913-914; Paul Henderson to Holland, 24 November 1925, Air Mail folder (1925-31), box 276; Holland to Henderson, 21 December 1925, folder 4C (2), box 181, both in Holland Papers; *Kansas Citian*, 2 February 1926, 109.

13. Holland to Luther K. Bell, 17 December 1925, folder 4C (2), box 181,

Holland Papers.

14. Holland to A. D. Simpson, 25 August 1926, folder 4C (1), box 181; Luther K. Bell to Lester Armour, 16 March 1926, folder 4C (5), box 182, both in Holland Papers; *Kansas Citian*, 2 February 1926, 109, 116; 4 May 1926, 355; *Kansas City Times*, 12 May 1926.

15. *Kansas Citian*, 4 September 1928, 659.

16. *Kansas City Times*, 20 October 1926; *Kansas Citian*, 20 December 1927, 912; 25 September 1928, 730; 27 November 1928, 897.

17. Rae, *Climb to Greatness*, 15.

18. Minutes, meeting of the Chamber of Commerce New Industries Committee, 16 June 1925, Chamber of Commerce folder (1925), box 177, Holland Papers; *Kansas City Post*, 16 July 1925.

19. Minutes, meeting of the special subcommittee of the New Industries Committee, 22 June 1925, Chamber of Commerce folder (1925), box 177; copy of syndicate agreement, Fokker Aircraft Corporation, 15 July 1925; folder 5C, box 182, both in Holland Papers; *Kansas City Post*, 16 July 1925.

20. Holland to Fokker, 27 November 1925, folder 5C, box 182, Holland Papers.

21. Memoranda on the Chamber of Commerce Aviation Census, 21, 22 April 1930, folder 10C-P, box 199, Holland Papers.

22. John T. Nevill, "The Story of Wichita," *Aviation* 29 (September 1930): 166-170; (November 1930): 291-295; (December 1930): 353-357; "Exhibit B," report of C. B. Elliott on aviation in Wichita, [March 1928], Industrial Committee Minutes folder, box 178, Holland Papers.

23. Harry J. Freeman, "Establishment of Municipal Airports as a 'Public Purpose,'" *National Municipal Review* 18 (April 1929): 263-266; D. R. Lane, "Recent Developments of Municipal Airports in the West," *American City* 37 (July 1927): 1-5; Austin F. MacDonald, "Airport Problems of American Cities," *The Annals* 151 (September 1930): 225-283; H. M. Olmsted, "The Airport and the Municipality," *American City* 38 (January 1928): 117-119; "Who Shall Own and Operate the Airports?" *American City* 39 (December 1928): 110; O. J. Swander, "Exceptional Site, Landscaping, Lighting and Building Characterize Wichita Airport," *American City* 44 (April 1931): 109-110.

24. Holland to Henderson, 29 September 1926, Henderson folder; General B. A. Poore to Holland, 11 January 1927, Personal folder (January-March 1927), box 92, Holland Papers; *Kansas City Star*, 19 February 1927.

25. Holland to William P. MacCracken, 4 February 1927, Personal folder (January-March 1927), box 92, Holland Papers; Airport Survey of the Army Air Corps Reserve Officers Association, [January 1927], Lou Holland Collection, Union Station/ Kansas City Museum, Kansas City, MO; *Kansas City Star*, 19 February 1927.

26. The best study of the Pendergast organization is Lyle W. Dorsett, *The*

Pendergast Machine (New York: Oxford University Press, 1968). A. Theodore Brown, *The Politics of Reform: Kansas City's Municipal Government, 1925-1950* (Kansas City: Community Studies, 1958), is also useful.

27. Holland to B. W. Rose, 14 December 1951, Personal folder (E-K), box 128; Holland to Colonel Tenney Ross, 20 January 1927, folder 4C (2), box 181, both in Holland Papers.

28. *Kansas City Times*, 23 February, 15 July 1927; *Kansas Citian*, 1 March 1927, 195; Holland to MacCracken, 24 February 1927, folder 4C (2), box 181, Holland Papers.

29. Holland to Harold M. Bixby, 21 June 1927; Holland to Henry F. McElroy, 21 June 1927, both in folder 29C, box 189, Holland Papers; *Kansas City Post*, 17 August 1927; *Kansas City Times*, 18 August 1927.

30. *Kansas Citian*, 15 November 1927, 828; 21 February 1928, 157-158; "Exhibit A," William E. Morton to Arthur Hardgrave, [March 1928], Industrial Committee Minutes folder, box 178, Holland Papers; *Kansas City Star*, 9 May 1928.

31. *Kansas City Star*, 19 June 1928.

32. Smith, *Airways*, 142-145; Report of the Subcommittee on Aeronautics, 18 June 1928, Industrial Committee Minutes folder, box 178, Holland Papers.

33. G. Hall Roosevelt to Holland, 8, 16 June, 3 July 1928; Holland to Roosevelt, 5 July 1928, all in folder 46C, box 191, Holland Papers.

34. Recommendations of the Subcommittee on Aeronautics, 18 June 1928; minutes, meeting of the Industrial Committee, 19 June 1928, both in Industrial Committee Minutes folder, box 178, Holland Papers; *Kansas City Star*, 19 June 1928; *Kansas Citian*, 26 June 1928, 504.

35. *Kansas City Journal*, 20 June 1928; McElroy to Hardgrave, 21 June 1928, folder 73C, box 195, Holland Papers; *Kansas City Star*, 21 June 1928; *Kansas Citian*, 26 June 1928, 504.

36. *Kansas City Times*, 10 July 1928; report on the organization of the Airport Bond Committee, n.d., folder 73C, box 195, Holland Papers; *Kansas City Star*, 8 August 1928; *Kansas Citian*, 14 August 1928, 609.

37. *Dysart v. City of St. Louis* (1927), 11 S.W. 2d, 1045; *Ennis v. Kansas City* (1927), 11 S.W. 2d, 1054.

38. *Kansas Citian*, 25 June 1929, 23; letter from an unidentified National Air Transport pilot to ?, n.d., folder 10C-P, box 199, Holland Papers.

39. James P. Wines, "The Airport on a Paying Basis," *Aviation*, 21 June 1930, 1217-1221; *Kansas Citian*, 18 December 1928, 973.

40. Henderson to Holland, 18 April 1929, Personal folder (April-June 1929), box 96, Holland Papers; Holland to William B. Stout, 3 August 1929, Holland Collection; Wines, "Airport on a Paying Basis," 1219-1220.

41. Holland to Matthew Murray, 22 March 1929, folder 4C (2), box 181, Holland Papers; *Kansas City Times*, 9 December 1929; *Kansas City Star*, 3 August 1969.

42. Memoranda on the Chamber of Commerce aviation census, 21, 22 April 1930, folder 10C-P, box 199, Holland Papers. Scenic Airways collapsed financially before it initiated operations and thus never serviced Kansas City.

43. Smith, *Airways*, 167-181.

44. Ibid., 175-181.

45. Holland to D. M. Sheaffer, 2 January 1931, Holland Collection; Holland to Henderson, 9 January 1931, Personal folder (January-April 1931), box 99, Holland Papers; McElroy to Shaeffer, 11 February 1931, Holland Collection.

46. Ted Everett to Holland, 6 February 1931, Personal—Chamber of Commerce folder, box 101, Holland Papers.

47. Telegram, Holland to Mann, 12 February 1931; Holland to Mann, 16 February 1931; Holland to McElroy, 17 February 1931, Holland Collection.

48. Holland to Henderson, 19 March 1931, Personal—Chamber of Commerce folder, box 101, Holland Papers; *Kansas City Times*, 19 June 1931.

49. T. B. Clement to Holland, 13 May 1931, Personal folder (May-July 1931), box 100, Holland Papers.

50. Holland to Sheaffer, 15 May 1931; Sheaffer to Holland, 20 May 1931, Holland Collection.

51. *Kansas City Star*, 25, 27 May 1931; Ray Wilson, *Where These Rocky Bluffs Meet* (Kansas City: Chamber of Commerce, 1938), 260-261.

52. Telegram, Holland to Eric Matchette, 16 June 1931, Holland Collection; Holland to Mann, 19 June 1931, Personal folder (May-July 1931), box 100, Holland Papers; *Kansas City Star*, 17 June 1931; McElroy to Jack Maddux, 4 August 1931, Holland Collection; *Kansas Citian*, 25 August 1931, 7.

53. Richard W. Robbins to the author, 15 January 1971.

54. *Kansas City Times*, 25 May 1945.

Criminal Aspects of the Pendergast Machine

LAWRENCE H. LARSEN and NANCY J. HULSTON

The Pendergast political organization in Kansas City and Jackson County, Missouri, lasted from the 1880s until the 1950s. Alderman James Pendergast, a first-generation Irish American who grew up in St. Joseph, founded a faction, the Jackson Democratic Club, in Kansas City's First Ward. Located in the West Bottoms packinghouse area and the heavily Italian North End, the First Ward also included Kansas City's red-light and entertainment districts. "Big Jim" Pendergast, a saloonkeeper by vocation, was a major figure in Kansas City Democratic politics until his death from Bright's disease in 1911. His youngest brother and successor as head of the "Goat Democrats," Thomas Joseph Pendergast, through firm leadership, ruthless tactics, and a highly developed instinct for politics, transformed the family's political operation into one of the most powerful city machines in United States history.[1]

Tom Pendergast, born of Irish immigrant parents in 1872, was a tough operator. While usually appearing psychologically sound, he also displayed a ruthless side, with a quick and sometimes violent temper. He easily intimidated those who dared to disagree with him, often with acts of violence. In one incident in an elevator at the 1932 Democratic State Convention in St. Louis, he struck a prominent delegate from Springfield.[2]

With little patience for small talk, Pendergast could be very querulous. His coarse, gravelly voice made him sound all the more menacing; his whole demeanor left little doubt about who was the boss. Demanding efficiency and fast results, Pendergast prided himself on making quick and correct decisions.

Pendergast's Control of Crime as Depicted by St. Louis Post-Dispatch Editorial Cartoonist Daniel Fitzpatrick

With a dark view of human nature, he believed that most people were capable of dishonesty if they believed they could get away with it.[3]

Under a new 1925 city charter, which greatly weakened the power of the mayor by placing municipal administration in the hands of a city manager hired by the city council, Pendergast solidified his control over Kansas City. The boss's influence with the council proved powerful; the first city manager chosen under the new charter was Judge Henry McElroy, a machine-made politician who retained the post until 1939.[4]

Pendergast claimed to be both a professional politician and a successful business leader. During Prohibition and through the Great Depression, he governed Kansas City, a municipality of four hundred thousand people, as his own private business while directing his machine from the second floor of a modest building at 1908 Main Street, a busy commercial thoroughfare running through the heart of the downtown area. No matter how they personally felt about the boss, hundreds of people, from unemployed laborers to gubernatorial candidates, went before Pendergast, hat in hand, to plead for jobs or favors. His unpretentious office, the headquarters of the Jackson Democratic Club, was one of the most significant political addresses in the state of Missouri.

Even though he never again held public office after resigning as alderman in 1915, Pendergast administered Kansas City through an enormous network of subordinates. Thousands of people, the vast number of them on the municipal payroll, worked for the Pendergast machine.[5] Pendergast's political and business sides proved impossible to separate. His most obvious holdings were the T. J. Pendergast Wholesale Liquor Company and the Ready-Mixed Concrete Company. The liquor concern, which marketed soft drinks during Prohibition, enjoyed a virtual monopoly in the city. Ready-Mixed, one of the first companies in the nation to deliver to the site, furnished the concrete for most local public projects, including the City Hall, the Jackson County Courthouse, and the Municipal Auditorium. Pendergast owned sizable open or concealed stakes in many other firms, including Centropolis Crusher and Eureka Oil, but no matter how hard they tried, federal investigators never uncovered the full extent of his holdings.[6]

Pendergast required a great deal of money to support a lavish standard of living. With his wife and three children, he resided in a mansion on Ward Parkway, a grand boulevard in the wealthiest part of Kansas City. He frequently took his family on extensive tours of Europe. During extravagant trips to New York, he rented luxurious hotel suites, and his wife and two daughters shopped at the most fashionable stores in town. He enjoyed the social whirl at upscale resorts such as Saratoga Springs, New York, during the racing season and always attended the Kentucky Derby. In Missouri, he owned thoroughbred horses and even a jockey club, but for him, horse racing loomed as more than a hobby of the rich and famous.[7] Pendergast admitted in 1939 to being a hopelessly addicted horse race gambler. In the depths of the Great Depression, he bet millions of dollars a month, sometimes losing a hundred thousand dollars in a single day. Under the circumstances, it is not surprising that he tried to turn Kansas City into his own personal money machine.[8]

Pendergast obtained immense profits from payoffs, kickbacks, and bribes. Anyone doing business with the city, all the way down to the street cleaners, needed to be on approved lists. Kansas City was a wide-open town in which all gambling and illegal entertainment establishments paid tribute to the machine. One "sin place" paid ten thousand dollars monthly. On a sliding scale, all honest businesses paid 5 to 10 percent of their annual gross income to the machine. All monies from an annual motor vehicle tax paid to the city revenue collector went directly into Pendergast's coffer. In return, Pendergast claimed to provide Kansas Citians with a lively and well-ordered city, free of debt. Honest audits made following his downfall, however, showed the city to be almost twenty million dollars in debt—at that time the greatest per capita deficit ever accumulated by an American municipality.[9]

"The Boss," Tom Pendergast [St. Louis Post-Dispatch]

Pendergast's power rested on popularity, votes, and threats. He ran an urban Democratic organization during a time of national ascendancy for the party of Franklin Roosevelt. Machine officials acknowledged having "bad actors" in the ranks but took pride in supporting attractive and popular politicians, including Harry S. Truman, in their rise through the political ranks. Even so, Pendergast was never an ideologue, rather he placed vote totals ahead of all other considerations. In the 1930s, just to be on the safe side, he also held sway over the local Republican Party organization. Yet, as politically involved as he was, he seldom listened to campaign speeches or attended political functions.[10]

The Pendergast machine consistently delivered majorities in excess of 100,000 votes in Kansas City. This was accomplished in a variety of ways, including padding the election rolls with fictitious or deceased "ghost" voters.[11] In 1936, Kansas City had 270,000 registered voters, a statistical impossibility in a city of 400,000 when the legal voting age was twenty-one. In the final analysis, however, the most direct means of control was the implied or actual use of force by professional thugs. Conditions became so extreme that honest citizens feared the consequences of speaking out against the machine. Like a bad dream, Kansas City evolved into a city in which gangsters and machine politics appropriated virtually all power.

A link between the Pendergasts and the gangster element existed throughout the long life of the machine. Founder James Pendergast claimed to have gotten his start in the saloon business with money won in a horse race. More likely, he obtained a loan from gamblers. Throughout his political career, he did favors for gaming elements, sanctioning "police protected gambling." That translated into protection for operators of illegal games of chance. In return, he received enough money to hand out welfare to unfortunates, especially in the depression that followed the Panic of 1893, furthering support for his organization.[12]

Tom Pendergast routinely used enforcers at the polls, as illustrated by the 1918 general election in Kansas City. Underworld characters—plug-uglies, ruffians, thugs, ex-convicts, hardened women, and other assorted low life—intimidated election officials, challengers to ballots, and any citizen who complained about voting practices. A highly respected former state supreme court justice, John Kennish, acted as an accredited challenger for an anti-Pendergast candidate. Upon arriving at a polling station, he was verbally abused by machine election judges while a police officer stood and watched. When Kennish challenged a voter, the judges cursed him and ignored the challenge. With studied contempt, they threw the ballots of many anti-Pendergast voters into a wastebasket and replaced them with preprepared ones favoring the machine slate. When a voter had the audacity to complain,

"Hitched On"

ruffians beat him senseless in front of a horrified Kennish as the police stood aside.   Outside, thugs menaced reporters who sought to gather evidence of irregularities.[13]   Given the presence of Justice Kennish as a restraining influence, what transpired was probably relatively mild.   The Pendergast machine ran an invisible government under which the sanctity of the secret ballot meant nothing.

Supporters hailed Pendergast as a veritable saint and a generous protector of the poor, but a federal judge, Albert L. Reeves, portrayed him much differently in what he called a "pen portrait."

> The man who became the emperor of an underworld empire . . . was a unique figure. He was squat, heavy set, thick necked, large jowled, and porcine in appearance. He was a perfect picture of the political boss as envisioned by cartoonists. He thoroughly understood the psychology of the underworld and the habitues of the shadow kingdom followed him blindly as well as devotedly. He protected them from prosecution for their misdeeds and granted them commissions to sin against the laws of God and man. His past experiences had qualified him to lead and rule the refuse of society. He understood the life of the brothel and houses of ill fame. The characters there looked to him for protection in their way of life and stood in readiness to serve him in his political plans.[14]

Reeves stressed the impossibility of understanding the Pendergast machine without considering its criminal side. In short, Pendergast's organization was not a typical urban political machine. Rather, even compared to Chicago's, it had a unique relationship to the underworld. The powerful Democratic machine in Chicago allegedly had ties to a crime organization led by the notorious Alphonse Capone.

Pendergast preferred homegrown criminals. By Prohibition, Pendergast drew upon a cadre of able and intelligent young first-generation Italian American men in strengthening his enforcement section.   As the men matured and learned increasingly nefarious skills, they coalesced into their own organization and loosely allied themselves with other regional criminal affiliations, notably in Chicago, while zealously guarding their own territory. For special purposes, primarily for helping at the polls on election day, they allowed the temporary importation of hoodlums from other areas.[15]

As Pendergast's control over Kansas City politics swelled with the passage of the 1925 city charter, a rising crime figure, Johnny Lazia, the son of Italian immigrants, sought a broader policy role in machine affairs. Early in his career, Lazia had served time for highway robbery, somehow gaining an

212 of Kansas City, America's Crossroads

early release. Posing as a legitimate politician, he used force to oust a close associate and took over the Democratic faction in the city's heavily Italian North End. In 1928, as a direct challenge, he held a roomful of Pendergast's key lieutenants captive while he negotiated with the obviously frightened boss.[16] This incident convinced Pendergast that it would benefit him to work with Lazia rather than risk losing control to the rising and charismatic young gangster. Lazia, once welcomed into the leadership of the machine, soon assumed a very visible presence in Kansas City. In 1929 his Cuban Gardens, a lavish nightclub and gaming palace, took in as much as $8,000 on weekend nights from gambling alone.[17] Through his arrangement with Pendergast, Lazia held considerable control over the police department and even recruited applicants of his choice for the force, including seventy-five newly released convicts from Leavenworth.[18] Pendergast, at least outwardly, got along well with Lazia and supported his influence in the police force.

In some cases, the police helped cover up murders. An investigator for the state and a future federal judge, William Becker, recalled an incident at the notorious Chesterfield Club, a downtown "sin place" famous for its comely nude waitresses.

> One incident that occurred at the Chesterfield Club that I helped investigate involved a girl who was in the dancing girl line. On one particular evening this girl went to the madam who had brought the girls over there and said, "I just looked out, and I see my brother out there. I'm from the country, as you know, and my family thinks I'm working as a secretary. Would you please excuse me for the night so my brother won't see me and I won't get in trouble?" The madam said all right, and the girl put on her street clothes and started to leave. There were men wearing tuxedo-type clothes standing around, and they were the criminal managers of the Chesterfield Club. One of them saw this girl leaving and asked her what she was doing. She said she had been excused. He told her to get back in the dancing line. She said no and started to walk out and he hit her and knocked her down. One of the cattlemen in the club saw that and thought it wasn't nice. He went over and knocked down the criminal who had hit the girl. The rest of the criminal managers of the Chesterfield Club saw it, and they just jumped on that cattleman and beat him to death. They knocked him to pieces. They called the Police Department. The police picked up the dead man and took him over into Kansas City, Kansas, where he was listed as a hit and run victim. That was the way that the cattleman's life was ended. We learned about that incident, and it was typical.[19]

This was a side of Kansas City's vibrant nightlife seen by few visitors or residents of the city. In any event, organized crime's unholy alliance with Pendergast proved a turning point for the machine.[20]

During one thirteen-month period, three major events—the so-called "Holy Trinity"—brought widespread attention to the critical situation in Kansas City. On the morning of June 17, 1933, three men carrying submachine guns, sometimes identified as Charles "Pretty Boy" Floyd, Adam "Machine Gun" Richetti, and Verne C. Miller, made a spectacular and unsuccessful attempt to free a colleague, Frank Nash, in the parking lot of the Union Station. Nash, a convicted bank robber recaptured following an escape from Leavenworth, was in transit back to prison, escorted by several unarmed federal agents. Before the automobile carrying Nash could drive away, the gunmen appeared, and after one said, "Let 'em have it," they opened fire. In a hail of bullets, four peace officers and Nash died. Lazia hurried to the crime scene and took charge of the investigation. He supervised the search for evidence and later arranged for the killers to leave town. The media called the affair the "Union Station Massacre."[21]

The second major event of the Holy Trinity grew out of a challenge to the Pendergast organization by a coalition of reformers in the 1934 city election. On election day, March 27, 1934, the machine demonstrated its domination with enforcers present in unusual strength. Ruffians killed four people at the polls and injured dozens of others.[22] The bloody election, won as usual by Pendergast candidates, drew additional national attention to the lawlessness in Kansas City.

Four months later, at 3:00 a.m., on July 10, 1934, gunmen ambushed Lazia and shot him at least eight times as he and his wife returned to their fashionable midtown apartment building near Armour Boulevard and Gillham Road. Emergency attendants rushed the mortally wounded Lazia to an area hospital where he lingered for a few hours and died. As he lay on his deathbed, he supposedly said, "If anything happens, notify Tom Pendergast, my best friend, and tell him I love him."[23] Pendergast reportedly sped to the hospital and unsuccessfully exhorted the best physicians available to save Lazia. The gangland-style murder made headlines for days, and the police tried to link it to Oklahoma and Minnesota gangs attempting to establish themselves in Kansas City. This scenario made the fallen Lazia appear as a gallant knight who had died defending his beloved city from interloping philistines.

At least in a public sense, Lazia appeared sorely missed. Several thousand people witnessed his funeral, which featured a procession of 120 "official" vehicles, one carrying T. J. Pendergast. The boss appeared openly grieved at the loss of his close associate.[24] Some, however, believed that the boss himself may have been responsible for the premature death of Kansas City's first true underworld kingpin. In the end, the killing went unsolved.

After the untimely demise of Lazia in 1934, and with the onset in 1936 of serious health problems for Pendergast, the machine began to unravel. A major heart attack, stomach surgery, and a colostomy operation impaired Pendergast's effectiveness, and he relied increasingly on his nephew and political heir apparent, James Pendergast, to run the everyday operations of the organization.[25] The difficulties continued when United States Attorney Maurice Milligan moved against vote frauds connected with the 1936 election in federal contests. In 1937 and 1938 juries brought in guilty verdicts involving 259 machine functionaries named in 39 indictments for conspiracy to interfere with the right of citizens to vote. Charges against 19 other defendants were dismissed. Despite threats, the two federal judges in the Western District of Missouri, Albert L. Reeves and Merrill E. Otis, sentenced over 200 of the vote fraud criminals to prison. A new state voting registration act in 1938 resulted in the striking of over 60,000 "ghosts" from the rolls in Kansas City. Although opposition to the machine by Governor Lloyd Stark—who owed his own election to Pendergast—received much publicity, it was the vote fraud trials that fundamentally damaged the organization.[26]

Governor Lloyd Stark (right) openly denounced the machine in 1938 despite his close political alliance with Pendergast during his successful 1936 bid for office. [St. Louis Post-Dispatch]

Senator Harry S. Truman, a past vice president of the Jackson Democratic Club, unsuccessfully attempted to block Milligan's nomination to a second term as U.S. attorney and used senatorial immunity to assail Reeves and Otis on the floor of the Senate. In a prepared speech, Truman proclaimed, "The Federal court at Kansas City is presided over by two as violently partisan judges as ever sat on a Federal Bench. . . . A Jackson County Democrat has as much chance of a fair trial in the Federal District Court as a Jew would have in a Hitler court or a Trotsky follower before Stalin."[27] Judge Reeves passed it off to the media as "a speech of a man nominated by ghost votes, elected with ghost votes, and whose speeches probably are written by ghost writers." Reeves wrote years later, "Subsequent developments convinced the author that all three of these were true." Commenting further on Truman's role, Reeves said, "By this attitude he upheld the conduct and practice of the political machine in Kansas City, and though the revelations of fraud were astonishing, yet he decried such revelations and upheld the practices of the machine."[28] Milligan, who wanted to indict Truman, gave up, concluding he was "money honest," implying that he was not involved in the machine's criminal activities.[29]

Pendergast fell with startling suddenness. On April 7, 1939, a carefully selected federal grand jury, exclusive of Jackson County residents, indicted him for tax evasion. At an arraignment on Good Friday he pleaded not guilty. Claiming persecution, he compared his plight to that of Jesus Christ of Nazareth. A surly Pendergast told reporters: "There's nothing the matter with me. They persecuted Christ on Good Friday, and nailed him to the Cross."[30] Milligan, however, had built an airtight case around Pendergast's failure to pay taxes on a fee of several hundred thousand dollars he had received to help many large insurance companies gain a favorable settlement in a complex rate hike case. He had needed quick cash to settle large gambling debts owed to big New Jersey bookies. Gambling had become such a mania with him that he made some careless decisions.

Pendergast ultimately changed his plea to guilty, and on May 22, 1939, he sat impassively as Judge Otis imposed a sentence of fifteen months in the penitentiary, a $10,000 fine, and five years probation. The terms of probation prohibited him from gambling, leaving Kansas City without court permission, taking part in political affairs, or visiting his office at 1908 Main.[31] Even though the sentence was in line with others imposed on older first-time offenders with serious health problems, numerous newspaper editorials denounced its leniency.[32] Friends of Pendergast claimed that the sentence was too harsh, that a man in his poor physical condition either should not have been imprisoned at all or should have been sent to the federal medical

"Who Me?"

detention center in Springfield, Missouri. Released for good behavior after a year behind bars, he returned to the solitude of his mansion, living quietly and outwardly avoiding any participation in politics. Tom Pendergast died in Kansas City on January 26, 1945. Vice President Harry S. Truman, among other notables, attended his funeral.

After his death, the Pendergast organization collapsed at the municipal level. Over three hundred people were convicted of machine-related crimes. In April of 1940, a "reform" government came to power in Kansas City, headed by business leaders and members of a Democratic faction long allied with Pendergast. While James Pendergast, a close friend and World War I friend of Truman, tried to keep the machine together, true leadership for the discredited organization failed to emerge from a complex power struggle. Pendergast's son, Tom Jr., although close to his father, had no interest in politics and preferred to let the machine die. "It started with a James Pendergast, let it end with a James Pendergast," longtime business associate and family friend Phil McCrory advised him after a 1943 meeting with Democratic leaders.[33] The last remnants of Tom Pendergast's once powerful organization lost any hope of a comeback in 1956 when its slate went down to resounding defeat. Even though old Pendergast factions remained active for many more years in Kansas City, the great machine passed into history.

By most standards, Pendergast was not a career criminal. Of course, to keep power, he used and cooperated with criminal elements throughout his long career, as his symbiotic relationship with Johnny Lazia demonstrated. Illegal ventures in Kansas City yielded vast profits. With Pendergast gone, open vice became less visible. After the death of Lazia, Charles Carollo attempted to lead the Italian faction, but he too went to the federal penitentiary, and authorities eventually deported him to Sicily. Following World War II, a local mobster, Charles Binaggio, sought to reopen Kansas City to widespread vice; however, those plans died with his 1950 gangland-style murder. After that, relationships between crime and politics took different forms. As a direct result of Lazia's corruption of the police, control of the department was taken from the city and given to the state in 1939, where it remains today.[34]

Surprisingly, even fifty years after the death of Thomas J. Pendergast, the memories of power and corruption endure from generation to generation. Scarcely a week goes by when there is not some reference to Pendergast and his political machine in the local newspapers. While the historical consensus is that Kansas City's government probably has never functioned more efficiently than under Pendergast's Democratic organization, citizens exhibit strangely emotional responses to any such public statements, as if the specter of the boss still haunts 1908 Main Street.

NOTES

1. For a general account of the organization's origins, see Lyle W. Dorsett, *The Pendergast Machine* (1968; repr., Lincoln: University of Nebraska Press, 1980).

2. "Psychological," Thomas J. Pendergast File, Notorious Offender Case Files, Records of the Bureau of Prisons, RG 129, National Archives, Washington, DC (hereinafter cited as Notorious Offender Case Files). See Maurice M. Milligan, *Missouri Waltz: The Inside Story of the Pendergast Machine by the Man Who Smashed It* (New York: Charles Scribner's Sons, 1948), 32-33. The St. Louis incident is in William M. Reddig, *Tom's Town: Kansas City and the Pendergast Legend* (1947; repr., Columbia: University of Missouri Press, 1986), 200-214.

3. Harry S. Truman, "Pickwick Papers," Family and Business Affairs File, Harry S. Truman Papers, Harry S. Truman Library, Independence, MO.

4. See Donald Oster, "Kansas City, Missouri Charter Movements: 1905-1925" (master's thesis, University of Kansas City, 1962).

5. No exact figures exist on the number of people who worked for the machine.

In 1938, City Manager Henry McElroy said Kansas City had 3,750 full-time and 5,000 part-time employees. Jerome Beatty, "A Political Boss Talks About His Job," *American Magazine* 115 (February 1933): 113.

6. For an indication of the extent of Pendergast's holdings, see Milligan, *Missouri Waltz*, 188-190. *Kansas City Times*, 27 January 1939.

7. Reddig, *Tom's Town*, 165-166. See Herb Phipps, "Bill Kyne of Bay Meadows," Thomas J. Pendergast Jr., Papers, Western Historical Manuscript Collection, University of Missouri-Kansas City (hereinafter cited as WHMC-Kansas City).

8. *Kansas City Times*, 27 January 1939.

9. See A. Theodore Brown, *The Politics of Reform: Kansas City's Municipal Government, 1925-1950* (Kansas City: Community Studies, 1958); Reddig, *Tom's Town*, 338; and Alan Hynd, *The Giant Killers* (New York: R. M. McBride, 1945), 192-193.

10. Beatty, "A Political Boss Talks," 114.

11. Ewing Young Mitchell, "The Four Horsemen of the Pendergast Machine," Thomas J. Pendergast Vertical File, Truman Library; "Ghosts in the Heart of America: Daylight Ghosts in Kansas City," Notorious Offender Case Files, RG 129.

12. The standard general accounts about the Pendergast machine are Dorsett, *Pendergast Machine*; Reddig, *Tom's Town*; and Milligan, *Missouri Waltz*.

13. Albert L. Reeves, "The Shame of a Great City," 41, Albert L. Reeves Papers, Archives of the United States District Court for the Western District of Missouri, Kansas City (hereinafter cited as Western District Archives). Reeves wrote this manuscript sometime between his retirement in 1954 and his death in 1971.

14. Ibid., 42.

15. Ibid., 31-39, 77-79.

16. Unsigned letter to James A. Reed, 10 May 1928, James A. Reed Papers, WHMC-Kansas City.

17. Reddig, *Tom's Town*, 166, 251; "Transcripts of Records and Briefs," *Lazia v. United States*, C, no. 10019, May Term, 1934, United States Court of Appeals for the Eighth Circuit, Records of the United States Courts of Appeals RG 276, National Archives-Central Plains Region, Kansas City, MO. (hereinafter cited as NA-CPR).

18. Samuel S. Mayerberg, *Chronicle of an American Crusader: Alumni Lectures Delivered at the Hebrew Union College, Cincinnati, Ohio, December 7-10, 1942* (New York: Block, 1944), 161.

19. William Becker, biographical interview, by Frederick Spletstoser, 17, 21 April, 12 May, 16 June, 7, 9 July 1989, 120-121, Western District Archives.

20. *Kansas City Star*, 18 July 1984; Reddig, *Tom's Town*, 250-252.

21. A good account of the crime is Reddig, *Tom's Town*, 254-259. See "Conspiracy to Deliver a Federal Prisoner: The Kansas City Massacre," 29 May

1940, Federal Bureau of Investigation, NA-CPR. For a revisionist account, see L. R. (Larry) Kirchner, *Triple Cross Fire! J. Edgar Hoover & the Kansas City Union Station Massacre* (Kansas City: Janlar Books, 1993).

22. See Reddig, *Tom's Town*, 237-243, and Milligan, *Missouri Waltz*, 198.

23. Quoted in *Columbia Daily Tribune*, 10 July 1934.

24. *Kansas City Times*, 11 July 1934. See Reddig, *Tom's Town*, 261-263.

25. Reddig, *Tom's Town*, 279-281.

26. Lawrence H. Larsen, *Federal Justice in Western Missouri: The Judges, the Cases, the Times* (Columbia: University of Missouri Press, 1994), 172-175; Milligan, *Missouri Waltz*, 158-159; Reddig, *Tom's Town*, 287; Reeves, "Shame of a Great City," 68.

27. *Congressional Record*, 75th Cong., 1st sess. (15 February 1938), 83: 1962-1964. The best account of Truman's rise in Jackson County politics is in Richard Miller, *Truman: The Rise to Power* (New York: McGraw-Hill, 1986). See Eugene Powell, *Tom's Boy Harry: The first complete, authentic story of Harry Truman's connection with the Pendergast Machine* (Jefferson City, MO: Hawthorn Publishing, 1948).

28. Quoted in Reddig, *Tom's Town*, 292; Reeves, "Shame of a Great City," 262.

29. Lawrence H. Larsen, meeting with William H. Becker, 2 October 1987, Western District Archives.

30. Quoted in Reddig, *Tom's Town*, 327.

31. "Statement of Facts to the Court" and "Sentence," *United States v. Pendergast*, C, 14, 567-KC, RG 21, NA-CPR. See Larsen, *Federal Justice*, 181-185.

32. "Memorandum," 19 August 1939, *United States v. Pendergast*, 28 F. Supp. 601 (W.D. Mo. 1939). The memorandum is part of the case file. See Lawrence H. Larsen, "A Political Boss at Bay: Thomas J. Pendergast in Federal Prison, 1939-1940," *Missouri Historical Review* 86 (July 1992): 396-417.

33. Thomas J. Pendergast Jr., draft of letter to Margaret Truman Daniels, 1973, Pendergast Papers.

34. Galen I. Johnson, "Policing in Kansas City: Reform, Reorganization, and the Crime Fighting Image, 1939-1961" (master's thesis, University of Missouri-Kansas City, 1991); Larsen, *Federal Justice*, 184-185. For information on conditions in the police department, see Lear B. Reed, *Human Wolves: Seventeen Years of War on Crime* (Kansas City: Brown-White-Lowell Press, 1941).

Chester A. Franklin and Harry S. Truman: An African American Conservative and the "Conversion" of the Future President

THOMAS D. WILSON

In his insightful and controversial essay, "The Conversion of Harry Truman," William Leuchtenburg argues that Truman's transformation from bigot to civil rights protagonist resulted from his 1940 tour of southern military bases and his view of the Constitution as a "sacred text." Other historians, most convincingly Larry Grothaus, assert that the future president's concern for African Americans began during his years on the Jackson County Court. Still others, Richard Miller and Harold Gosnell among them, question whether Truman "converted" at all, arguing instead that his attention to civil rights was a result of paternalistic racism and political expediency.[1]

These contradictory interpretations of Truman's attitudes toward African Americans illustrate a situation common to historiographical debates: everyone is partially right. Truman's tour of the South did alter his feelings about discrimination, he did view the Constitution as a "sacred text," he did attend to the needs of the Kansas City African American community in the twenties and early thirties, and his actions did appear paternalistic and politically expedient. How did these factors fit together?

An examination of Truman's personal and political relationship with Chester Arthur Franklin, the African American publisher of *The Call*, a black Kansas City newspaper, reveals a possible answer to this question. The evolution of their relationship also reveals the shifting attitudes of black conservatives during a crucial period in African American political history—that is, from the rise of Republican lily whitism through the New Deal and Truman's presidency.

Chester A. Franklin
[Kansas City Call]

C. A. Franklin, as his friends and readers called him, was born June 7, 1880, in Denison, Texas.[2] In 1887 he and his parents headed north, intending to settle in all-black Nicodemus, Kansas. While enroute, they changed their plans and located in Omaha, Nebraska, where Franklin's father, George, opened a barbershop. George sold his shop in 1891 and began publishing the *Omaha Enterprise*, a weekly newspaper that prospered. C. A. finished high school and attended the University of Nebraska for two years before returning home to assist his ailing father in the publication of his paper.[3] In 1898, George's poor health caused the family to sell the *Enterprise* and move to Denver, hoping that the drier, cooler climate of the foothills would invigorate the elder Franklin.

Shortly after arriving in Denver, the Franklins bought the *Colorado Statesman*, which they renamed *The Star*. George's health continued to deteriorate, and his wife, Clara, and son, C. A., soon took charge of the paper's operation. When George Franklin died in 1901, the serious and sometimes volatile C. A. became publisher and editor, while his mother worked as bookkeeper and circulation manager. The team proved quite successful, and *The Star* grew in size, circulation, and reputation even though Denver had a relatively small black population.

As his paper prospered, C. A. Franklin joined Booker T. Washington's National Negro Business League, the Prince Hall Freemasons, and the Republican Party. Like many African Americans at the turn of the century, Franklin suspected that the Democrats were little more than ex-slaveholders who wanted to return to the ways of the antebellum South. He actively campaigned for Colorado Republicans in local and state elections and demanded that African Americans be allowed to share in the spoils of victory. According to his friends, the young publisher opened government jobs in Colorado to blacks. Despite his success in Denver, Franklin decided that a community with a larger African American population would offer him greater opportunities, and in 1913 he left for Kansas City, Missouri. His mother joined him two years later.

Upon his arrival in Kansas City, Franklin opened a printing shop, and he earned a reputation as a hard-working, reliable businessman. His journalistic desires remained strong, however, and on May 6, 1919, he published the first issue of *The Call*.[4] Few subscribers, paper shortages, inadequate printing equipment, and a formidable rival paper, *The Sun*, all threatened the four-page newspaper. But Franklin—with the help of his contacts in the Business League, the Freemasons and the YMCA—managed to make his publication the leading black newspaper in Kansas City.

C. A. Franklin's mother, Clara, provided business and bookkeeping support for both her husband's newspaper in Denver and, later, her son's paper, The Call. [Kansas City Call]

The Call mirrored the editorial tone of other early twentieth-century African American newspapers. Black publishers, like white publishers, shared a penchant for attention-grabbing headlines; as businessmen, they had not missed the market value of Hearst-style sensationalism. For example, Franklin used forty-point block letters to proclaim "LEPER WIFE MURDERER ESCAPES PUNISHMENT" and "PRETTY GIRL KILLS HER CAVE MAN LOVER." The stories under such headlines rarely ran more than two column inches, but they usually rated front-page coverage. Many African American publications, Franklin's included, also donated front-page space to churches that wished to advertise upcoming revivals. These advertisements, juxtaposed with the often sensational headlines, make the editors of these newspapers appear more shallow than they actually were. More importantly, however, most publishers of African American weeklies preferred to emphasize the accomplishments of their race and the importance of self-reliance, not the negative aspects of segregation.[5] In 1922, Franklin wrote:

> Our business used to center around 12th Street in what is near down-town territory now. We did not buy and we were shoved back. We moved to Eighteenth and again as renters we have been dispossessed. If we do not see tomorrow with all its wondrous growth we are not worth-while citizens. We must be builders of greatness if we would share it. Let us buy homes and then investment property too. Too many dollars are going into the froth of life. Too much social furbelows, too little savings accounts. Too many empty honors, too little hardy businesses. Too much common labor, too little craftsmen. Our grip on the industries of our section cannot be strong, if we are content with anything less than a man's share of responsibility. Kansas City does not owe us a living nearly as much as we owe it a real benefit from our living here.[6]

Franklin believed that civil rights depended on economic success, and economic success depended on the Protestant work ethic. When African Americans failed to display this ethic, he chastised them. "Negro labor in Kansas City is being less and less desired, because it is not responsible," wrote Franklin. "When the labor market, the labor market as created by the demands of white capital, is closed against the Negro, we are destroyed."[7]

If one accepts the standard categories for post-World War I African American politics—Booker T. Washington's nonconfrontational and "self-help" conservatism, W. E. B. Du Bois's aggressive and integrationist liberalism, and Marcus Garvey's separatist radicalism—Franklin fits neatly in the first category. He regularly preached the tenets of Washington's Business League

Despite early setbacks, The Call *became the foremost black newspaper in Kansas City.* [Kansas City Call]

in his editorials, he openly disagreed with the National Association for the Advancement of Colored People's (NAACP) *Crisis* on numerous occasions, and when Marcus Garvey spoke in Kansas City in March 1922, Franklin's coverage of the event might best be described as "cool."[8] Clearly, the early editorial tone of Franklin's paper places him squarely within the conservative camp.

Franklin's conservative approach to civil rights and his belief in the necessity of economic success reinforced his faith in the GOP. For decades, Republicans had recommended policies that benefited all businessmen, regardless of race, and Franklin invariably supported candidates who favored such policies, sometimes at the expense of more immediate racial concerns. For example, during the 1920 presidential campaign, Republican candidate Warren Harding had promised to appoint a number of African Americans to key positions in the federal government. When President Harding failed to keep this pledge, members of the African American press, led by W. E. B. Du Bois in the NAACP's *Crisis,* vigorously criticized him. Franklin, however, did not share Du Bois's opinion: "This paper has not been so lugubrious as most of the race press over the failure of President Harding to make many appointments in the national service. . . . The achievements of today are hundreds of thousands of home owning and farm owning citizens, insurance companies with millions of dollars in assets, businesses that serve whole districts, banks, newspaper plants, and other substantial results of our own efforts."[9] Franklin did inform the president of the disappointment that many African Americans felt because of his failure to appoint blacks to key jobs, and he published Harding's carefully worded response on the front page of *The Call*. "It is quite impossible," Harding wrote, "to meet up with the excessive demands for patronage. We are working out a program of consistent recognition and I hope in the end it will be entirely satisfactory."[10] This noncommittal reply satisfied Franklin, who continued to support the president.

Franklin's pro-Republican stance appeared even more strident in his coverage of local politics. Two rival Democratic factions dominated the Kansas City political scene from 1900 to 1930: James and Tom Pendergast's "Goats" and Joe Shannon's "Rabbits." Although these groups sometimes split the spoils of office fifty-fifty, their truces rarely lasted, and the rivalry continued until Kansas City Democrats elected Shannon to the U.S. House of Representatives in 1930, leaving Tom Pendergast in firm control until he went to prison nine years later. Pendergast and Shannon were brazenly corrupt—"now is the time for all good cemeteries to come to the aid of the party" was a popular joke in their day—and Franklin relished in exposing their sins. In the weeks before the 1922 municipal election, Franklin accused the Pendergast machine of vote fraud, bribery, favoritism, police brutality, gambling, prostitution, and bootlegging. On election eve, he reminded voters that during the previous election, "white ruffians wearing police badges beat Negro Republicans away from the polls, while Negro repeaters voted the Democratic ticket." Franklin also published a six-by-ten-inch sample ballot with instructions for voting a straight Republican ticket.[11]

Ward-heeler Casimir Welch proved particularly important for Kansas City African Americans during the Pendergast years. As a youngster, he had made a name for himself as a street fighter, and Joe Shannon had recognized that Welch's personal and physical qualities would make him a successful organizer. Shannon assigned him the unenviable task of drawing the Republican African Americans of the "Bloody Sixth" Ward into the Democratic camp. Welch combined friendliness, intimidation, and spoils to achieve his objective, and in the process, he became popular enough to win several terms as municipal judge, even though he had dropped out of school at age nine. In 1924, Welch left the Rabbits when Shannon secretly enjoined the Ku Klux Klan (KKK) to help defeat a young Goat, Harry Truman, in his reelection bid to the eastern seat of the Jackson County Court. Welch threw his support to the Goats and regularly delivered African American votes to the Pendergast machine until his death in 1936. In spite of Welch's break with the apparently racist Rabbits, Franklin detested the man. Before the 1931 municipal elections, he placed this headline on the front page of *The Call*: "$100 FOR ELECTION FRAUD

Political boss Joe Shannon led the "Rabbit" faction of the Kansas City Democratic Party until he was elected to the U.S. House of Representatives in 1930. This left Tom Pendergast in control of local Democrats.

PROOFS: Limited to Precincts of Sixth Justice of Peace District."[12] No one accepted the offer, and Welch won in a landslide.

Despite rampant corruption, local Democrats clearly demonstrated a concern for the African American community. By 1926, Democratic administrations had appointed hundreds of blacks to various positions in city and county government and built the Home for Aged Negroes, the Home for Negro Boys, and two hospitals for African Americans.[13] But Franklin's hatred of Pendergast, Shannon, and Welch blinded him to these contributions, and he continued to support Republican candidates in municipal and county elections throughout the 1920s.

Franklin's allegiance to state and national Republicans weakened in 1924. In the early twenties, southern GOP leaders attempted to take advantage of spreading racial conservatism (fostered in part by the reemergence of the KKK) by removing African Americans from key advisory positions—a policy known as "lily whitism." Although initially limited to Dixie, lily whitism spread rapidly to other parts of the country, and by 1924 rumors of a Klan-Republican alliance were rampant enough to be included in Kansas City Democratic advertisements. Franklin generally ignored these rumors—one linked Joe Shannon to a Republican-Klan coalition aimed at defeating Harry Truman in the 1924 campaign for eastern county judge—and he endorsed

Republicans for all but one elective office.[14] By 1928, however, Franklin could no longer deny that GOP leaders were changing the party's goals.

Three months before its national convention in Kansas City, the Republican Party announced that it intended to house black and white delegates separately. Franklin responded with a threat of sorts: "Republican chances in the national election are being threatened by what is going on in Kansas City." Party chieftains ignored Franklin's and other black leaders' protests and held the convention as planned. When the party denied seats to black delegates, Franklin reported, "G.O.P. Leans to Southern Lily Whites." And when the convention concluded without promising substantial racial reforms, the front page of *The Call* blasted the party: "Lily Whitism Now Official Republicanism" and "One Sentence on Lynching in Platform: Appeal is Buried by Heavy Vote Favoring the Lily Whites."[15] Franklin appeared ready to abandon the party of Lincoln.

The fall of 1928 proved to be a difficult time for Franklin. He was arrested in July for assaulting Willa Dwiggins, a woman active in local fund-raisers, at a benefit for the Negro Orphan Home. Franklin had become upset when Dwiggins insisted on giving the welcoming address—a speech he expected to deliver. After she refused to discuss the matter on the stage, Franklin had dragged her outside while calling her a variety of names. Not surprisingly, *The Call* ignored Franklin's indiscretion, but a new rival black newspaper, Felix Payne's *Kansas City American*, gave the story front-page attention. Although Dwiggins eventually dropped the charges against Franklin, the negative publicity had taken its toll. The publisher took an extended vacation in the fall, and upon his return, he ignored the threat of lily whitism and endorsed Herbert Hoover for president and Republicans for most county and state offices. Franklin did support Democrat Francis Wilson's failed attempt to win the governor's seat in Missouri, which brought his total number of Democratic endorsements to two.[16]

Significantly, Franklin's 1928 pro-Republican editorials lacked the fervor of his earlier writings. He concluded his lukewarm election-eve defense of Hoover with this sentence: "We are wise to vote for our friends no matter under what party label."[17] These words, combined with the outrage he expressed during the GOP national convention, suggest that Franklin was leaning away from both dogmatic Republicanism and Booker Washington's accommodative approach to civil rights. He appeared ready to embrace the Democratic Party and pursue a more aggressive approach to civil rights. While this shift was common among African American conservatives after the spread of lily whitism, Franklin never quite made the leap. Although the publisher of *The Call* subsequently attacked segregation with a vigor more reminiscent of

Du Bois than Washington, he could not bring himself to abandon Washington's business tenets or Republicanism in general. He did, however, moderate his positions on these and other issues.

By 1928, *The Call* frequently ran twenty-four pages and had twenty thousand subscribers in more than a dozen states; the paper also reflected Franklin's new-found moderation.[18] Although he still used sensational headlines, they appeared less frequently and seemed less lurid than those of his early issues. He continued to donate space for invitations to fundamentalist revivals, but he displayed these advertisements more discreetly. Washington's ideas still appeared in Franklin's editorials, and Republicans still received the vast majority of his endorsements, but he devoted more space to the evils of segregation and no longer published sample ballots with instructions for voting a straight GOP ticket. And as illustrated in the gubernatorial elections of 1924 and 1928 in Kansas and Missouri, respectively, Franklin endorsed more Democrats for elective office.

This moderation did not result from lily whitism alone; three people in particular appear to have played roles in "softening" the publisher's positions. In 1923, Franklin hired Roy Wilkins, a journalism graduate from the University of Minnesota and an active member of the NAACP. By expressing Du Bois's ideas in a sarcastic style similar to H. L. Mencken, Wilkins quickly won a following with his column "Talking It Over." This bright, young journalist openly contradicted Franklin in the pages of *The Call*, and he probably exasperated his mentor in private as well. Wilkins remained with *The Call* for nearly a decade, and Franklin undoubtedly learned as much from his employee as Wilkins learned from his boss.[19]

In 1925, Franklin married Ada Crogman, a young actress with a dramatics degree from Emerson College. According to contemporary accounts, this energetic and cosmopolitan woman tempered his manic work habits and soothed his volatile demeanor. According to Franklin himself, his wife instilled an open-mindedness in him that he had lacked in his earlier years.[20]

During the late twenties, a third person appears to have reinforced the moderating influences of Wilkins and Crogman. Harry Truman, a Pendergast Democrat and the presiding judge of the Jackson County Court from 1927 to 1934, ran a remarkably honest administration despite the corruption that surrounded him. He regularly awarded construction contracts to the lowest bidder rather than to the highest briber, and he did not demand monthly kickbacks from the thousand or so county employees—rather novel behaviors in Pendergast's domain.[21] Truman's integrity won him many supporters, including C. A. Franklin.

Ada Crogman Franklin proved to be a moderating force in her husband's life. [Kansas City Call]

By modern standards, Truman was not a champion of civil rights during his eight years as presiding judge, but he willingly and energetically pursued racial policies that Franklin found attractive. By 1928, African Americans made up one-third of the county's payroll, many in white-collar jobs, and near the end of his second term, Truman used his power as state commissioner of the Federal Reemployment Board to increase the number of federally financed jobs available to blacks. Truman also actively supported the county's "Negro" institutions. In fact, *The Call* reported in 1928 that, due to Truman's influence, "the Jackson County Home . . . is so human in its dealings with the inmates, that for comfort and security, they are as well off as if in the best private homes for the aged in the east," and "the Home for Boys," meanwhile, "has become a first class industrial institution for delinquent and neglected Negro boys." The presiding judge also proposed a bond issue in 1928 to build a home for Negro girls. The bond passed, and the home was completed a year later, but staffing it proved to be a problem. Cas Welch, boss of the "Bloody Sixth," insisted that Truman hire Welch's cronies, but the presiding judge refused. Truman's overwhelming reelection in 1930 and Shannon's election to the U.S. House of Representatives left Welch with little bargaining power. Jackson County opened the Home for Negro Girls in early 1931, and Truman's appointees operated the home.[22]

County budget records show that despite efforts to cut funding to these institutions, Truman managed to maintain their allotments at pre-depression

C. A. Franklin admired Harry Truman's honesty and integrity during his eight years as presiding judge of the Jackson County Court. [National Archives, U.S. Office of War Information 208-PV-201c-34]

levels into the thirties. Perhaps most importantly, Truman offered moral as well as financial support to residents of these facilities. According to Robert Sweeney, who later became the first African American supervisor at the Kansas City Post Office, the presiding judge frequently visited each institution, and after students "had left the Home [for Negro Boys] and gone to Howard, Fisk, or other universities Mr. Truman contributed to their support."[23]

The fact that these were segregated institutions appears not to have bothered Franklin. Instead, he seems to have been genuinely grateful to Truman for his financial and moral support of Jackson County's disadvantaged African Americans. A 1928 article, "Jackson County Shows Its Great Heart of Love," included a three-by-five-inch portrait of the presiding judge, and Franklin entitled a 1930 editorial, which endorsed Truman's bid for reelection, "County Cares for Sick."[24] Truman's obvious paternalism, described admirably by Richard Miller, did not disturb Franklin. After nearly two decades of Cas Welch's arbitrary favoritism, the presiding judge's concern for blacks, paternalistic as it was, must have seemed refreshingly genuine. This sincerity, combined with Truman's administrative integrity, proved to Franklin that a Democrat could be both honest and empathetic—a realization that solidified Franklin's new pragmatism.

Truman's actions on the county court were undoubtedly politically expedient, but that does not, as some have argued, necessarily imply duplicity.

Roy Wilkins, for example, recalled Truman as "politically astute on the race question before he ever came to Washington, because the Pendergast machine was politically astute on the race question. They weren't the fair-haired boys and they didn't believe in good government and they didn't necessarily love the Negro, but they believed in machine control and in marshalling whatever votes it took to keep the machine in power." In an attempt to demonstrate that Truman lacked "firm convictions on civil rights," Harold Gosnell quotes Truman in a private conversation: "You know that I am against this bill [the 1938 antilynching act], but if it comes to a vote I'll have to be for it. All my sympathies are with you but the Negro vote in Kansas City and St. Louis is too important."[25]

Such arguments apparently offer compelling evidence of Truman's duplicity, but an examination of how Truman defined "political expediency" suggests he did not attempt to "dupe" anyone. In his last "Pickwick Memo," written on the eve of his 1934 announcement to run for the U.S. Senate, Truman argued that actions cynics label "expedient" are in reality the most honorable because "the ultimate responsibility of an elected official is to represent the interests of the voters regardless of his own position."

Hence, to represent interests that conflict with one's own is not "politically expedient," it is doing one's job. While it can be argued that this line of reasoning was little more than a shameless rationalization, several of Truman's later letters suggest that his concern for African Americans was genuine—expedient, but genuine.[26]

Truman's concern for minorities was comparatively new. As the son of "an unreconstructed rebel mother," he had developed a dislike for all minorities at an early age. His lack of contact with these groups exacerbated his prejudices, and his early letters to his future wife, Bess Wallace, are filled with racial slurs. Truman's wartime experiences in the largely Irish Catholic D Battery of the 128th Infantry Division made him more sensitive to the position of minorities and offered him proof that non-WASPs deserved his respect.[27] His business partner after the war was Jewish, his political mentor was Catholic, and his record as presiding judge demonstrated a remarkable empathy for the twenty thousand Jackson County African Americans.

What or who convinced Truman that he represented Jackson County African Americans? At first glance, Tom Pendergast and Cas Welch seem to be likely candidates, but the "Pickwick Memo" suggests otherwise. Truman harbored grave doubts about Boss Tom's methods and ends, and he wrote that Welch "is a thug of the worst water, he should have been in the pen twenty years ago." If Truman learned anything from these men, he learned how to fix elections. Probably local African American leaders, not machine politicians, convinced Truman that he should consciously and sincerely attend to the needs of minorities. The presiding judge had extensive contact with several local black representatives, and all of them likely played a part in Truman's "conversion." Truman's personal correspondence files infer that his relationship with Franklin was perhaps most influential. While no other Kansas City African American wrote the senator on a regular basis, Franklin and Truman corresponded frequently (sometimes more than once a week) throughout his first Senate term. The content of these letters is primarily political, but the tone reveals the writers' respect for each other: Franklin repeatedly voiced admiration for the senator's work, and Truman often complimented the editor's judgment and integrity. This mutual respect shows up in other writings as well. Not surprisingly, Franklin continued to support Truman in *The Call*, and Truman often commended Franklin in his notes to other government officials.[28]

Lucile Bluford, who replaced Roy Wilkins as news editor at *The Call* in 1932, contends that this mutual respect led to friendship. Despite differences in race, temperament, and party affiliation, Bluford recalls that Franklin and Truman had a great deal in common: both were Freemasons, both believed in fiscal accountability, and both thought that citizens, not government, held ultimate responsibility for their own well-being. These shared beliefs led to a friendship that Bluford describes as "personal first, political second."[29] To

Truman recorded his personal observations on political and Jackson County events in his secret office at Kansas City's Pickwick Hotel.

assert that Franklin was the primary cause of Truman's "conversion" would be foolish; this transformation began long before they met, involved countless men and women, and ultimately was the result of the future president's own cogitations. To deny, however, that these unlikely friends exerted some influence on each other would be equally foolish.

With Pendergast's blessing, Truman entered the Democratic primary for the U.S. Senate in 1934. He faced stiff competition from John Cochran, a representative of William L. Igoe's St. Louis machine, and the St. Louis papers were ruthless:

> It's hard to believe . . . that Boss Pendergast really means it when he comes out for a candidate for the United States Senate whose only experience in public life has been to sit ten years as a member of the Jackson County Court. . . . To ask that County Judge Truman be elected for six years to the nation's highest lawmaking body on a record of O-K-ing county supply bills and seeing that the county clerk's books are properly kept is taking too much risk with inexperience.[30]

On the eve of the primary, Franklin wrote, "If ever a man deserved public confidence on the basis of the record made in the public's service, that man is Harry S. Truman." Because of rampant vote fraud on both sides, Franklin's role—any publisher's role—was negligible. Truman won the August primary by 40,000 votes, largely because Jackson County voters, both alive and dead, cast more than 137,000 votes for Truman and only 1,525 for Cochran.[31] Truman easily won the November general election and moved to Washington the following month.

Many of Franklin's letters to Truman illustrate his inexperience with the political realities of Washington. Assuming that the freshman senator could easily secure Reconstruction Finance Corporation (RFC) funds, Franklin asked Truman in late 1937 to obtain RFC loans for African American homebuilders. "This is right down your alley," wrote Franklin. Truman replied: "I am sure that when the new housing policy is worked out, that we will have an opportunity to come in on it. . . . As you know, several efforts have been made to get projects started there, but nearly every time that is done, somebody throws a monkey wrench in the machinery."

Franklin wrote to Truman again in 1939, repeating his request for federally funded housing. This time he included a copy of a two-page letter he had written to Eleanor Roosevelt, explaining housing conditions in Kansas City. Still unable to alleviate the problem himself, Truman arranged a meeting between representatives of the Kansas City African American community and

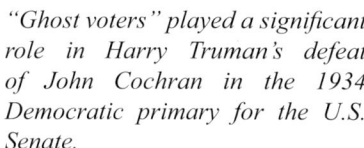

"Ghost voters" played a significant role in Harry Truman's defeat of John Cochran in the 1934 Democratic primary for the U.S. Senate.

Stewart MacDonald of the Federal Housing Authority (FHA).[32] Nothing grew out of this meeting.

Franklin's request that Truman secure a change in the policies of the U.S. Postal Service also failed. In early 1939 the publisher founded the Colored Mail Order Corporation of America, the first African American mail-order business in the United States. To save on postage costs, Franklin wanted to send catalogs to blacks only, but the postal service refused his request unless the corporation placed specific names on the address labels. Franklin wrote to Truman explaining the situation and asked him to contact the appropriate official. Truman forwarded Franklin's proposal to William Howes, first assistant postmaster general, who denied the appeal. An obviously disappointed Truman informed Franklin of the decision.[33]

Not all of Franklin's requests went unfilled. For decades, Missouri's governors had staffed the state's black college, Lincoln University, with political favorites. The University of Missouri did not admit African Americans. Franklin had repeatedly argued in his paper against the use of patronage in hiring Lincoln's staff, but until he forwarded his complaint to Senator Truman, no administration had taken these arguments seriously.[34] Truman convinced Governor Guy Park (a Pendergast man) that he should remove jobs at Lincoln from the spoils list, and Park complied.[35]

Segregation at the University of Missouri was not so easily resolved, but it led to a key episode in the Franklin-Truman relationship. The U.S.

Supreme Court ruled in *Gaines v. Canada* (1938) that Missouri had to provide professional schools for blacks within the state. In an attempt to avoid integrating the University of Missouri, the state legislature and Governor Lloyd Stark (originally a Pendergast man) enacted the Taylor bill, allotting Lincoln University $200,000 to create a professional school. Stark's position on the Taylor bill, which in effect maintained the segregated system that Gaines had sought to end, infuriated Franklin, and in May 1939 he wrote to Truman about it. In his reply, Truman acknowledged that the bill was simply a way to avoid integration, but concluded that there was little he could do.[36]

As events unfolded in the summer of 1939, Franklin realized that the senator could do something—end Stark's political career. Stark had spent the preceding two years diligently dismantling the Pendergast machine, and with his former benefactor, Pendergast, now in prison, the governor began to campaign openly for Truman's seat in the Senate. Truman's ties to the discredited machine (and the absence of eighty-five thousand "ghost voters") significantly reduced his chances for victory, and he considered not running. In October, Franklin joined Truman's advisers in urging the senator to remain in the race and beat Stark at the polls—a defeat that would almost certainly end the governor's political career and possibly provide an opportunity to integrate the University of Missouri. Truman, who had his own reasons for wanting to crush Stark, agreed to run.[37]

These two letters perhaps constitute the most enlightening Franklin-Truman exchange, not because Franklin "convinced" Truman to run for reelection, but because they reveal how the two men dealt with the political realities of their time. Franklin, a politically astute man, described in his letter how a Truman attack on Stark might initiate a "clean-government" backlash and how an African American attack on the governor might initiate a racist backlash—either of which would lead to Truman's defeat. Consequently, Franklin argued that Truman should run a positive campaign, appealing specifically to Missouri's black voters. "To keep up the good work, we must now turn to selling you. Be thinking of your points of contact with our voters so that when you come back home, we can map a course of action." Intriguingly, Franklin voiced his concern over Truman's reputation among his racist colleagues in Washington. If Truman's stance on African American issues appeared too liberal, he would earn the label "nigger lover"—a label that would hamper his effectiveness in the Senate. If Truman's positions were not liberal enough, however, he would lose the black vote and, in all likelihood, the election. In short, the senator would have to walk an impossibly thin line. Truman, a politically astute man as well, agreed with Franklin on all counts: "In matters of this kind, your judgement is always good."[38]

Truman officially announced his candidacy in March 1940, and his first major campaign engagement took place in Sedalia at the ground-breaking ceremony for a new African American hospital.[39] After citing his first-term voting record—his support of the antilynching bill, the office of Recorder of Deeds of Washington, DC (which provided hundreds of jobs to African Americans), and the antidiscrimination amendment to the Selective Service Act of 1940—Truman set the tone for his campaign rhetoric:

> Negroes have never had much choice in regard to work or anything else. By and large, they work mainly as unskilled laborers and domestic servants. They have been forced to live in segregated slums, neglected by the authorities. Negroes have been preyed upon by all types of exploiters, from the installment salesmen of clothing, pianos and furniture to the vendors of vice. The majority of our Negro people find but cold comfort in shanties and tenements. Surely, as free men, they are entitled to something better than this.[40]

One month later, in a speech before the National Colored Democratic Association, Truman stated flatly, "We should recognize his [the African American's] inalienable rights as specified in our Constitution."[41]

Senator Truman maintained a Sedalia office during the 1940 senatorial campaign; his first campaign engagement took place at the ground-breaking for a local African American hospital. [Harry S. Truman Library]

These statements appear to support Leuchtenburg's contention that Truman's conversion largely resulted from his view of the Constitution as a "sacred text." Leuchtenburg, however, ignores a salient fact: during the 1940 campaign, Truman limited such comments to African American audiences, while his speeches to whites concentrated on the need to continue the New Deal. Does this imply that Gosnell's assessment of duplicity is closer to the truth? Possibly, but when one considers Truman's record on the county court and in the Senate, his October 1939 exchange with Franklin, and his subsequent actions as senator and president, another possible explanation emerges: Truman acted duplicitously not with blacks, but with racists. By limiting his civil rights rhetoric to African American audiences, Truman could, for the most part, limit the publication of his comments to the African American press—publications not widely read in racist crowds—and thereby avoid the backlash that he and Franklin feared. As implausible as this may sound, it explains Truman's actions in the 1940 campaign and some rather odd denials he made one year later.[42]

Truman defeated Stark in the Democratic senatorial primary by only 7,476 votes, and in a letter to Franklin, the senator attributed his victory to African American voters. While Truman's assessment was a bit simplistic—he received a key endorsement from St. Louis boss Robert Hannegan as well—Franklin played a major role in the victory. In all likelihood, Kansas City and St. Louis blacks would have voted for Truman regardless of Franklin's position—they had voted solidly Democratic for years—but Missouri's rural African Americans had not supported Truman in 1934, and they did in 1940. Much of this new support was anti-Stark and pro-Roosevelt, but almost certainly, some of it was a result of Franklin's paper. By 1940 nearly one-third of *The Call*'s fifteen thousand Missouri subscribers lived outside of Kansas City and St. Louis, and Franklin's paper informed many of these traditional Republicans of the senator's contributions to the African American agenda.[43] To assert that Franklin was the key in Truman's primary victory would be wrongheaded, but he was certainly a key. Truman won the November general election and returned to Washington.

In late December 1940, Franklin complained to Truman that the builders contracted to expand housing at Fort Riley, Kansas, refused to employ African American carpenters: "This will happen at Lake City as well." Without revealing how he planned to halt the discrimination, Truman replied that he would "look into it as soon as possible." Within a week, every Fort Riley builder except the Missouri-based Long Construction Company had hired African Americans. In early January, Franklin asked for "one more shove, [then] Negroes will be integrated into the defense industries."[44]

The first weeks of the 77th Congress were hectic for the second-term senator, and he apparently delayed action on Franklin's request while pursuing other concerns. Since 1939, Truman had heard rumors of fraud and waste on the part of defense contractors at Fort Leonard Wood, Missouri, and these reports prompted him to visit dozens of military bases in 1940. He was appalled. Upon his return to Washington, he met with Franklin Roosevelt to discuss the issue and soon began working on a proposal to create a Senate select committee to investigate defense contractors.[45] Consequently, Truman's workload increased dramatically in January 1941, and it became even heavier in March when the Senate established his committee and appointed him chairman.

Franklin, unaware of (or ignoring) Truman's busier schedule, reminded the senator of the "Long Construction problem" in his next letter, this time including the address of the company. Truman, clearly in a testy mood, wrote: "I am not acquainted with the Long Construction Company and therefore am not in any position to discuss with them whom they ought to hire in Kansas. If they were [contracted to work] in Missouri, it might be different. It seems to me that with two Republican senators in Kansas who supported Willkie, as you did, you ought to get some results in that quarter."[46]

Truman was right. Franklin had supported Wendell Willkie in his presidential campaign against Roosevelt, and Truman's letter revealed his irritation. Franklin did not miss the senator's consternation. "Did you smile," wrote Franklin, "when you wrote that last paragraph? I hope so. . . . One interpretation of this paragraph is that I am to look elsewhere in the future. Is that your meaning?"[47]

Another interpretation—and considering subsequent events, a more reasonable one—is that Truman was simply being sarcastic. Frustrated by Long, and perhaps feeling the pressure of his growing responsibilities, Truman's suggestion that Franklin "ought to get results" from Republican senators seems to have been an unsuccessful attempt at cynical humor. Franklin's failure to perceive the senator's sarcasm is not surprising; Roy Wilkins, news editor of *The Call* until 1931, wrote that Franklin was a humorless, "intense man [who] was all business."[48] Despite Truman's eventual success in correcting the "Long Construction problem"—the company hired African Americans within two weeks—the rift created by this misunderstanding did not end.

In Franklin's next letter, he acknowledged Truman's work and asked for more of the same. "I am most happy to report to you that 25 Negro carpenters went to work last week (at Fort Riley) and an additional number is going to find work there in the immediate future. We now face the task of getting a share of the work in the bomber plant at Fairfax [the North American Aviation factory in Kansas City, Kansas] and the ammunitions plant at Lake City."[49]

Truman wrote that he would see that the same reforms were carried out at Lake City (though he strangely failed to mention Fairfax) and included an apology of sorts for his testy letter of two weeks earlier: "I was morally certain that they would be put to work, but it did seem to me that those Kansas fellows should be willing to do something about it, just as well as us from Missouri. I pulled every wire possible to get the job done."[50]

During the succeeding months, Franklin reiterated his request for Truman's help in ending discrimination at the Fairfax plant and asked for assistance with discrimination at several midwestern training programs for defense industry workers. Although it is not clear how Truman convinced contractors to employ African Americans, the fact that most contractors began hiring blacks soon after Franklin's letters arrived in Washington suggests that the senator was doing something. If Truman was abusing the power of his new committee to achieve his ends, Franklin appears not to have cared: "When I returned from a visit to Washington a couple of years ago, I said of you that you were rising fast. I have that impression confirmed by the statesmanlike manner in which you are conducting your committee."[51]

Truman's conduct, however, was not statesmanlike enough to sustain Franklin's respect and support. Their rate of correspondence dwindled after May 1941, and after 1942, Franklin rarely wrote Truman. When the publisher of *The Call* felt compelled to contact Truman, he wrote not to the senator (or

An active member of the NAACP, Roy Wilkins was more liberal than his mentor, C. A. Franklin. Despite their differences, Wilkins worked for The Call *for nearly a decade.* [Kansas City Call]

In 1955, after the death of C. A. Franklin, Lucile Bluford succeeded him as editor and publisher of The Call.

president) but to his secretary, Victor Messall, or to his brother, Vivian. This estrangement, though perhaps precipitated by their tense exchange in January 1941, was not due solely to Truman's failed attempt at sarcastic wit. Rather, it resulted from three factors, two that emerged in the summer of 1941 and one that had been brewing since 1933.

In late 1940, Boss Tom returned to Kansas City after serving his fifteen-month prison sentence in Leavenworth, and Truman assisted in rebuilding his machine. During the spring and summer of 1941, the second-term senator—who once vowed never to "desert a ship that is going down"—found a variety of federally financed positions, including jobs at Lake City, for loyal Pendergast men. To Franklin, who supported the anti-Pendergast reform coalition in the local 1940 elections, Truman's actions must have smelled like the old days.[52] Franklin, however, was accustomed to patronage, and while Truman's attempts to revitalize the machine certainly irritated the publisher, this alone cannot account for his break with Truman.

After May 1941, Truman seemed to ignore pleas to end discrimination in defense industries. Although he acknowledged the problem's existence, he refused requests for a public hearing on racial discrimination and claimed that such a hearing would not and could not achieve the desired result. "When we try to get the facts and the sworn testimony to prove it [racial discrimination], it evaporates into thin air, because the people affected are afraid of assault and battery, and you can't blame them much. The gang that does that sort of thing . . . are [*sic*] the thug class and are very difficult to run to earth."[53]

Although a reasonable position for a man whose official actions depended on the accumulation of evidence, some African Americans believed Truman's reluctance to attack discrimination stemmed from political expediency. They thought he was tempering his activism to maintain the support of his racist colleagues in Washington. The senator's private response to such attacks was both remarkable and revealing: "I have never heard of any race prejudice existing either at Lake City or the bomber plant."[54] This strange denial supports the contention that his inaction was the result of expediency. In October 1939 both Franklin and Truman expressed fear of a racist backlash in the 1940 election, and Truman planned his campaign strategy accordingly: he limited his civil rights rhetoric to African American audiences (and hence, the African American press), and his strategy worked. By the fall of 1941, however, the success and popularity of his committee had made Harry Truman a household name, he was no longer an obscure junior senator from some midwestern state, he was chairman of the Truman Committee. His fame in a racist society and his desire to maintain his carefully constructed alliances in the Senate made him particularly vulnerable to the label "nigger lover." In short, political expediency may account for both Truman's "activism" regarding African American interests in the 1920s and his inaction in late 1941.

In the meantime, Franklin had become rather intolerant of inaction. In 1940 he backed Lucile Bluford's failed lawsuit against segregation at the University of Missouri, applauded Wendell Willkie's attempts at integration in Ohio, and organized a series of demonstrations against discrimination at Fort Riley, Fairfax, and Lake City in December 1940 and January 1941.[55] By the start of Truman's second term, Franklin—who had ignored segregation in Jackson County ten years earlier—had replaced Booker T. Washington's accommodation with W. E. B. Du Bois's activism. Franklin pursued equality of opportunity, not equality of condition; he demanded equal education and employment, not handouts. Truman's expedient inaction in the summer and fall of 1941, particularly in the area of job discrimination, must have disappointed the publisher. Like Truman's attempts to revitalize the Pendergast machine, his inattention to discrimination cannot by itself account for Franklin's estrangement from Truman. The fissure had been growing for years.

Franklin, who had internalized the free enterprise tenets of the National Negro Business League, found in Roosevelt's New Deal a mortal and moral enemy, and *The Call*, like many other major black weeklies, aggressively and repeatedly attacked the Democratic president and his policies. Aid programs would sap the will of poor African Americans by allowing them to make a living from government-sponsored work programs, a living that would be, in Franklin's opinion, illusory. "Some sober sense," wrote Franklin, "must save the Negro from being like the dog who, while crossing a stream, saw his reflection and dropped the bone he had to try to get another."[56]

As much as aid programs disturbed the publisher of *The Call*, the indignities suffered by businessmen bothered him even more. Franklin believed that the private sector alone was responsible for economic growth and government should limit itself to spurring private investment by rewarding capitalists. Roosevelt, though hardly a socialist, did not share Franklin's faith in unbridled capitalism, and after 1932 businessmen paid an increasing share of taxes as the federal government saddled them with unprecedented regulations. Like many businessmen, Franklin lashed out: "Roosevelt will have to do more than deny any intention of becoming communistic or wanting the support of Communists. . . . What the people want to know is does he agree with [Rexford G.] Tugwell and [Harry] Hopkins, head of the PWA, in their declaration that this is a war between the Haves and the Have-Nots. If he does not, he should either silence them or get rid of them."[57]

In addition to alleging that Roosevelt was pink, if not red, Franklin attempted to prove that the New Deal endangered the freedom of African Americans. When Roosevelt threatened to pack the Supreme Court to uphold the constitutionality of New Deal programs, Franklin argued that his actions would threaten the Thirteenth, Fourteenth, and Fifteenth amendments. If the president could pack the court to manipulate the Constitution in favor of the New Deal, Franklin reasoned, what will keep him from packing it against civil rights? Four years later, as war neared, Franklin added treason to his list of charges against the president. "That the President is swapping safety of the nation for votes is the grave charge made. Congress has voted a defense program. It is Franklin D. Roosevelt's sworn duty to see that it is carried out. Instead of doing his sworn duty, he is accused of giving workers of CIO affiliation free hand to strike through cessation of work, tying up the plants producing essential defense materials."[58]

Franklin ignored Roosevelt's contributions to the African American agenda—for example, his numerous black advisers and the Civilian Conservation Corps' literacy classes for blacks—and endorsed Alf Landon in 1936, Wendell Willkie in 1940, and Thomas Dewey in 1944. In each presidential campaign, Franklin mixed racial issues with economic policy, but his primary concern appeared obvious: "Alf Landon, with his faith in private initiative, is the safer choice for the nation's highest office," and "Dewey Will Ease Your Tax Load."[59] Franklin could not tolerate the left-leaning policies of President Roosevelt, and after 1941 he would not endorse a senator who supported the president.

Truman's liberal position on government intervention was comparatively new. As presiding judge in Jackson County, Truman had shared Franklin's faith in fiscal conservatism and individual responsibility, but during his first term in the Senate, Truman had backed Roosevelt on virtually every major New Deal proposal. Franklin tolerated Truman's new liberalism as long as he could, partly because of friendship and partly because of the senator's growing influence. In late 1941, however, Congress created the Federal Employment Practices Commission to enforce Executive Order 8802, which outlawed discrimination in federal training programs, and this agency offered Franklin a more direct route for attacking discrimination.[60] Although the Truman Committee continued to grow in importance, it was no longer significant for Franklin, and the advantage of supporting a New Dealer was gone. Their correspondence effectively ended after 1942, and Franklin's paper rarely mentioned the senator again until he became the Democratic vice presidential candidate.

Rumors of a "southern deal" raged during the 1944 Democratic national convention. Roosevelt allegedly dumped the liberal Henry Wallace in favor of the more conservative Truman to win southern support. Two weeks before the election, the headline of *The Call*'s lead story read "Truman's Alliance

After Franklin D. Roosevelt chose Harry Truman as his vice presidential candidate in 1944, The Call *lambasted the senator and accused him of KKK involvement.*

With South Proven," and on election eve, Franklin's paper participated in a smear campaign directed at Truman. Four witnesses claimed that the vice presidential candidate had been involved with the KKK while he was eastern county judge. Truman replied, and rightly so, that "the Klan fought me and I fought the Klan. The Klan is repugnant to every policy and every principle I have advocated and struggled for." Franklin knew Truman was no Klansman, and he wrote in the same issue that "whether or not Truman belonged to the Klan in 1922 is inconsequential."[61] He ran the story anyway, effectively ending any chance for a political reconciliation with Truman.

Roosevelt won his fourth presidential election and died shortly after his inauguration. The man from Independence became president, and for those who believed the hysterical accusations of KKK involvement, it must have been a traumatic transfer of power. Franklin, however, knew that Truman had made a number of contributions to African Americans during his eight years as presiding judge and his ten years in the Senate. He did not fear a return to slavery, but rather a continuation of the New Deal. Although Franklin initially approached the Truman administration with tolerance—he titled a 1945 editorial "Let's Help, Not Hinder the President"—his optimism faded when the president continued the programs of his predecessor.[62]

During the 1948 campaign, Franklin chose an odd strategy to attack his former ally: Truman became a nonperson in the pages of *The Call*. Not once during the three months prior to the election did Franklin mention Truman in an editorial, and few front-page stories appeared regarding the president. Franklin chose to act as though Republican Thomas Dewey were the only man running for president. The publisher ran headlines from the previous campaign ("Dewey Will Ease Your Tax Load"), and he added new reasons to vote Republican ("Joe Louis to Vote for Dewey"). Interestingly, when Franklin attacked the Democratic Party, he blasted the dead Roosevelt, not the living Truman. "Bureaucracy, introduced in America by F.D.R. under the name 'New Deal,' goes on though it challenges the traditional American way of life. . . . We can decide to go further toward bureaucracy or turn back to free enterprise. Republicans are champions of the latter."[63]

Whether Franklin avoided direct attacks on Truman out of respect for the president or out of some interesting application of campaign psychology remains a mystery, but the strategy clearly failed. Truman secured a surprise victory over Dewey and Democratic defectors Strom Thurmond and Henry Wallace and spent four more years in the White House—four years that earned the Democratic Party, rightly or wrongly, the label "the party of civil rights."

Shortly after Truman's victory, C. A. Franklin semiretired. Sixty-eight years old, he had inherited his father's infirm health, and though he retained

C. A. Franklin [Kansas City Call]

the title of editor/publisher, Lucile Bluford assumed a larger role in running *The Call*. In spite of the obvious ideological break between Franklin and Truman and the absence of substantive correspondence after 1942, they appear to have harbored no ill feelings toward each other. They exchanged Christmas greetings throughout the late forties, and Franklin invited Truman to his seventieth birthday party in 1950.[64] Franklin died in 1955.

The Franklin-Truman story addresses two significant questions. First, what factors influenced Harry Truman's changing attitudes toward African Americans? And second, how did conservative African Americans adapt to the changing political climate of the twenties, thirties, and forties? Their relationship suggests that Truman's "conversion" or "evolution" began during his first term as presiding judge and that it was the result of several factors: political expediency, his sense of fairness, and his contact with Kansas City's African American leaders, especially C. A. Franklin. Truman and the publisher shared a number of beliefs—most notably a faith in fiscal conservatism and a traditional, accommodative approach to civil rights—and they became friends. But the depression, or more precisely, Roosevelt's response to the depression, prompted a rift between the two men. While Franklin retained his belief in unfettered free enterprise, Truman abandoned fiscal conservatism in favor of the New Deal. From 1933 on, Truman combined fiscal liberalism with government intervention on behalf of African Americans—a combination that would become standard in later Democratic platforms and virtually synonymous with civil rights.

Franklin's faith in the Republican Party, shaken but not destroyed by lily whitism, actually deepened during the 1930s; higher taxes, increased regulation, and "illusory" handouts pushed him back into the GOP camp for good. Consistent with fiscally conservative Republicanism, Franklin pursued equality of opportunity, not equality of condition. This combination, representative of middle-class African American attitudes in the thirties and forties, would later become rare.

Ironically, Franklin appears partially responsible for the failure of African American conservatism to gain adherents. There was no reason in the mid-forties to believe that Democrats would become the "party of civil rights." But Harry Truman, the "converted" border-state bigot whose political career nearly ended in 1940, won the 1948 election, placing a Democrat in the White House during the infancy of the civil rights movement. By playing a role in Truman's "conversion" and supporting the future president in the critical 1940 campaign, Franklin inadvertently helped the Democrats take the lead in civil rights, consequently insuring the decline of his own philosophy.

NOTES

1. Truman's tour of the South was part of a thirty-thousand-mile trip to investigate rumors of fraud and waste in defense spending. William Leuchtenburg, "The Conversion of Harry Truman," *American Heritage*, November 1991, 55-68; Larry Grothaus, "Kansas City Blacks, Harry Truman and the Pendergast Machine," *Missouri Historical Review* 69 (October 1974): 65-82; Richard Miller, *Truman: The Rise to Power* (New York: McGraw-Hill, 1986), 325-329; Harold Gosnell, *Truman's Crises: A Political Biography of Harry S. Truman* (Westport, CT: Greenwood Press, 1980), 108-109, 134-136.

2. The following biographical account, except where noted, was compiled from the program written for Franklin's seventieth birthday celebration. President's Personal File, box 548, folder 2328, Harry S. Truman Library, Independence, MO.

3. William H. Young and Nathan B. Young, *Your Kansas City and Mine, 1850-1950* (Kansas City: W. H. Young, 1950), 12.

4. *Kansas City Star*, 25 December 1983.

5. For an accurate description of early twentieth-century African American

periodicals see Vishnu Oak, *The Negro Newspaper* (Westport, CT: Negro Universities Press, 1948), 124-128. The headlines appeared respectively in the *Kansas City Call*, 1 November, 29 February 1924.

6. *Kansas City Call*, 4 February 1922.

7. Ibid., 18 July 1924.

8. Hanes Walton Jr., "Blacks and Conservative Political Movements," in *Black Political Life in the United States: A Fist as the Pendulum*, ed. Lenneal J. Henderson, Jr. (San Francisco: Chandler, 1972), 218. *Kansas City Call*, 18 March 1922. Garvey was extremely popular among the poor urban African Americans who, in 1922, made up the majority of Franklin's subscribers. One may reasonably infer—though there is no evidence to do so—that Franklin tempered his anti-Garvey rhetoric to avoid alienating his readers. When a federal grand jury indicted Garvey for mail fraud one year later, Franklin was less forgiving.

9. *Kansas City Call*, 25 February 1922.

10. Ibid., 4 March 1922.

11. Lyle Dorsett, *The Pendergast Machine* (New York: Oxford University Press, 1968), 91; *Kansas City Call*, 25 March, 1 April 1922.

12. William Rockhill Nelson, publisher of the Republican *Kansas City Star*, offered Welch an office job after he saw him beat up a rival paperboy. William Reddig, *Tom's Town: Kansas City and the Pendergast Legend* (New York: J. B. Lippincott, 1947), 109-111; *Kansas City Call*, 31 December 1930.

13. *Kansas City Call*, 22 October 1926.

14. Ibid., 21 March 1924. Franklin supported a Democrat in the Kansas gubernatorial election because Republican candidate Ben Paulen was, according to *The Call*, a "thorough-going Klan assistant." Paulen won, and interestingly enough, Franklin wrote an editorial two years later titled "Negroes of Kansas Should Support Governor Paulen." Ibid., 19 September 1924; 22 October 1926.

15. Ibid., 16, 23 March, 8, 15 June 1928.

16. *Kansas City American*, 19 July 1928. The competition between Franklin and Payne grew more heated as time passed. The rivalry peaked in October 1932 when Payne, with the support of Joseph LaCour, a minority stockholder in *The Call*, and Dr. William Thompkins, whom Franklin Roosevelt would later name as recorder of deeds in Washington, DC, attempted to acquire control of *The Call* by proving in court that Franklin had mismanaged his paper. Unfortunately for Payne, LaCour, and Thompkins, the court ruled in favor of Franklin. A federal grand jury had indicted Payne the previous week for conspiracy to violate the Prohibition Act, and two unknown assailants beat Payne nearly to death only one week later. *Kansas City Call*, 21, 28 October, 2 November 1932.

17. *Kansas City Call*, 2 November 1928.

18. Noel Wilson, "The *Kansas City Call*: An Inside View of the Negro Market," (PhD diss., University of Illinois at Urbana-Champaign, 1968), 395.

19. Roy Wilkins, *Standing Fast: The Autobiography of Roy Wilkins* (New York: Viking Press, 1982), 56. Wilkins left *The Call* in 1931 for a position in the headquarters of the NAACP. He replaced Du Bois as editor of the *Crisis* in 1934 and eventually became president of the organization, but he and Franklin remained friends until Franklin's death in 1955. Ibid., 108, 155.

20. *Kansas City Star*, 25 December 1983; Young and Young, *Your Kansas City*, 12.

21. The Jackson County Court was an administrative, not a judicial, body, primarily responsible for maintaining roads, bridges, and public buildings. Truman, with support from the Pendergast machine, had won the eastern seat on the court in 1922. Out of 228 miles of road paved in 1928, Tom Pendergast's Ready-Mixed Concrete Company paved only three-fourths of a mile. Dorsett, *Pendergast Machine*, 72.

22. *Kansas City Call*, 27 July 1928; Philip H. Vaughan, *The Truman Administration's Legacy for Black America* (Reseda, CA: Mojave Books, 1976), 2. Truman proposed that the home be named in honor of Hiram Young, an African American blacksmith on the Santa Fe Trail, but his idea was not adopted. *Kansas City Call*, 4 May, 27 July 1928; 31 October 1930; 26 October 1934.

23. "Jackson County Budget 1932" and "Jackson County Budget 1933," Papers of Harry S. Truman, Presiding Judge, 1927-1934, box 1, folder 1, Truman Library; "Robert Sweeney: An Oral History," 8, 11, Truman Library.

24. *Kansas City Call*, 27 July 1928; 31 October 1930.

25. Wilkins quoted in Gosnell, *Truman's Crises*, 108. Wilkins was not alone in his assessment of Truman's real motives; for a more fully developed contemporary African American view of Truman's "duplicity," see Jay Franklin, "What Truman Really Thinks of Negroes," *Negro Digest*, June 1949, 65. Gosnell, *Truman's Crises*, 135.

26. The purpose of the "Pickwick Memos" is not entirely clear. Written over a three-year span on stationery from Truman's secret office in the Pickwick Hotel, they are certainly not letters, and with such questions as "What chance is there for a clean, honest administration . . . when a bunch of vultures sit on the sidelines and puke on the field?" Truman clearly did not intend for them to become public while Tom Pendergast was alive. Apparently he used the memos to clarify in his own mind what his political career was all about and, perhaps, to document for posterity that he may have been a "Pendergast boy" but not a Pendergast fan. Truman Presiding Judge Papers, box 2, folder 9.

27. Truman quoted in *Kansas City Call*, 20 October 1944. See Robert H. Ferrell, ed., *Dear Bess: The Letters from Harry to Bess Truman, 1910-1959* (New York: W. W. Norton, 1983) or Harry S. Truman, *Letters Home*, ed. Monte M. Poen (New York:

Putnam, 1984). Truman's letters home reveal how proud he was to be a part of the D Battery and how well he and his men worked together. Truman, *Letters Home*, 51-52.

28. Truman Presiding Judge Papers, box 2, folder 9. In a January 26, 1939, memo to FHA official Stewart MacDonald, Truman wrote, "He [Franklin] is one of the sharpest colored editors in the Midwest." Senatorial Papers, box 60, folder 1, Truman Library.

29. Lucile Bluford, personal interview with author, 3 July 1991.

30. *St. Louis Star-Times*, 16 May 1934.

31. *Kansas City Call*, 3 August 1934. Estimates vary, but Truman apparently received votes from approximately 85,000 "ghost voters." A subsequent investigation removed these 85,000 ghosts from the rolls in 1936. Eugene Powell, *Tom's Boy Harry* (Jefferson City, MO: Hawthorn Publishing, 1948), 71-74.

32. Franklin to Truman, 20 November 1937; Truman to Franklin, 23 November 1937; Franklin to Truman, 23 January 1939; Truman to Franklin, 30 January 1939, all in Senatorial Papers.

33. Franklin to Truman, 17 May 1939; Truman to Franklin, 7 June 1939, both in ibid.

34. As late as 1932, the governor's office kept lists of the party affiliations of every Lincoln University employee, from professors to groundskeepers. Guy B. Park Papers, folder 1224, Western Historical Manuscript Collection-Columbia, MO. Based on Franklin to Truman, 19 October 1939, Senatorial Papers, Franklin made this request in late 1934—before Truman left for Washington.

35. *Kansas City Call*, 4 December 1936.

36. Lloyd Gaines, an African American, had applied to the University of Missouri School of Law in 1935. S. Woodson Canada, university registrar, denied his application, prompting Gaines and the NAACP to file a suit. Shortly after his victory in the U.S. Supreme Court, Gaines disappeared from his rooming house in Chicago and was never heard from again. See Edward T. Clayton, "The Strange Disappearance of Lloyd Gaines," *Ebony*, May 1961, 26. Franklin to Truman, 15 May 1939; Truman to Franklin, 18 May 1939, both in Senatorial Papers.

37. Stark had been elected governor in 1936 with the support of the Pendergast machine, but in 1937, when federal investigators began to unearth evidence of Tom Pendergast's complicity in bribery, tax evasion, and election fraud, Stark quickly turned against his former benefactor. The Great American Insurance Company of Chicago, Illinois, had paid Pendergast $750,000 in return for city and county insurance contracts, and the governor, eager to replace Pendergast as the boss of Missouri's Democratic Party, called in federal investigators. Elmer Irey, chief of the intelligence unit of the U.S. Treasury Department, wrote, "It was Stark who asked us to put Pendergast in jail." Quoted in Dorsett, *Pendergast Machine*, 129. Franklin to

Truman, 19 October 1939; Truman to Franklin, 25 October 1939, both in Senatorial Papers. Truman disliked Stark personally and wanted revenge for what he considered an unfair and politically motivated attack on Pendergast. In a letter to Bess, Truman wrote, "I'm going to lick that double crossing lying governor if I can keep my health." Quoted in Miller, *Rise to Power*, 315.

38. Truman, though he subsequently wavered during the fall and winter of 1939, had made the decision to run several months earlier. Miller, *Rise to Power*, 315. Franklin to Truman, 19 October 1939; Truman to Franklin, 25 October 1939, both in Senatorial Papers.

39. Truman based the decision partly on his belief in numerology. In a letter to Joel Pelofsky dated March 5, 1959, Truman's secretary, Victor Messall, recalled that he knew Truman viewed certain combinations of numbers as omens. Consequently, Messall suggested to Truman that he officially announce his candidacy on March 6 at 9:00 a.m. Truman apparently believed that an announcement involving such a lucky series of numbers—3-6-9—improved his chances of winning. The senator followed Messall's advice. Victor Messall Papers, box 6, folder 12, Truman Library.

40. Quoted in Vaughan, *Truman Administration's Legacy*, 3.

41. Donald R. McCoy and Richard T. Ruetten, *Quest and Response: Minority Rights and the Truman Administration* (Lawrence: University Press of Kansas, 1973), 15.

42. In the winter and spring of 1940-1941, Franklin wrote to Truman on numerous occasions to ask for help in integrating various defense contractors. The evidence suggests that Truman helped rectify the situation in each case. Yet, the senator later denied knowing about any cases of discrimination.

43. Reddig, *Tom's Town*, 381; Truman to Franklin, 18 November 1940, box 131, "Negroes" folder, Senatorial Papers; William E. Pemberton, *Harry S. Truman: Fair Dealer and Cold Warrior* (Boston: Twayne, 1989), 31. Hannegan also played a major part in Truman's vice presidential nomination four years later, and Truman "managed to reward Hannegan with appointment as Democratic National Committee chairman." Miller, *Rise to Power*, 384; Grothaus, "Kansas City Blacks," 81. The author extrapolated the figures from Wilson, "*The Kansas City Call*," 395.

44. A munitions plant was then under construction at Lake City, approximately five miles east of Independence. Franklin to Truman, 20 December 1940; Truman to Franklin, 27 December 1940; Franklin to Truman, 2 January 1941, all in Senatorial Papers. Truman's method for convincing contractors to hire African Americans remains a mystery, but it seems reasonable to assume that he threatened to investigate them for fraud if they refused.

45. Gosnell, *Truman's Crises*, 154-155.

46. Franklin to Truman, 9 January 1941; Truman to Franklin, 14 January 1941, both in Senatorial Papers.

47. Franklin to Truman, 18 January 1941, in ibid.

48. Wilkins, *Standing Fast*, 57.

49. Franklin to Truman, 21 January 1941, Senatorial Papers.

50. Truman to Franklin, 31 January 1941, in ibid.

51. Franklin to Truman, 19 May 1941, in ibid.

52. Quoted in Miller, *Rise to Power*, 313; ibid., 347-348; *Kansas City Call*, 3 April, 25 October 1940.

53. Truman to E. J. Wallace, 22 December 1941, quoted in Miller, *Rise to Power*, 503.

54. Quoted in Miller, *Rise to Power*, 359. Chester Stovall of the *St. Louis Call* argued that Truman was "whitewashing" the situation.

55. The federal district court upheld the Taylor bill in *Bluford v. Canada* (1940). See Diane Loupe, "Storming and Defending the Color Barrier at the University of Missouri School of Journalism: The Lucile Bluford Case" (unpublished paper, University of Missouri-Columbia, 1989), Black Archives of Mid-America, Kansas City, MO. For Franklin's position on Willkie, see *Kansas City Call*, 11, 18, 25 October 1940. For accounts of antidiscrimination demonstrations, see *Kansas City Call*, 23 December 1940; 19 January 1941.

56. Approximately one-half of America's black newspapers with more than ten thousand subscribers were anti-Roosevelt. Oak, *Negro Newspaper*, 135; *Kansas City Call*, 9 October 1936.

57. *Kansas City Call*, 9 October 1936.

58. Ibid., 16 October 1936; 11 October 1940.

59. Ibid., 9 October 1936; 3 November 1944.

60. McCoy and Ruetten, *Quest and Response*, 14.

61. *Kansas City Call*, 28 July, 20 October, 3 November 1944. According to Miller, Truman paid his $10 membership fee. When the Klan asked the judge to ignore Catholics in appointments, Truman asked that his membership fee be refunded. The Klan returned his money. Miller, *Rise to Power*, 62.

62. *Kansas City Call*, 21 December 1945.

63. Ibid., 15, 29 October 1948.

64. The president could not attend. President's Personal Files, box 548, folder 2328, Truman Library.

"Just Like the Garden of Eden": African American Community Life in Kansas City's Leeds

GARY R. KREMER

For more than two decades a growing number of American scholars have devoted their research to uncovering the ways in which African Americans forged rich and rewarding lives during the late nineteenth and early twentieth centuries within a society often committed to the devaluation of people of color.[1] Despite this intellectual effort, our understanding of African American community life during the age of segregation is incomplete, especially in regions of the country outside the Deep South.

The border state of Missouri witnessed creative and energetic efforts by African Americans to achieve dignity and autonomy in the face of racial oppression during the so-called "Jim Crow era."[2] Indeed, an in-depth look at black life in the Kansas City, Missouri, community of Leeds from approximately 1915 to 1960 adds detail and texture to the story of the African American response to segregation.

Kansas City's African American population grew dramatically during the last decade of the nineteenth century and the first two decades of the twentieth century. In 1890, 13,700 African Americans called Kansas City home. Thirty years later, that number had more than doubled, to 30,719.[3]

The growth of Kansas City's black population was part of a larger story of African American migration from southern to midwestern and northern states, and from rural to urban areas in Missouri. In 1890, 47 percent of Missouri's black population lived in cities; by 1900 the figure had jumped to 55 percent. By 1910 nearly 67 percent of Missouri's African Americans lived in the cities, almost three times the national average.[4]

Newlyweds Lawrence and Erma Joe Jackson and Lawrence's sister, Myrtle Jackson, pose with Bill Mitchell's jitney in the Leeds neighborhood. [JoAnn Jackson]

White Kansas Citians, much as their urban cousins across the state in St. Louis, responded to this influx of African Americans by restricting them from living in white residential neighborhoods. Thus, during the first two decades of the twentieth century, Kansas City blacks increasingly concentrated in what historian Sherry Lamb Schirmer calls the "Vine Street Corridor," a strip several blocks wide, extending from about Tenth Street on the north to Nineteenth Street on the south.[5]

Although this neighborhood quickly became crowded and, as Schirmer writes, "developed many of the earmarks of a ghetto," it had much to offer its African American residents. The high concentration of blacks in the area resulted in the building of a number of important social, cultural, and commercial institutions. Crispus Attucks School, named for the African American killed by British soldiers at the Boston Massacre in 1770, was erected at Eighteenth and Brooklyn in 1893. Fourteen years later, black population growth in the Vine Street area prompted the building of a new Attucks School at Nineteenth and Woodland, only two blocks east of Vine. Additional elementary schools for African American students were built in or near the Vine Street Corridor over the next several years. The city erected a black high school—Lincoln High—just to the west of Vine Street, at Nineteenth and Tracy, in 1906. Black churches also anchored themselves in this neighborhood, which by 1912 had perhaps as many as three thousand residents.[6]

Despite the advantages of living in a predominately African American neighborhood with strong black cultural and social institutions in the Vine Street area, not all black Kansas Citians wanted to live there. During the era of World War I (1914-1918), an alternative, if smaller, African American community began to develop west of the Blue River, south of Raytown Road.

Incorporated into the city in 1909, this area was not platted and laid out into lots until 1915. On October 29 of that year, J. W. Couch and his wife, Laura, filed a plat for what became known as "Couch's 1st Addition." The neighborhood extended from Thirty-third Street on the north to Thirty-sixth Street on the south, and from Raytown Road to Hardesty Avenue. Although white, the Couches began building houses in their new subdivision and selling them exclusively to African Americans.[7]

Roughly a decade later, during the mid-to-late 1920s, the demand for housing in this area led to two more subdivisions being opened for African Americans, just east and southeast of Couch's 1st Addition. Known collectively by local residents as "Allen's Addition," this neighborhood extended to the Blue River on the east.[8] By the late 1920s, residents of Couch's and Allen's additions had begun to refer to the joint neighborhoods as Leeds, a name that also referred to a white industrial community east of the Blue River.[9]

What attracted African Americans to this area that lay roughly two miles east of the Vine Street Corridor, and even farther from the heart of downtown Kansas City? Interviews with longtime residents of Leeds provide insight into the motivations of early settlers. First of all, property proved far more affordable in the Blue River area than in the Vine Street Corridor. In addition, the white owners of the property would sell the land to blacks on installment plans. This allowed African Americans to become landowners rather than renters, as was the case with a majority of the residents in the Vine Street area. Taking advantage of this option, some early Leeds residents moved to the Blue River area from the Vine Street Corridor. Dolly Mosby Malone, for example, born in 1911 in the 2500 block of Woodland, two blocks east of Vine Street, moved with her parents to Couch's Addition in 1917. She recalled in an interview that "the rent in Kansas City caused them [her parents] to move."[10]

Thus, the Leeds community, and the opportunity to buy land there, provided Kansas City blacks with the chance to own their own homes, a possibility that had been extremely important to African Americans since the early post-emancipation period.[11] The 1920 federal census reveals that 96 of the 108 households in the community at the time were occupied by residents who lived in homes they owned, an astonishing 89 percent. Only twelve of the households were listed as renters.[12]

The houses in Leeds were not, by any stretch of the imagination, elaborate or extravagant. A majority of the early houses erected in Couch's Addition were two-room, frame, shotgun structures built by the white developers who owned the land. Malone remembered, "Regardless of how large your family was, you got a two-room house." Most of the houses included porches, which served as bedrooms in the summer. To ward off mosquitoes, a large tub filled with smoldering rags would be kept nearby.[13]

The houses lacked bathrooms, central heat, even foundations—they were built on wooden piers sunk into the ground. At least some of the houses had dirt floors. Gertrude Gillum, who moved to Leeds in 1921 at the age of six, mentioned that "some [women] would sweep designs in the floor and they did not want you to mess up their floors." Buyers "paid some money down and then you paid so much a month." The developers "came through on Sunday" to collect the money due them.[14] The Reverend Kenneth E. Ray, born four years after his parents moved to Couch's Addition in 1928, said his father told him that he paid $100 down on the family's first house.[15] The houses in Allen's Addition, built during the late 1920s and 1930s, tended to be more substantial than the early houses in Couch's. Most were built as single-story, front-gable, frame bungalows, featuring full basements and full-length screened-in front porches.[16] Mary Garth, whose family was among the first to move to Allen's Addition, recalled that at the entrance to the neighborhood

Yvonne Starks Wilson grew up in the Allen's Addition of Leeds. She represented District 42 in the Missouri House of Representatives, 1999-2005. [John Viessman, Missouri Department of Natural Resources]

from Raytown Road, "there was a big sign . . . and it had a house on it and under it was printed 'exclusively for colored.'"[17]

In addition to providing African Americans with an opportunity to own their own homes, many migrants to the community thought Leeds offered a better way of life than they could attain in the city. Parents, especially, found Leeds' wide-open spaces, where children could run and play, inviting. The Reverend Kenneth Ray summarized the attitudes of many when he reported that his father moved from Arkansas to Leeds because he was "looking for a place where he could raise his family and have a garden and not have to worry about the inner city."[18] Comments such as this underscore the fact that the people who chose to make Leeds their home were very family oriented. The 1920 federal census indicates that 105 of the 108 households in the community had both a father and a mother living in the home.[19]

The fact that so many of the Leeds residents came either from the South or from rural Missouri was another important reason why they congregated in the area. Although within the city limits of Kansas City, the area remained very rural. Southern and rural blacks quickly discovered that they could replicate their Southern semi-subsistent lifestyle. Stories about gardens and livestock in Leeds are woven tightly throughout the community's collective memory.

Abandoned shotgun house located in the 3400 block of Denver Avenue. The house has a later addition, but the original two-room shotgun can still be seen. [John Viessman, Missouri Department of Natural Resources]

Annie Mason feeding her chickens in her yard at 5620 East 36th Street, circa 1964 [Hazel Mason Nicholson]

Longtime residents recalled that most neighborhood families established large vegetable gardens in which they raised a variety of items, including mustard greens and collards, sweet potatoes, green beans, asparagus, and corn. Residents also raised fruit such as peaches, pears, blackberries, and raspberries. Harvest time was a time of sharing with neighbors. The Reverend Kenneth Ray's father "had one of the biggest gardens in Leeds and at that time people would not only plant for their families but they would also have enough left to help people in need." Food grown in gardens and not consumed in season would be preserved for the winter months through canning, with the canned goods usually stored in cellars dug beneath family homes.[20]

In addition to the ubiquitous vegetable garden, many residents raised chickens, not only to ensure a supply of eggs, but also to provide meat for the family table. Other residents raised ducks and guineas for the same purposes. Thinking back, Rosa Mae Gillespie said, "There was a man named Gillman and he had cows . . . and we used to get milk from those cows."[21] Easter Hubley, born in Leeds in 1923, remembered the community as a place where "the Lord took care of everybody. I can say I never did have a hungry day. Everybody shared things. Where we lived we had hogs and chickens and every October we had a big hog kill and everybody was there. Everybody would bring their hogs to our house and kill them. The people would go around to the homes and collect garbage and that is what they would feed to their hogs. After they killed the hogs they would separate the meat and salt some and smoke others."[22]

To augment their diet of homegrown food and meat, community residents hunted and fished. They also gathered fruits, nuts, and greens growing in the countryside beyond the houses. "Leeds was just like the Garden of Eden," reminisced Mary Garth, who moved there when she was about six years old, during the early 1920s. "You could go over that hill at Leeds and find all kinds of fruit and some of the sweetest strawberries over there."[23] Charles Jones, whose family moved to the area in the 1930s, recalled that a number of community men, including his father, made wine from wild berries and grapes.[24]

Jones also stated that most Leeds residents relied on fish and wild game for food. Men and boys in the community hunted rabbits and squirrels in the nearby woods. "Back then you could walk out of your back door and hunt," Jones said. Wild game not only supplemented his family's diet but also provided him with spending money. He sold the rabbits he killed with a .22 caliber rifle for twenty-five cents apiece.[25]

As with other foodstuffs, neighbors shared fish and wild game with each other. The Reverend Thomas McCormick noted, "There were a lot of

Raised in Leeds, Vivienne Smith has worked to ensure the history of her childhood neighborhood is documented. [John Viessman, Missouri Department of Natural Resources]

[neighborhood residents] who lived for hunting in the winter and fishing in the summer and our family would always share in the results. Nobody went hungry unless you did not like fish or rabbit or squirrel." Those children who claimed not to like rabbit often found themselves eating it anyway, disguised as hamburger. Hunting in the area continued into the era of World War II and beyond.[26]

For those few residents who did not grow, gather, or hunt their own food, or for those who wanted to supplement their fare with store-bought goods, there were several neighborhood grocery stores. The dominant grocery store in Couch's Addition during the pre-World War II era and beyond was O. M. Scott's Grocery Store, located at 3400 Hardesty Avenue. Scott, an African American, lived with his family in the upstairs of the large two-story building that housed the store. Turner's Grocery Store on East Thirty-sixth Street Terrace was the most popular store in Allen's subdivision. Like Scott's, Turner's was also a black-owned and -operated business. All of the neighborhood grocery stores allowed patrons to buy on credit.[27]

At the far eastern edge of the black Leeds community, near the intersection of White Avenue and Raytown Road, Denzil Maple, a white man, operated a grocery store. Located just west of the Blue River, Maples Grocery served a large black clientele from Leeds. Across the Blue, several blocks east of White Avenue, a Jewish-owned grocery store known as Friedmans also attracted some black Leeds shoppers. Although African Americans were welcome at Friedmans and Maples, Vivienne Starks Smith recalled, "A lot of people didn't go [to either one]. . . . You had a lot of black people just as prejudiced as white people."[28]

The residents of Leeds lived a semi-subsistent lifestyle. Jobs with a steady income proved hard to find in the community, especially during the early 1920s. The most common occupation recorded for heads of household in the 1920 federal census of the area is "laborer," with the place of employment listed as "working out."[29]

Gertrude Gillum recalled, "Until they built the Chevrolet plant out in Leeds [in late 1928], most of the men worked in construction."[30] Men often traveled into downtown Kansas City to work on construction sites as day laborers. In the 1920s, Lella Jo Birks's father, a construction day laborer, "would go to the corner and a truck would come by and pick him up" and take him to a job site.[31]

During the early 1920s, it appears that most men had to leave the neighborhood to find work. A few found employment at one of Kansas City's packinghouses, and some worked as elevator operators, cooks, or janitors in downtown hotels or office buildings, but they, like the construction

James "Doby" Nelson standing in front of the railroad tie treating plant from which he retired in 1954. The operation produced 100,000 ties per month in 1925. According to Lawrence Jackson who worked there as a young man, the work was hard, but the pay was good. "You usually made $100 a month or better since you were paid by the piece." [JoAnn Jackson]

workers, had to leave Leeds. The most common way to go downtown was to walk to Thirty-first Street and Raytown Road, at the northwest edge of the neighborhood, and catch a streetcar. In later years, during the early 1930s, at least one enterprising Leeds resident operated a cab or "jitney" service that carried those who could afford it to and from the streetcar stop. Cab fare ranged from five to fifteen cents, depending upon the distance traveled.[32]

The streetcar served as a stark reminder to Leeds residents of the reality of racism that surrounded their island community. Although the streetcars were not segregated, African Americans usually found themselves outnumbered by whites on the cars. They were often subjected to racial epithets and derogatory comments. Sometimes white riders would not move over in a seat, thereby refusing to allow black riders to sit beside them. Added to the irony of being forced to face racial hostility on a supposedly integrated public transportation vehicle, the streetcar took Leeds riders from their friendly, collegial community to an area of the city stratified on the basis of race and class.[33]

A minority of Leeds women joined the men for the trek downtown each day, largely to work as maids in private homes. The majority of neighborhood women, at least during the 1920s, remained behind with their children and busied themselves with the day-to-day chores of housekeeping and childrearing. These chores were made difficult by the absence of "modern" conveniences in the community. For example, no running water existed in the houses. The bulk of the water used in the homes came from community hydrants located in each block. According to Hazel Nicholson, "You had to go out into the garden where there was a water faucet and we would have to bring the water into the house and heat it on the stove to wash the dishes." The absence of running water also made it difficult to do laundry. Ruby Robinson remembered her mother boiling the laundry in a large iron pot in the yard.[34]

Not only was there no running water in Leeds homes during the 1920s and early 1930s, there was also no electricity or natural gas. Kerosene lamps provided lighting, and wood or coal heating stoves furnished warmth during the winter.[35] Refrigeration came in the form of iceboxes, cooled by large blocks of ice delivered by men who hauled their product in horse-drawn wagons through the unpaved streets of the neighborhood. Coal and milk were delivered in the same manner. According to Ruby Robinson, "The coal man would bring the coal and the ice man would bring the ice and the milk man would bring the milk. We had a man for everything."[36]

Church attendance was important in Leeds. The Reverend Kenneth Ray reported, "Church was always an important part of our lives. Our parents and grandparents were there and they saw that we had a good religious education." One of the earliest neighborhood churches was Gilbert Memorial AME (African Methodist Episcopal). Organized in 1918 at 3608 Bellaire Avenue by the Reverend A. A. Gilbert, the congregation moved from house to house until they built a church at 3704 Topping Avenue in 1920.[37]

Other early churches included the Green Grove Baptist Church, at 3300 Oakley Avenue, and Pilgrim's Rest, a Baptist church organized in September 1918 at 3400 Hardesty Avenue.[38] *The Call*, an African American newspaper established in Kansas City in 1919, regularly published accounts of activities at these churches during the early 1920s. In January 1922, for example, *The Call* reported on "watch meeting services" at Pilgrim's Rest that lasted "throughout the old year, into the New Year." *The Call* noted that "the Services were well attended Sunday all day and night," and the "offering for the entire day [was] $27.90." Likewise, "a glorious watch meeting was observed" at Green Grove Church, where "a large number partook of the Lord's Supper."[39]

According to Hazel Nicholson, churches provided the major social outlet for Leeds residents in her youth. She and her family attended Sunday school and worship services every Sunday morning and then returned in the evening for Baptist Youth Training Union (BYTU). Church attendance was important to Hazel's parents. If she did not attend Sunday morning services, her parents would not allow her to go downtown to the Lincoln Theatre for a Sunday matinee, a favorite activity.[40]

Young Carl Edward Hurt stands on a chair next to his older cousin, Lawrence Jackson, circa 1926. [JoAnn Jackson]

Churches held social activities throughout the year that were often attended by community members who may or may not have belonged to the church. Gilbert Memorial AME Church, for example, always held a children's fashion show on the Monday after Easter so that, as Nicholson remembered, "every kid could strut his or her stuff." Gilbert Memorial also held popular "Tom Thumb Weddings," presided over by child ministers.[41]

The significance of the churches was reflected in the fact that ministers were among the most highly respected members of the community. Often they would be invited into the homes of congregants for Sunday dinner. In a circa 1950s late-life reminiscence, Ruby Robinson still marveled "at how fast [the preacher] could eat and talk."[42]

Because all of the neighborhood's schoolchildren attended the local public school, it was probably a more important community institution. The school opened in September 1917 in the Green Grove Church with an initial enrollment of about twenty-five. By the end of the first school year, enrollment had climbed to thirty-nine students. Whitfield Ross, the first teacher and principal, lived in Leeds until his accidental death on December 20, 1929. In September 1919, Ross hired a second teacher, Annie C. Goins. By the end of the 1919-1920 school year, enrollment at the Green Grove School had grown to ninety-six students. In June 1920 the Kansas City Board of Education voted to erect a new eight-room schoolbuilding on the crest of a hill on East

Thirty-sixth Street, between Oakley and Hardesty avenues.[43] Vocational education students from Lincoln High School, under the supervision of their instructor, W. T. White, did much of the building of the new school. The Reverend Thomas McCormick recalled, "My father related to me he was on the crew that came out from Lincoln High School that built Dunbar School."[44] The new school was named Dunbar in honor of the prominent African American poet Paul Lawrence Dunbar, born in Dayton, Ohio, in 1872. Dunbar was at the height of his popularity in the United States during the second decade of the twentieth century.[45]

On November 16, 1920, the day that Dunbar opened, the entire student body marched in a parade from Green Grove Church to the new school. "I was happy," Dolly Mosby Malone said, "because it was a big improvement. We did not have to have school in the church with those hard benches. Also, the new school had better bathroom facilities." The "bathroom facilities" were still outhouses with a wooden partition dividing boys' and girls' toilets.[46]

As more families with children moved into the Leeds community, the school grew dramatically. By the close of school in 1921, enrollment had jumped to 151 students. At the end of the next year, 231 students attended Dunbar. Seven faculty members were employed by 1922, including Bessie Taylor, who oversaw the department of sewing and a school garden that was maintained as part of a vocational training program.[47]

Each school day began with a prayer, usually the Lord's Prayer recited in unison, followed by a recitation of the Pledge of Allegiance to the flag. Often the pledge was followed by a song—"Good Morning to You." The students sat in desks discarded by white schools and arranged in rows. They often

Pilgrim's Rest Baptist Church Women's Group, circa 1950s [Philip and Gloria Mathis]

used hand-me-down materials, including textbooks from the white schools. There was no school lunch program. Students either returned to their homes for lunch and then went back to school for afternoon classes or carried their lunches to school in paper bags. Former students who attended Dunbar stated that they had been taught by "excellent teachers" who took a keen interest in them, both as students and as people. One former student commented, "[The teachers] just did not let you fail. They made you learn."[48]

Although many Dunbar teachers lived outside the community, in or near the Vine Street Corridor, they tended to remain at the school for long periods of time, and they got to know their students' families well. Parents trusted teachers and thought of them as partners in the shaping of the neighborhood's children. This partnership extended to discipline. Corporal punishment was common at Dunbar, and according to the Reverend Ray, "If the teacher would paddle you at school . . . that meant you would also get one at home." On one occasion, Ray's father came to school and whipped his son in front of the whole class for talking back to a teacher. Community monitoring of truancy minimized the incidence of skipping school.[49]

One of the high points of the school year for Dunbar children was the day of the Christmas program, when each class put on a performance. Parents

Adults help students load newspapers onto a truck outside Dunbar School during the Junior Officer Council paper drive in 1945. [Missouri Valley Special Collections, Kansas City (MO) Public Library]

helped to make costumes, and children practiced their programs to perfection. The most eagerly anticipated day of each school year, however, was May Day, which featured an outdoor picnic on the playground behind the school. Students participated in square dancing, foot races, and an assortment of games. Each class put on a program or performed a dance, often wearing costumes made of paper that fit over outer clothing. A flagpole in the middle of the schoolyard was transformed into a Maypole, with long streamers extending from its top. One former student remembered, "Each child got hold of [a] streamer and [would] go round and round the May pole and we would sing."[50]

A large vacant lot across the street from the school served as a neighborhood playground. Widely known by the neighborhood children as "Big Dusty," this site hosted baseball games throughout the summers. Girls and boys alike played baseball, the neighborhood's dominant sport. Ground rules specifying how many bases could be taken on errant balls traveling into adjacent yards governed the playing of games.[51]

Liberty Park, bordered on the north by Raytown Road and on the west by Thirty-fourth Street Terrace, provided another place for public gatherings and entertainment. The seventeen-acre park opened with great fanfare in mid-June 1922. Described by advertisements in *The Call* as "'The Negroes' Playground" and "The Only Place of its Kind in the United States that is Run for the Exclusive use of Negroes," the park became a popular gathering place for both adults and children, especially on weekends.[52] Gertrude Gillum said, "[Liberty Park] was a regular amusement park and they had merry-go-rounds, ferris wheels, concession stands [and] a dance hall." Delores Ray remembered, "You always had to pay to get in but the kids had a place they could slip in by the fence and they did not pay nothing." Lawrence Jackson summed up many residents' view of the park: "That park was jumping."[53]

The Call proclaimed that the park had "the finest dancing pavilion in Kansas City," adding that "the music for dancing is furnished by George Lee's Orchestra." In addition, *The Call* reported, a radio was being installed so that "free Radio Concerts" could be held at the park. This was especially popular with area residents who did not own radios. African Americans from throughout the city found Liberty Park an attractive place to gather. It provided a welcome alternative to Kansas City's Swope Park, where blacks were confined to a segregated area commonly referred to as "Watermelon Hill."[54]

Liberty Park also featured a lake that served as a swimming pool in the summer and an ice skating rink in the winter. Occasionally, a baptism was held in the lake. The park had a baseball field, as well, where teams comprising young men from Leeds challenged teams from other parts of the city. One of

Advertisement in the Kansas City Call [Gary Kremer]

the most popular community teams was the Leeds Clowns. Among the most beloved annual activities at Liberty Park was a Fourth of July celebration that included the shooting of fireworks.[55]

Gypsies found Liberty Park a favorite camping place in the summer, sometimes staying for weeks at a time. Each evening, the Gypsies performed a musical for all who wished to attend. Although the gatherings attracted sizeable crowds, some area residents remained in their houses, fearing that other Gypsies might steal from neighborhood homes during the nightly performances. Dora Craven was warned, "Don't go down there [to the park]. [The Gypsies] will steal you and make slaves out of you."[56]

Across Raytown Road from Liberty Park, near Thirty-fourth Street, stood a neighborhood bar known as the Liberty Tavern. A favorite gathering place for men of the community, women sometimes frequented the tavern as well. Rosa Mae Gillespie recalled, "We all went down to that tavern and that is where we learned to drink." The Reverend Kenneth Ray, however, remembered the tavern as "the only place we could not go in Leeds when we were kids."[57]

In May 1929, Sarah Rector, a wealthy African American woman, opened a dance hall called Del Ray Gardens on Thirty-fourth Street, near the southern border of Leeds. An article in the *Kansas City American* announced the opening and explained that "special permission from city authorities will allow the Garden to remain open all night."[58] Rector's dance hall attracted well-known bands and a large clientele from the Vine Street Corridor; Leeds residents who could afford the admission also went there for entertainment. At one point during this period, the rowdy reputation of Del Ray Gardens seems to have attracted a vigilante group of whites, remembered by a number of people as members of the Ku Klux Klan. The group marched through Leeds toward Del Ray Gardens in an apparent effort to intimidate community members into "cleaning up" the dance hall.[59]

Children and adults also sought entertainment in their own homes and yards and in the streets of Leeds. Young people depended upon each other when it came to having fun. Hazel Nicholson recalled that children often gathered at her house because her mother "was always home and would look out for all of us." They played jacks, marbles, cards, school or church, or made mud pies. Yvonne Starks Wilson loved to play school: "I used to teach school on the front porch. . . . I had the kids on our front porch and I would try to teach them math. . . . We spent a lot of time on the front porch." According to Delores Ray, "In the winter time we used to sleigh ride down those hills and some of the boys would . . . build a fire to keep us warm. Everybody had sleds. We even had a pulley rigged up so you could pull yourself back up the hill."[60]

Often in the evenings, after dinner, family members gathered to sing and play music. Dolly Mosby Malone remembered, "My father played the mandolin, my brother played the drums and my sister played the piano. And my mother played the mandolin and piano . . . and I had another brother that played the horn."[61] Sometimes in the evenings, families gathered to study the

Dolly Malone holding her father's mandolin. He worked for Barnum and Bailey Circus, playing and singing. [John Viessman, Missouri Department of Natural Resources]

Bible or listen to the radio. Few people, for example, missed listening to a live broadcast of a Joe Louis fight during the 1930s or early 1940s.[62] Indeed, one could walk through the streets of Leeds during the broadcast of a Louis fight and hear the play-by-play coming from radios perched on porches and in living rooms throughout the neighborhood. The recounting of community interest in Louis's fights calls to mind the one described by Maya Angelou in her autobiography, *I Know Why the Caged Bird Sings*. Angelou described how neighborhood blacks gathered in a store to hear a Louis fight:

> The last inch of space was filled, yet people continued to wedge themselves along the walls of the Store. Uncle Willie had turned the radio up to its last notch so that youngsters on the porch wouldn't miss a word. Women sat on kitchen chairs, dining room chairs, stools and upturned wooden boxes. Small children and babies perched on every lap available and men leaned on the shelves or on each other. The apprehensive mood was shot through with shafts of gaiety, as a black sky is streaked with lightning.[63]

Joe Louis was a source of racial pride for African Americans all over the country, and his popularity in Leeds prompted neighborhood women to form a social club known by a variation of the heavyweight's nickname, the "Brown Bombers."[64]

Dolly Mosby Malone and her teenage friends "had a club called 'The Gays' and we would get together for socials and dances, all the young people. . . . We went from house to house." Parents were not fearful of crime or criminals. Consequently, they allowed their children to roam all over the neighborhood. Mary Woods recalled, "In the summertime we would go crawdad fishing in the Blue River." Gertrude Gillum allowed her son Ronald to roam at will without concern about his well-being: "I remember we had a next door neighbor that had four boys all about the same size and Ronald would get up, eat a bowl of cereal, and leave the empty bowl on the table and go with these neighbor's boys and be gone all day and when they came home about 5-6 o'clock they always smelled like dogs." A favorite place for the boys to play was a wooded area between their neighborhood and a city-run correctional center, the Kansas City Municipal Farm, widely known as the Leeds Farm.[65]

While most parents seemed to have had little fear for their children so long as they stayed in the Leeds neighborhood, some parents were reluctant to allow their children to go into the city for fear that they might get into trouble. Dolly Mosby Malone's parents did not permit her to attend movies downtown

As adults, Leeds residents remembered fondly their childhoods spent playing in the neighborhood and the nearby woods. [JoAnn Jackson]

when she was a child. She "did not get to see a movie until I was eighteen years old. The superintendent of the Sunday School . . . took me downtown to the Gem Theater to see 'Moon Over Israel' and I never forgot that. It was a silent movie." Likewise, the Reverend Thomas McCormick remembered, "My father was not too keen on us going to town."[66]

Graduation from Dunbar School, for those who went on to high school, meant a daily trip out of the neighborhood to attend Kansas City's racially segregated Lincoln High. Some students experienced discrimination and ridicule because they lived in Leeds. A number of city students regarded Leeds, with its absence of running water, electricity, and paved streets, as a backward, even primitive, place to live. They sometimes made fun of and picked on students from Leeds.

Leeds students devised a variety of strategies to deal with the situation. They tended to travel together and to remain in groups at school whenever they could, hoping thereby to ward off taunts and verbal and physical threats. Students who owned two pairs of shoes wore one pair for the walk from their home to meet the streetcar at Thirty-first Street. There, they changed shoes before boarding the streetcar, leaving behind the dust- or mud-covered shoes that signaled they lived in Leeds. The soiled shoes would be retrieved in the afternoon after school and worn home.[67]

Some Leeds students at Lincoln High claimed that the negative treatment extended also to teachers and administrators. Ronald Gillum recalled, "The high school counselors did not encourage the Leeds kids to go to college. [If you were from Leeds,] you were encouraged to go to a trade school." Gillum also remembered occasional announcements: "All kids from Leeds [should] report to the auditorium." Once in the auditorium, students would be told "how bad we were and they said we were lower than 'pine scum' and he said 'you are all living out there in squalor.'"[68]

Dating exacerbated the tension between Kansas City youths and their "country cousins." Leeds boys, in particular, resented city boys who tried to date girls from the neighborhood. As the Reverend McCormick said, "We did not appreciate the boys from town coming out to Leeds to see the girls."[69]

The self-subsistent, cooperative lifestyle of the Leeds residents, no doubt, helped to sustain them through the Great Depression. One manifestation of the willingness of community members to help each other was what Dora Horn Craven remembered as "tax parties." When someone could not afford to pay their property taxes, and was threatened with the loss of their property, friends raised money by throwing a party, charging admission, and giving the proceeds to the person(s) who needed money for taxes.[70]

The community's connection to Kansas City's Democratic political boss, Tom Pendergast, also proved beneficial. African Americans throughout the country were moving from their traditional alliance with the party of Abraham Lincoln, "the Great Emancipator," toward the party of Franklin D. Roosevelt during the 1930s.[71] Tom Pendergast openly courted African American support

According to Lawrence Jackson, "In the 30s, you wore clothes until they wore out, and then you wore them some more." (Left to right) Edgar Fletcher, Lawrence Jackson holding daughter JoAnn, and Clarence whose last name is unknown. [JoAnn Jackson]

in Kansas City, including Leeds. Isola Richardson recalled that "you could always tell when it was election time. They would come down and grade and oil Hardesty Street." Pendergast's principal lieutenants in Leeds appear to have been Mary Evans and Darie Richardson. A precinct captain, Richardson and his wife, Myrtle, lived at 3316 Oakley Avenue and operated the Liberty Tavern on Raytown Road. Evans and the Richardsons, said Dolly Malone, were "with Pendergast." Isola Richardson stated that Darie Richardson "was over the garbage trucks for Pendergast." Lawrence Jackson called Richardson "a pretty big shot guy."[72]

Malone and others also remembered that Evans traded clothing for votes: "After the election [she] would bring clothes out to Leeds to give away." Mary Garth said that Pendergast would have bread and milk delivered to community members in exchange for political support. Alvin Brooks remarked, "During the Pendergast days if you were a precinct captain you got coal and food but if you were not on the list of some captain, you might not get anything." Others remember Tom Pendergast coming to Leeds, especially just before elections. Often accompanied by a milk or bread truck, he dispensed milk and bread to all who approached him. His favorite stops seemed to have been on Raytown Road, near Darie Richardson's tavern, and on the playground behind the Dunbar School.[73]

No doubt the community's connection to Pendergast made Leeds a focal point of Works Progress Administration (WPA) projects, which brought improvements to the community while providing much-needed jobs for the men of the neighborhood. As historians Lawrence Larsen and Nancy Hulston have pointed out in their biography of Pendergast, the Kansas City boss influenced the allocation of WPA funds throughout Missouri by virtue of the fact that one of his associates, Matthew Murray, was in charge of WPA projects for the state.[74] Thus, Pendergast was in a position to make sure that some WPA money was funneled into the African American community of Leeds.

Longtime residents recalled multiple WPA projects in the area during the mid-to-late 1930s, including the paving of several streets, the widening of the Blue River, and the building of a new bridge across the river. Easter Hubley recalled with great clarity the widening of the Blue River. Her father worked on the project until he drowned in an accident on the job in June 1938.[75]

World War II brought many changes to the Leeds community. Robert White, born in 1930 and reared in Leeds, recalled the war years as a prosperous time: "Everybody had a job and cars were beginning to show up." In addition, running water and indoor toilets were installed in many neighborhood houses during the early war years. Many men of the community, at least those not called into the armed services, went to work either at the Lake City Arsenal or at Pratt & Whitney, war industry plants outside of Leeds.[76] Women also worked in the defense plants, expanding upon a trend that had become increasingly apparent during the Great Depression—the tendency of Leeds women to work outside the home. During the depression, neighborhood women found jobs as domestics, seamstresses, and child-care providers in the homes of Kansas City whites. Extended family members or neighbors cared for these women's children. Yvonne Brooks Bullock recalled, "Mrs. Nelson took care of me because my mother worked. Back then in Leeds people never had to hire babysitters. There was always somebody to look after the children for you. Mrs. Nelson was a neighbor. She lived right across the street from us."[77]

A relative prosperity continued in Leeds after World War II. By that time, most of the men worked either at the Chevrolet factory east of the Blue River or in the railroad tie plant near the Chevrolet plant. Continued employment combined with the opening of housing in formerly all-white areas of Kansas City during the late 1950s led many Leeds residents to leave the community for better homes. One Leeds resident recalled, with perhaps only slight exaggeration, "The best house in Leeds wasn't as nice as some of the worst houses in white neighborhoods."[78]

Nevertheless, life in Leeds left a huge imprint upon the people who grew up there in the period between and during the world wars. According to Clara Horne Walker, one of the greatest legacies of Leeds was that it was a place where young people learned self-sufficiency. In Leeds, "boys learned to be men." They learned to do chores and to accept the responsibility of helping out their families, which,

After a successful strike in 1947, African Americans were able to move up from janitorial positions to higher paying jobs on the assembly line at the Chevrolet plant in Leeds. Photo from the mid-1950s. [Missouri State Archives]

in turn, helped them to become good providers as adults. Consequently, Robert White asserted, "The word [was] out that if you marry a Leeds man, you have a good man." In addition, Walker recalled, girls learned to fill the roles of wife and mother by learning to cook and keep house.[79]

Just as importantly, life in Leeds taught residents to think of their neighbors as members of a large, close family. Yvonne Brooks Bullock recalled, "That was the best time in my life [living in Leeds]. My friends say to me 'you just love Leeds,' and I say, yes, everybody out in Leeds was just like a family." The Reverend Kenneth Ray commented, "Almost everybody from Leeds is my sister and brother and whenever someone dies in Leeds it is just like someone in our family." Ray summarized what was perhaps the greatest legacy of Leeds when he said, "Love in Leeds ran like water. . . . Everybody loved everybody."[80]

NOTES

1. For a good summary of much of this research, see Leon F. Litwack, *Trouble in Mind: Black Southerners in the Age of Jim Crow* (New York: Vintage Books, 1999).

2. The term "Jim Crow era," as used here, refers to the period from the end of Reconstruction during the 1870s to the beginning of the modern-day civil rights movement during the mid-1950s.

3. Sherry Lamb Schirmer, *A City Divided: The Racial Landscape of Kansas City, 1900-1960* (Columbia: University of Missouri Press, 2002), 29.

4. Lorenzo J. Greene, Gary R. Kremer, and Antonio F. Holland, *Missouri's Black Heritage*, rev. ed. (Columbia: University of Missouri Press, 1993), 107-113.

5. Schirmer, *City Divided*, 39-41.

6. Ibid., 42-45.

7. Plat for Couch's 1st Addition, County Recorder's Office, Jackson County Courthouse, Kansas City, MO.

8. Plat for Hollie Addition, ibid. Although the legal name was "Hollie Addition," named for the owner, Hollie B. Allen, Leeds residents referred to it as "Allen's Addition."

9. "Leeds" vertical file, Missouri Valley Room, Kansas City Public Library.

10. Interview with Dolly Mosby Malone, 14 November 2001. All interviews cited in this article were conducted by the author. Tapes and transcripts of the inter-

274 ~ Kansas City, America's Crossroads

views are housed in the Missouri State Museum, Jefferson Landing State Historic Site, Jefferson City.

11. Leon F. Litwack documents this intense desire on the part of African Americans to own land. In addition to his book, *Trouble in Mind*, see his *Been in the Storm So Long: The Aftermath of Slavery* (New York: Knopf, 1979).

12. U.S. Census, Fourteenth Report, 1920, *Population Schedules*, "Jackson County, Kaw Township, Ward 14, District No. 238."

13. Malone, interview.

14. Interview with Gertrude Gillum, 10 May 2001.

15. Interview with Kenneth E. Ray, 16 May 2001.

16. Interview with Vivienne Starks Smith, 24 July 2002.

17. Interview with Mary Garth, 24 May 2001.

18. Interview with Delores Louise Ray, 24 May 2001; Gillum, interview; Kenneth Ray, interview.

19. U.S. Census, Fourteenth Report, 1920, *Population Schedules*.

20. Interview with Clara Horne Walker, 28 June 2001; interview with Rosa Mae Gillespie, 19 April 2001; interview with Lois Kinney, 16 August 2001; interview with Isola Richardson, 19 April 2001; Kenneth Ray, interview.

21. Gillespie, interview.

22. Interview with Easter Hubley, 10 May 2001.

23. Garth, interview.

24. Interview with Charles Jones, 16 August 2001.

25. Ibid. Charles Ward also remembered his family relying on wild game; interview with Charles Ward, 17 October 2001.

26. Interview with Thomas McCormick, 12 December 2001; Richardson, interview.

27. Smith, interviews, 13 April 2001, 24 July 2002.

28. Interview with Ruby M. Robinson, 25 April 2001; Smith, interview, 24 July 2002.

29. U.S. Census, Fourteenth Report, 1920, *Population Schedules*.

30. Gillum, interview.

31. Interview with Lella Jo Birks, 15 August 2001.

32. Telephone interview with Lawrence Jackson, 11 October 2002.

33. Smith, interview, 24 July 2002.

34. Interview with Hazel Nicholson, 31 May 2001; Robinson, interview.

35. Garth, interview.

36. Robinson, interview.

37. Kenneth Ray, interview; "The History of Gilbert Memorial A.M.E. Church, Kansas City, MO," Missouri State Museum.

38. "Pilgrim's Rest Baptist Church History," Missouri State Museum; *Kansas City Missouri City Directory* (Kansas City: Gate City Directory Co., 1918), 1101.

39. *Kansas City Call*, 7 January 1922.

40. Nicholson, interview.

41. Interview with Betty Holt, 7 June 2001; Nicholson, interview.

42. Robinson, interview.

43. Malone, interview; Whitfield Ross, "History of Dunbar School," Missouri State Museum.

44. McCormick, interview.

45. Ross, "History of Dunbar School."

46. Malone, interview.

47. Ross, "History of Dunbar School."

48. Gillum, interview; interview with Yvonne Brooks Bullock, 2 May 2001; Kenneth Ray, interview.

49. Kenneth Ray, interview; McCormick, interview; Richardson, interview.

50. Malone, interview; McCormick, interview; Delores Louise Ray, interview; Birks, interview.

51. McCormick, interview.

52. *Kansas City Call*, 24 June 1922.

53. Gillum, interview; Delores Louise Ray, interview; interview with Lawrence Jackson, 11 December 2002.

54. *Kansas City Call*, 17, 24 June 1922.

55. Kenneth Ray, interview; Ward, interview; Jones, interview.

56. Ward, interview; interview with Dora Horn Craven, 24 July 2002.

57. Gillespie, interview; Kenneth Ray, interview.

58. *Kansas City American*, 23 May 1929.

59. Craven, interview.

60. Nicholson, interview; interview with Yvonne Starks Wilson, 16 August 2001; Delores Louise Ray, interview.

61. Malone, interview.

62. Wilson, interview.

63. Maya Angelou, *I Know Why the Caged Bird Sings* (New York: Bantam Books, 1971), 111-112.

64. Craven, interview.

65. Malone, interview; interview with Mary Woods, 31 May 2001; interviews with Gertrude and Ronald Gillum, 10 May 2001. The Kansas City Municipal Farm was established in 1909 as a "progressive" institution where "vagrants, mendicants, and petty criminals" could be reformed. *Kansas City Times*, 19 January 1909. Kristine Stilwell, "'If You Don't Slip': The Hobo Life, 1911-1916" (PhD diss., University of Missouri-Columbia, 2004).

66. Malone, interview; McCormick, interview.

67. Malone, interview.

68. Ronald Gillum, interview.

69. McCormick, interview.

70. Craven, interview.

71. Lawrence H. Larsen and Nancy J. Hulston, *Pendergast!* (Columbia: University of Missouri Press, 1997), 103-105. Larsen and Hulston document Pendergast's efforts to bring African Americans into the Democratic Party.

72. Richardson, interview; Malone, interview; Jackson, interview. Isola Richardson and Darie Richardson are not related.

73. Malone, interview; interview with Lynthia V. Ponder, 16 August 2001; Garth, interview; interview with Alvin Brooks, 28 June 2001; Craven, interview.

74. Larsen and Hulston, *Pendergast!*, 117.

75. Ward, interview; Robinson, interview; Hubley, interview.

76. Interview with Robert L. White, 10 May 2001; Richardson, interview.

77. Bullock, interview.

78. Ibid.; Jones, interview; Craven, interview.

79. Walker, interview; White, interview.

80. Bullock, interview; Kenneth Ray, interview.

It Finally Happened Here:
The 1968 Riot in Kansas City, Missouri

JOEL P. RHODES

On April 9, 1968, the rising tide of mid-1960s urban racial violence engulfed Kansas City, Missouri. Many in the city expressed dismay when it finally happened, yet during the week preceding Easter, Kansas City's predominately African American east side joined south-central Los Angeles's Watts neighborhood, Cleveland's Hough district, Newark's Central Ward, Detroit's west side, and nearly three hundred other American cities that experienced urban violence during the mid-1960s. For the four days following the funeral of Martin Luther King Jr., normal societal restraints in the city could not contain the rage that eventually left six people dead and cost close to four million dollars in damages.

The Kerner Commission, appointed by President Lyndon B. Johnson in 1967, concluded that nearly all previous riots had been ignited by community-specific incidents associated with local racial conflicts. In Kansas City, the indignities of school segregation and police racism eventually channeled generalized hostility and precipitated a riot. The confrontation at city hall between angry blacks and police, which sparked the disorder, was the culmination of a protest march following King's assassination. From there the violence escalated, and Kansas City blacks took part in the national phenomenon that left 7,942 wounded and 191 dead, destroyed millions of dollars in property, decimated ghettos, and perplexed white society between January 1964 and May 1968.

When the civil rights movement became fragmented after the 1965 march in Selma, Alabama, the events in the Watts neighborhood planted a seed in

April 9, 1968 [Kansas City Star]

the minds of many disillusioned northern African Americans. With many still enduring the nearly insurmountable problems of poverty and discrimination, rioting now seemed to be a legitimate form of social protest.[1] The civil rights movement raised their expectations, and faced with the reality that permanent subordination and segregation could be a distinct possibility, a significant minority of urban blacks found no other viable strategy for implementing continued change. By 1965 northern blacks stood ready to use riots as a form of communication with the white power structure in much the same way southern blacks had earlier used nonviolent protest. The disorders varied from city to city, but in general, all displayed similar patterns of rioting, looting, arson, and assault—often in the form of restrained and articulate protests against the most immediate grievances.

By the spring it became apparent that 1968 would be a very traumatic year for the United States. As the antiwar movement intensified, the strain over Vietnam exploded on streets and campuses across the country. In February the Tet Offensive stunned even the most staunch war supporters and exposed the nation to the reality that something had gone terribly wrong in Southeast Asia. The once formidable Lyndon Johnson, broken by Vietnam and the division within the nation, announced his decision not to seek reelection. Rage in America's ghettos had ignited during three consecutive "long, hot summers," and nothing indicated that emotions would subside in 1968. As former activist Todd Gitlin said, America seemed to be at war with itself, and by Easter, so was Kansas City.[2]

The extensive publicity given to the major riots surrounding Newark and the increasingly volatile nature of the anti-Vietnam War movement engendered a nationwide "rebellious consciousness" while producing a climate conducive to social imitation.[3] Continued exposure to civil rights activists and antiwar protestors who risked their well-being for ideological goals weakened the ghetto inhabitants' concern for personal safety. In addition, the activism of the period had proven that if the cause was just, arrest was an honor not a stigma. With television and other media broadcasting the urban carnage, Kansas City blacks understood how to conduct a riot and what roles could be taken. An unidentified African American maintained that once violence erupted, "the kids picked up the tools they had seen on TV."[4] "The whole television image, starting with John Kennedy, gave us an image of a product," ventured the Reverend James Blair, "and regardless of what that product was, it sold." Blair thought that media sensationalism magnified militancy and made it appear more attractive among the young. "They [the militants] got the most press and pretty soon they began to believe what they saw."[5]

On April 4, 1968, the assassination of Martin Luther King Jr. in Memphis stripped the civil rights movement of its most charismatic leader. The intensity of bereavement felt by African Americans may have been impossible for others to fathom, and as the news spread across the nation, violence spontaneously erupted in several urban centers. The fourth "long, hot summer" had arrived two months early. As one young black Kansas Citian predicted: "This is going to bring out the most violent people. . . . People are ready to tie up America."[6]

Yet, the initial mood in Kansas City was one of stunned and somber shock, rather than of immediate violence. A profound sense of righteous indignation simmered among young African Americans. While one moderate black leader vainly hoped that the senseless act would ultimately bring the community together, younger blacks like Vernon Thompson, the first person arrested during the disorder, prophesied: "There are going to be a lot of changes, a whole lot of changes. The older people who have been for non-violence are changing their attitudes. This is going to change the attitudes of even the Uncle Toms." "People are mad," declared fellow activist Bernard Powell, "The young are even madder. The older people who were against violence are now turning to violence."[7]

Over the weekend following the assassination, students in the Kansas City, Missouri, school district began to cultivate the idea of a peaceful march in memory of Dr. King. A teacher close to the students reported to the school

African Americans in Kansas City believed that the public school system displayed a lack of respect for Dr. Martin Luther King Jr. The administration's refusal to close schools in deference to King's funeral triggered the initial march. [Library of Congress. LC-U9-11696-9A]

board on the morning of April 8 that a march similar to the one held in Kansas City, Kansas, the previous week was being planned for the following day. Parents and civil rights leaders called the board of education and confirmed the planning of a Tuesday march. Despite the warning, the board decided to hold classes on Tuesday and broadened a one-minute observance to a districtwide school assembly.[8]

A pivotal moment in the city's race relations occurred later that afternoon when the school district discovered that their Kansas counterparts had decided to close schools on the following day. At this point, the district had an opportunity to avert disaster, but poor judgment and structural deficiencies undermined any meaningful reconsideration. The district maintained that regardless of the Kansas decision and the possibility of a march, students would be better off in an organized setting where emotions could be channeled and monitored, rather than sent back to possibly empty homes.[9]

At 7:30 a.m., on Tuesday, April 9, the African American radio station KPRS aired the list of schools that would close in deference to King's funeral, and those that would remain open. Years of disappointment and frustration with the school system now culminated in the district's apparent lack of respect for the black leader. Many African American students viewed the decision as a tangible sign that their schools did not care. According to Vernon Thompson, there was "no intent to riot" on the morning of April 9, but some students wanted to know why the schools did not close, "like for Kennedy."[10] This decision, in addition to the African American community's traditional hostility toward the police department, provided the precipitating event for the Kansas City riot and set in motion social forces that had been played out in schools nationwide over the preceding three months.

Almost immediately after broadcasting the school district's decision, KPRS received a phone tip that students from Lincoln High School would walk out and march south to Central High. Over two hundred students from both Lincoln and Manual high schools left their respective buildings on their way to Central. The groups eventually merged, and the march proceeded with enthusiasm and excitement through the city's predominately black eastern side, stopping on occasion for pictures. There is some dispute about the initial disposition of the marchers, but in general it was a peaceful event, and black police officers often moved freely through the crowds.[11]

Vernon Thompson, one of the march's organizers, characterized the group as cheerful and upbeat. "We were just getting together to do a little rap talking," he recalled, "The kids were peaceful, but demanding, before the cops got there."[12] The students contended that the school district had shown considerable disrespect for Dr. King, but in the early stages, no clear objective or ultimate destination for the march emerged. Some students wanted to stage a nonviolent demonstration at a park while others advocated a march to city hall, "like the kids in Kansas did." Word of the march spread rapidly throughout the African American community, and many nonstudents joined as the procession made its way south down Vine Street toward Twenty-fifth Street.[13]

Upon receiving the news of the march and of disturbances in and around Central Junior and Senior High, Police Chief Clarence Kelley decided to move into Tactical Alert—Phase II of Kansas City's riot control plan, which totally mobilized the city's force. The police then notified Mayor Ilus Davis, the highway patrol, and the school board about the possibility of a disturbance and their decision to mobilize. Local radio stations soon announced the mobilization to the public.

Following the Phase II announcement, reports from citizens and teachers about sporadic acts of vandalism and the menacing presence of young blacks moving through the streets began to pour in from all over the area. The crowd gathered around Central Junior and Senior High overturned several small cars and broke out the windows of others. Soon, one group looted a potato chip truck behind the school while others stoned and clubbed several cars driven by whites.[14]

With the march from Lincoln and Manual fast approaching the Central schools and the proliferation of violence around the campus, the administration quickly dismissed the students. Shortly after the Central students had been encouraged to go directly home, the marchers from Lincoln and Manual arrived on the scene. Nearly one hundred Central students joined the group to trek south toward Paseo High School, another predominately black school on the east side. Vandalism erupted sporadically up and down Indiana where rioters stomped on cars and threatened residents with baseball bats. A line of police confronted the marchers off Thirty-fourth and Indiana streets, and several officers used Mace for crowd control. Herman Johnson, president of the local NAACP chapter and one who had been with the march since its inception, screamed, "For God's sake don't do that," as four white officers drove by and sprayed the crowd with Mace. After this unprovoked attack, according to Johnson, "The bad ones got mad."[15] Infuriated, the main body broke north and returned to the Central High School campus to regroup and devise a plan. Now, some openly advocated violence.[16]

Understandably upset, most young marchers demanded that the police apologize for the use of Mace. After one policeman offered an explanation, rather than an apology, the crowd erupted and began hurling rocks at the police. Fury and anger rapidly replaced the holiday spirit noticed earlier among the young people. Several students complained that police confronted them everywhere they tried to march. "We want respect, to be able to march wherever we want without the police on our heels," affirmed an angry young activist. "The cops started it, they initiated it," recalled Thompson.[17]

Throughout the remainder of the morning, emotionally charged marchers perceived many of the police department's actions as unjust, insulting, and inflammatory.[18] The overall conduct of the police was the second precipitating event of the day. The idea of demanding an apology for their actions directly from Mayor Davis quickly began to gain acceptance. "If the police won't apologize for the use of mace, let's ask the Mayor to apologize," demanded a young marcher. Civil rights leaders on the scene agreed that a march to city hall might be a therapeutic release for the rage building in the crowd.[19] The marchers now had a proactive objective; they were headed to the mayor's office.

At the top, forces mobilized to suppress Kansas City's escalating disturbance. The Missouri Highway Patrol was placed on full alert while Chief Kelley requested troopers be sent to the downtown area. Mayor Davis and the chief had met in Kelley's office where Jackson County Sheriff Arvid Owsley was also briefed on the situation. By 10:00 a.m., Davis and Governor Warren Hearnes decided to activate one thousand Missouri national guardsmen.[20]

Activity rapidly intensified when police used Mace for crowd control. [Kansas City Star]

More and more police cruisers also entered the fray in an attempt to contain the disorder.

The march from Central High School continued to snake its way westward, leaving behind broken windows—including one in a police car—and plundered delivery trucks. Often, the excited marchers—numbering nearly a thousand by now—broke into a run, screaming and tossing rocks as they went, but many in the group remained peaceful. Leadership shifted periodically between ministers, established civil rights leaders, and young militants. One of the leaders who emerged nearly spontaneously during the march was Lee Bohanon, a twenty-three-year-old, self-described Black Power advocate. With his Afro haircut, dark glasses, and strong rhetoric, Bohanon exuded the image of black militancy that frightened many whites. "Lee was like Rap Brown," assessed Vernon Thompson, "he was very militant, not a negotiator like me."[21]

Although vandalism and minor assaults erupted all morning and some forty individuals were already in police custody, the disorder in Kansas City had not yet progressed to a major disturbance. Meanwhile, the downtown area braced for the impending arrival of one thousand aroused protestors. Impromptu "Closed in Memory of Dr. Martin Luther King" signs appeared in the windows of hurriedly closed stores. Busloads of police in riot gear quietly transformed the area around Eleventh and Thirteenth between Oak and Baltimore into an armed sector.

Shortly before noon on the steps of city hall, the city's second precipitating event came to a head as the restless throng gathered to listen to Mayor Davis and a host of other speakers. By this time it had clearly evolved into more than a student action. Because of a defective sound system, many could not hear the speakers' pleas that violence was out of order on the day of King's funeral. "You're forgetting everything Martin Luther King stood for," implored one black woman at the podium. "Violence don't get it. You think rioting is going to get it. No, no, man, you can't get it this way."[22] The energized crowd quickly became uneasy and bored, and the pressure mounted.

At the podium, militants and moderates struggled for possession of the microphone. Some of the more vocal activists incited the crowd and walked up and down the police line set up across Twelfth Street, goading the police with taunts and obscenities. Many were already in a disagreeable mood due to the earlier police action, and the sight of police and highway patrolmen in full riot gear further inflamed them. "No wonder we're losing the war in Vietnam, we've got all our troops here," declared one young black. Well aware of what had happened in other riot cities, the police decided to make a show of force. "The police wanted to assure us that a riot could be put down," recalled the Reverend James Blair.[23] Another African American believed: "The police

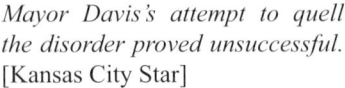

Mayor Davis's attempt to quell the disorder proved unsuccessful. [Kansas City Star]

were looking for a fight. They [had] been wanting it for a long time and this time they had an excuse."[24]

Cherry bombs exploding in the crowd further frayed nerves. Hundreds of people watched from downtown windows, anxiously awaiting the outcome. The kinetic energy reached a fever pitch when Davis left the podium and someone grabbed the microphone, declaring, "The 'man' has us outnumbered . . . we need to organize. Let's go home and organize." Alluding to the riots that had occurred throughout the country, another marcher shouted, "Why can't we have one here?"[25]

In an attempt to defuse the volatile situation, KPRS radio announced that a dance would be held at Holy Name Catholic Church and buses currently on the scene would provide transportation. Although the majority of marchers were no longer students who might be appeased by a church social, a couple hundred young marchers boarded the buses. Then, at 12:44 p.m., the violence escalated.

Police dragged off and struck a young man who had climbed on top of a sheriff's car. As the state troopers protecting city hall surged forward, the protestors hurled bottles and rocks. One older black shouted, "The niggers don't have no country, but before we're through this is going to be nigger town."[26] The Mayor's Commission never ascertained who threw the first canister of tear gas. African Americans insisted police had triggered the riot by instigating the use of gas; the police maintained that a black man heaved the first can of gas, stolen earlier when marchers had swarmed an unoccupied police cruiser at Parade Park. Amid the chaos and confusion, probably no one really knew. Regardless of who tossed the first one, the police immediately fired six more canisters into the mass. Engulfed in tear gas, the crowd bolted east and scattered, with the police in pursuit.[27]

Kansas City was one of thirty-seven American cities that experienced a riot whose precipitating events indirectly related to the death of Martin Luther King Jr. Unlike the cities where violence erupted immediately following the assassination, Kansas City's disturbance resulted from a combination of King's death and the local events that followed. Localized animosities and nuances played a large role in the nature and timing of these types of disturbances but were not the underlying causes. Each riot city experienced unique, community-specific, "precipitating" or "triggering" events that aggravated distinct local racial sensitivities. These precipitating events kindled frustrations and fury prompted by universal economic, political, and social conditions in the ghetto—conditions that in Kansas City "did not differ materially from other cities."[28]

Following sociologist Thomas Mason's model of the four phases of riot progression, the morning's events had been the first, or the crowd formation and "keynoting," phase of the Kansas City riot. According to Mason, this first phase, where crowds typically began to form and violence remained relatively light, was followed by a period in which the initial crowds disseminated information about the disturbance throughout the affected ghetto area. If sufficient support for the riot developed during the second phase, a third phase involving looting followed. In extreme cases, such as in Kansas City, looting sometimes escalated while law enforcement efforts intensified, and the disorder progressed to a fourth, or siege, phase where violence and destruction reached a peak.

In Kansas City, low intensity violence, destruction of property, and symbolic looting flared from time to time during the morning, but compared to later acts, it remained mild. During this first phase, as crowds began to grow, "keynoting" among members took place. Participants commented on and analyzed the events they were witnessing, and once a consensus was reached, the crowd developed the potential to riot.[29]

Throughout the morning, whether at Thirty-fourth and Indiana or Thirty-first and Prospect, many bitter blacks became convinced that "insensible" police were treating them with disrespect and contempt. Keynoting took place up and down the march and in particular when the crowd stopped at Parade Park and city hall. A handful of emerging militant leaders like Lee Bohanon and Vernon Thompson incited the marchers and aided the process. The incapacitating effects of tear gas are indiscriminate; thus its use in such a large crowd affirmed African American views that the police treated them all like criminals. In response to the tear gas, the crowd apparently reached a consensus to expand the protest. The Mayor's Commission later concluded that "persons with an inclination or desire for mass violence and lawlessness found themselves with a suitable emotional platform to give them support for their unlawful activities." At any rate, the events of the morning, and in particular at city hall, had "provided the emotional climate for the violence, looting and burning" that would follow.[30]

The use of tear gas at city hall marked the progression of the Kansas City riot into phase two of Mason's model. During this phase, the initial crowd dispersed into smaller groups throughout the ghetto, and word of the confrontations spread. By Tuesday afternoon, participation escalated, and while light looting occurred, the violence and destruction of property intensified.[31]

Almost immediately after the crowd bolted from the steps of city hall, groups of ten to twelve persons fanned out from Twelfth and Walnut streets

Riot activity occurred between Woodland and Indiana avenues,
with the most intense violence erupting along Prospect Avenue.
[Kansas City Star]

and shattered windows in the downtown area. Police reported large groups rampaging through the streets, throwing bricks and rocks through windows, and overturning cars. "They might as well know, it's going to be a long, hot summer," a defiant student notified a reporter. At Twelfth and The Paseo, broken glass completely exposed storefronts. One man, using a stolen walkie-talkie, shouted obscenities at police and informed the officers that they were witnessing "Black Power talking."[32]

Some store owners huddled in fear inside their shops. Police scrambled to contain the spread of violence, and most of the initial property damage came in the form of broken windows. Although rioters robbed a transit bus, they stole very little on Tuesday afternoon.[33]

Away from the spreading disorder, nearly 250 young African Americans attended the dance at the Holy Name Catholic Church at Twenty-third Street and Benton Boulevard. This spontaneously arranged event had the potential to be an effective antiriot tool but instead resulted in more violence. Most of the students at the dance had been bused from city hall shortly before the tear gas incident. And although the police department had advance notice of the event, officers did not know a dance was in progress in the church basement when they responded to a disturbance call at that location.

The students stoned the first policemen to arrive, and more police were summoned to the area. Officers again used tear gas to disperse the group, and after several students entered the church to escape, police fired gas into the basement. In the chaos that followed, police kicked in the windows and shot seven more canisters into the party. Panicked dancers, unaware of the events outside, searched for the exit through the dense clouds of gas.

Once outside, the students were livid. A rumor—later proven false—that police had killed an African American man further inflamed their passions. Police again became the targets of rocks and used additional tear gas to dispel the incensed students. For over half an hour, the tension at the church remained fierce.[34]

Many of those involved in the city hall and church incidents eventually returned to the area around Central High School. Along Indiana, between Thirty-first Street and Linwood Boulevard, people filled the streets. Large numbers of residents met to discuss the day's events and spread the word about the incidents at city hall and the church. Word of mouth proved a very effective type of media coverage: the Kerner Commission estimated that nearly 80 percent of ghetto blacks initially heard about or stayed informed of the riots by word of mouth. On Tuesday afternoon in Kansas City, news traveled fast across the ghetto's communication network.[35] Although Mayor Davis appeared on television to apologize for the use of tear gas and present an official version of the day's events, African Americans were already synthesizing their own opinions on the street.

An accurate picture of actual riot participation or the mood of those involved proves difficult to reconstruct. Once the riot became part of the ghetto's oral tradition, events could become distorted and often embellished. Since the rioters participated in illegal activities, the historian also has difficulty soliciting accurate accounts of roles and conduct. Yet, it is clear that a feeling of camaraderie and purpose developed among young militants on that April afternoon. In the opinion of Vernon Thompson, "Years of anger and oppression were coming out. . . . The media had glorified and sensationalized it [rioting]." And when violence broke out, some of those kids were "cheering."³⁶

Unlike their southern brethren, northern blacks often had difficulty identifying their oppressors amongst the shrouded forms of discrimination. In Kansas City they were now striking back at their chief tormentors. One young African American proclaimed, "I say if we can't have it one way, we're going to take it another way." "There is an intelligent way to achieve our goals," declared another militant, "but if we can't get it the right way it will be 'burn, baby, burn until the white man learns.'"³⁷

Kansas City blacks wanted an end, or at least honest improvement, to the effects of discrimination. They wanted formal recognition that intolerable discrimination remained the rule, and not the exception, in most aspects of the city's life. "We're not asking for something," one young militant declared, "we're free!"³⁸ In their eyes, they had attempted to express their feelings in a peaceful way on Tuesday morning. The use of tear gas confirmed their belief that the white community viewed them not as individuals, but as an untrustworthy class without legitimate concerns or grievances. For some emerging militants, the riot was an attempt, similar to nonviolent protest, to communicate with whites. Activist John Wesson believed, "Riot [was the] only method left to the Negro—the only way to get the white man to listen."³⁹

By 3:21 p.m. on April 9, the first shot had been fired, and by 4:17 p.m. the first Molotov cocktail had been thrown. To the battle cry of "Get Whitey," rioters beat or stoned numerous whites. The police spent much of the afternoon following rumors in the black community, but as nightfall approached, reports of looting, vandalism, and arson clogged the police radio. In most riot cities, night brought a dramatic proliferation of disorder, and Kansas City followed the pattern. The situation throughout the metropolitan area remained tense, and reports of violence began to exceed police manpower. Shortly after 5:00 p.m., two hundred national guardsmen, equipped with M-1 rifles, began patrolling the eastern side of the city in jeeps.⁴⁰

Mayor Davis declared Kansas City under a state of emergency at 5:20 p.m. and ordered all taverns, liquor stores, service stations, and gun shops within the city limits to close. Most had already done so on their own accord. At his request, the surrounding suburbs followed suit. Along with the declaration, Davis imposed the first emergency curfew in the city's history. As darkness fell, Kansas City progressed into the third phase of rioting. Militant blacks had thrown down the gauntlet. Over a stolen police radio came the challenge, "You best believe, boy, we're going to be downtown tonight, you better be there, we will."⁴¹

The riot entered the third phase when extensive looting began after 6:00 p.m. in the inner city. Over two hundred stores, mostly on the eastern side of town, were looted or damaged. Ninety-four fires, forty of which were confirmed arson, raged while crowds gathered to jeer and throw rocks at firefighters. Most of the looting took place from Twelfth to Forty-seventh streets between Independence and Troost Avenue. Consistent with other riot cities, small retail establishments suffered the largest losses, particularly the liquor, grocery, drug, and automobile parts stores along Twenty-seventh, Thirty-first, Troost, and Prospect.[42] During this third phase, the disorder temporarily outstripped normal law enforcement capabilities, and individuals interested in plunder could ignore the usual threats of incarceration. Normal social controls over theft vanished, and the activities of the crowds offered adequate cover for extensive looting. The afternoon looting had been symbolic, but overnight it became more conscious and deliberate, a kind of alternative income redistribution. One African American described it as "a selective operation."[43]

Following the national pattern, the acts of looting and arson in Kansas City were usually intentionally restrained and selective. Whites owned the vast majority of the targeted businesses considered exploitive by rioters. "You know most of the money they make down there [Thirty-first and Prospect] is off us," explained one confessed looter. "It's like that tire store. Most of their trade is with Negroes. He overcharges $5 a tire so we got him. That ----- drug

Auto parts, grocery, and liquor stores suffered the most damage in the riot. This grocery store at 2100 Prospect Avenue was looted on April 9, 1968. [Kansas City Star]

store. We burned them out because they don't have enough Negro employees. They follow you around like thieves—not all Negroes are thieves—so we got them. That ----- market. Have you ever been in that filthy place? That's the dirtiest place in town. We got him. That auto parts place. A lot of us have old cars and have to buy parts there. They charge twice as much as they should. We burned them."[44]

Taking a cue from other riot cities, some black businesses displayed "Soul Brother" or "Soul Sister" signs in hopes that the violence would pass over. In most cases, rioters spared black businesses; those hit generally shared a building with or were owned by whites. One arsonist who accidentally set fire to a home owned by African Americans helped extinguish the blaze and apologized to the owner.[45]

The emergency curfew did little to discourage African Americans from filling the streets or heckling police and firefighters. During the evening, residents implemented an impromptu signal system in the inner city. Many tied black cloth on their car antennas, honked their horns repeatedly, and raised their clinched fists in a Black Power salute.

The first confirmed shooting victim was Leonard Whitmore at Thirty-third and Woodland, but before the night ended, ten more African Americans, almost all under thirty, had been admitted to General Hospital for gunshot wounds. All had been shot by police or property owners. One man was shot in the back as he fled from Klein's Market at Thirty-first and Benton. Maynard Gough became the first fatality in the riot when police shot him as he held a case of whiskey in his hands outside Joe's Liquor Store on Nineteenth Street.[46]

Firefighters vainly attempted to respond to the avalanche of alarms, which sounded at a rate of one every two minutes. Travel through the streets proved difficult, and at nearly each location, firefighters became the targets of rocks and bottles, many times seeking shelter under their vehicles. At one call, two firemen, James Whitaker and Harley Hutchins, were injured by flying objects; a fire truck was set ablaze at Twenty-ninth and Prospect. Eventually, Fire Chief James Halloran shut down two inner-city fire stations for fear they would be overrun.

As Kansas City burned, the rules of the game had been redefined, and the law enforcement personnel struggled to contain the disturbance. The seven hundred police on duty were spread dangerously thin in the energized ghetto, and they remained the principal target of black fury. Although no sniping had yet occurred, rioters tear gassed police from a building on Highland Avenue. Even Chief Kelley conceded, "We do not have the control of the situation that we would like to have."[47]

In addition to those already on patrol in the eastern part of the city, reinforcements from the Missouri National Guard augmented beleaguered police throughout the night. By 10:00 p.m., soldiers had been issued live ammunition for their M-1 rifles but ordered not to fire unless engaged in a life-threatening encounter. By midnight 450 guardsmen had been deployed in the riot area.[48]

After midnight, the violence dissipated as quickly as it had accelerated. In the chilly overnight temperatures, the disorder subsided from apparently natural causes. One hundred and seventy-five persons had been arrested, most for curfew violations, and forty-four had been injured. Property damage was extensive. All of the talk about racial understanding in Kansas City—a city that prided itself on it—had been drowned out by looting, burning, and hundreds of soldiers.[49] Still, the uneasy ceasefire left many optimistic that the riot had run its course. But the worst was yet to come—on April 10, Kansas City entered phase four.

No immediate or spontaneous resumption of violence occurred in the city during the morning hours of April 10. Still, it did not take long to rekindle rage in the African American community. Provocative police action at Lincoln and Central high schools led to another round of tear gas, and by 11:00 a.m., these and three other schools had been dismissed for the day.

The renewed use of tear gas sent fresh feelings of resentment reverberating throughout the black community and reinforced the climate for violence. As nightfall approached, tension grew. Nervous business owners between Twenty-ninth and Thirtieth streets along Prospect boarded up their windows as rumors spread and crowds filled the streets declaring "Tonight we eat free."[50] Rumors ran rampant throughout the city. Some people talked about police shooting several blacks and hiding the bodies while others claimed to have heard of bank robberies, snipers, and people hoarding gasoline for bombs. A story about police searching an African American woman by raising her dress above her head began to circulate. In Johnson County, an affluent white suburb on the Kansas side that remained immune to violence throughout the riot, students at the fashionable Shawnee Mission East High School nearly panicked when word spread that the Plaza, the city's trendy shopping district south of downtown, had been looted and burned.[51]

The second night of violence began at 7:15 p.m. when a fire erupted at a Thirteenth and Prospect supermarket. At the same time, several caravans of cars raced along Thirty-first between Benton and Cleveland throwing Molotov cocktails. On the 2900 block of Prospect, snipers pinned down police and national guardsmen. From there, the disorder escalated, and Kansas City entered the fourth, or siege, phase of rioting. Conflicts and confrontations

Before the end of the riot, national guardsmen aided Kansas City law enforcement officials. [Kansas City Star]

intensified; damage and participation reached a peak. Violence such as arson, fire bombing, and sniping became more destructive while law enforcement efforts had escalated enough to present a serious physical threat to those involved. Attempts to control riots during this phase resulted in numerous arrests, injuries, and deaths. Once disorders reached this stage, their severity reflected the level of frustration among the black population. Only 5 percent of riots in the 1960s reached this critical phase.[52]

Confusion, rumors, anger, and bloodshed marked the evening of April 10. While many Kansas Citians watched Bob Hope host the Academy Awards, one journalist described the scene on the east side as a "battleground where snipers dueled with police and national guardsmen in the glow of high reaching flames from fire bombed buildings." Another would-be Edward R. Murrow reported from the front lines: "This was Kansas City, April 10, 1968. It seemed like Hue or Seoul or Berlin as the night grew darker and the fires grew brighter." Streets remained dark after lights were shot out and fires severed many power and telephone lines in the riot area. Police vehicles moved without headlights. Sentries challenged all pedestrians. Armed with

.30 caliber carbines and riot guns loaded with large caliber buckshot, police joined soldiers in "major battles" with snipers at nearly every intersection along Prospect between Twenty-seventh and Thirty-ninth.[53]

The bloodiest battle erupted at the Byron Hotel, near Thirtieth and Prospect. According to police, when officers used tear gas to disperse a marauding crowd looting the supermarket across the street, blacks quickly regrouped and began goading the police. Sniper fire believed to have come from the hotel wounded W. F. Jewett, a national guardsman. As a result, police and guardsmen directed heavy return fire in that direction. The battle scattered the crowd. Police saw muzzle flashes come from the top of a paint store, apartment house porches, and three other locations in and around the hotel. Frightened police and entrenched snipers exchanged intense gunfire. In the pandemonium, police fatally shot Charles "Shugg" Martin. Martin had been sleeping against a car when the shooting began, and upon waking he walked toward the police with his hand in his pocket. At nearly the same time, George McKinney and his son, George Jr., who had walked to the store for milk and had stayed to watch the fires, were also killed by police gunfire. None of the three was armed or had engaged in any criminal activities.[54]

While securing the hotel, police shot Julius Hamilton when he stepped onto the front porch of an apartment down the street. Unarmed, he appeared in response to police requests that he "come out." At the moment he emerged from the apartment, an unrelated shot rang out, and police instinctively fired on Hamilton.[55]

At the same time, the intersection of Thirty-first and Prospect "resembled a military battlefield." Upon hearing of the events at the hotel, Mayor Davis hastily ordered a 9:00 p.m. curfew, with an additional ban on all nonessential traffic and the possession and transportation of firearms, ammunition, or explosive liquids. The school board also announced that Easter break would start one day early.[56]

Under a bright moon, fires raged along with the cracks of sniper fire. Dense black smoke from a burning gas station at Thirty-first and Indiana dominated the skyline. Flames engulfed all four corners of the intersection at Thirty-fifth and Prospect, and young blacks at the scene applauded when the front of one of the buildings exploded. Three other major fires in the area burned out of control. Due to the sheer number of calls and increased violence against firefighters, some blazes were left unattended. At three locations, firefighters were pinned down and forced either to withdraw or seek shelter under their equipment.   Rioters also pinned down an ambulance driver attempting to reach a civilian. Two firemen and two policemen suffered injuries at

Thirty-fifth and Wabash, and a fire captain was later wounded south of the Byron Hotel. Even the Fire Department Academy was set ablaze.[57]

"This city is in a state of chaos," a National Guard colonel reported. "It was bad last night and it's a whole lot worse tonight," added a tired policeman.[58] Almost seven hundred national guardsmen warily patrolled the streets with over two thousand in reserve or on the way. Four hundred and fifty police, on twelve-hour shifts, along with thirty Jackson County sheriffs contributed to the coordinated effort.

At a police barricade near Thirty-first and Park, Albert Miller became the sixth and final fatality of the riot. Traveling at a high rate of speed, Miller's car approached the barricade with its lights off. A shot was reportedly fired from the vehicle, and when police returned fire, Miller was struck and killed.[59]

By midnight the violence had once again subsided. As temperatures dropped into the lower forties, two armored personnel carriers rumbled down dark and deserted Prospect Avenue. Although sporadic looting and burning continued until morning, the worst was over. The peak of violence in Kansas City had left five more blacks dead and sent twenty others to the hospital, somewhat low numbers considering the intensity of the violence. Well over one hundred persons had been arrested. Two national guardsmen, two firefighters, and a policeman had been wounded by sniper fire, while forty-five confirmed arson cases brought the two-day total to nearly 150 fires.[60] Thursday effectively marked the end of Kansas City's riot experience. Although unseasonably warm weather prevailed, only sporadic and isolated recurrences of violence broke out after April 11. True to form, the fourth phase had been extremely destructive. By April 18, when Kansas City was no longer under a state of emergency and the last vestiges of riot control had been removed, the human casualties and property damage had made a significant contribution to the most violent month of the 1960s rioting.

In the end, a striking aspect is not how Kansas City differed from other riot cities, but rather that it was a local manifestation of the larger historical and sociological forces involved in the riot phenomenon of the 1960s. The various features of the disorder, the general characteristics of the participants, and the phases of progression conformed to the national pattern. Conditions in the city prior to the riot mirrored national trends, and what Kansas City blacks found intolerable did not differ materially from other cities. The disorder, with only a few local nuances, represented the national experience.

Despite the proliferation of sociological paradigms and theories from both political scientists and historians regarding riot propensity, no scholarly consensus emerged to explain why some cities experienced riots while other cities with seemingly similar or worse racial conditions escaped unscathed.

According to sociologist Seymour Spilerman, when viewing the 1960s riots as a historical whole, the key components to riot proclivity were a city's northern location and a large enough black population to develop group consciousness and ensure a sufficiently large pool of potential rioters.[61] Spilerman determined that frustration, uniformly felt among all urban blacks irrespective of their individual community situation, combined with the zeitgeist, or extremist spirit of the mid-1960s, to create a volatile "tinderbox" status. This "tinderbox" status was higher in some cities than in others, but all northern cities with a large African American population had sufficient levels of frustration to fuel potential riots.[62] This may suggest why St. Louis, more closely resembling a southern city in racial mores and tradition, avoided a riot while northern ghettos burned.

Although for "far too many persons, it [the riot] was the first and only indicator of dissatisfaction," by 1968, Kansas City had all the earmarks of a riot waiting to happen.[63] Ominous storm clouds had been gathering on the city's racial horizon since the summer of 1967, and according to prominent African American community leader Alvin Brooks, the assassination of Martin Luther King Jr. was "simply the straw that broke the camel's back." If violence had been averted on April 9, 1968, it probably would have come eventually. In the opinion of Vernon Thompson, it was "just time" for violent action.[64]

In Kansas City hundreds, maybe thousands, of blacks joined the estimated five hundred thousand African Americans who participated nationwide in the 1960s riots. Roughly equal to the number of Americans who served in Vietnam, they too engaged in a noble, if not misguided, crusade. Due to rising expectations and the heightened activism brought about by the civil rights movement, the War on Poverty, and the Black Power movement, African Americans increasingly found intolerable the universal grievances regarding housing, employment, education, and the police. Yet these conditions proved insurmountable to traditional civil rights strategies and required an evolution of direct action. Because a significant minority of inner-city blacks viewed collective violence as what Alvin Brooks described as "direct action taken to another level," the riots of the mid-1960s were not violent aberrations but rather restrained and articulate protests, the goal of which was to draw attention to an aspect of race relations left virtually untouched by traditional civil rights gains: the northern urban ghettos. Still, judging from current ghetto conditions, if Kansas City blacks and thousands like them truly delivered a protest in the mid-1960s, many whites failed to see it.[65]

NOTES

1. Robert M. Fogelson, *Violence as Protest: A Study of Riots and Ghettos* (Garden City, NY: Doubleday, 1971), 107. The National Advisory Commission on Civil Disorders, headed by Illinois Governor Otto Kerner, determined that the riots were inevitable reactions to pervasive discrimination and segregation found in the nation's ghettos. In the Kerner Commission's judgment, intolerable conditions in housing, employment, education, and police relations, all "factors within the society at [large] . . . created a mood of violence among many urban negroes." Otto Kerner, *Report of the National Advisory Commission on Civil Disorders* (Washington, DC: Government Printing Office, 1968), 4.

2. Fogelson, *Violence as Protest*, 24; Todd Gitlin, *The Sixties: Years of Hope, Days of Rage*, rev. ed. (New York: Bantam Books, 1993), 243.

3. Seymour Spilerman, quoted in Gregg Carter, "Explaining the Severity of the 1960s Black Rioting: A City Level Investigation of Curvilinear and Structural Breaks Hypotheses" (PhD diss., Columbia University, 1983), 23, 42, 140.

4. David R. Hardy Papers, private collection. At the request of the Hardy family, the identities of those quoted have been withheld.

5. James Blair, telephone interview by author, Kansas City, 4 October 1995.

6. *Kansas City Times*, 5 April 1968.

7. Ibid.

8. David R. Hardy, *Mayor's Commission on Civil Disorders Final Report* (Kansas City, MO, 1968), 11.

9. Ibid., 34-35.

10. Vernon Thompson, telephone interview by author, Kansas City, 4 October 1995; "Chronology of Events," Lincoln Senior High School, 2, folder 296, Arthur Mag Collection, Western Historical Manuscript Collection, University of Missouri-Kansas City.

11. *Kansas City Star*, 10 April 1968.

12. Thompson, telephone interview.

13. "Chronology of Events," Lincoln Senior High School, 2; Hardy, *Mayor's Commission*, 13.

14. "Police Log," 3, folder 296, Mag Collection.

15. *Kansas City Star*, 10 April 1968.

16. "Chronology of Events," Central Senior High, 4, folder 2, Mag Collection.

17. *Kansas City Star*, 10 April 1968; Thompson, telephone interview.

18. Hardy, *Mayor's Commission*, 34.

19. Ibid., 15.

20. Ibid., 16.

21. Thompson, telephone interview.

22. *Kansas City Star*, 9 April 1968.

23. *Kansas City Call*, 19 April 1968; Blair, telephone interview.

24. Hardy Papers.

25. *Kansas City Times*, 9 April 1968; Hardy Papers.

26. *Kansas City Star*, 12 April 1968.

27. Hardy, *Mayor's Commission*, 20.

28. Ibid., 19.

29. David Mason, "Individual Participation in Collective Racial Violence: A Rational Choice Synthesis" (PhD diss., University of Georgia, 1982), 34.

30. Hardy, *Mayor's Commission*, 41.

31. Mason, "Individual Participation," 34.

32. *New York Times*, 12 April 1968; "Police Log," 20-21.

33. *Kansas City Star*, 10 April 1968.

34. Hardy, *Mayor's Commission*, 22-23, 39-40.

35. Kerner, *Report*, 207.

36. Thompson, telephone interview.

37. *Kansas City Times*, 10 April 1968; *Kansas City Star*, 11 April 1968.

38. *Kansas City Star*, 10 April 1968.

39. Hardy Papers.

40. *Kansas City Star*, 10 April 1968.

41. "Police Log," 21.

42. *Kansas City Times*, 10 April 1968.

43. Mason, "Individual Participation," 27, 36; Lee Rainwater, quoted in James Geschwender, "Civil Rights Protest and Riots: A Disappearing Distinction," *Social Science Quarterly* 49 (December 1968): 476; Hardy Papers.

44. *Kansas City Star*, 8 May 1968.

45. Hardy Papers. While cleaning up his ransacked grocery store on Twelfth Street, a white merchant found a "Soul Brother" sign, apparently left by sardonic rioters, hung on the outside of his shop.

46. *Kansas City Star*, 10 April 1968.

47. *Kansas City Times*, 10 April 1968.

48. Ibid.

49. *Kansas City Call*, 19 April 1968.

50. Hardy, *Mayor's Commission*, 27.

51. *Kansas City Star*, 10 April 1968.

52. Seymour Spilerman, "Structural Characteristics of Cities and the Severity of Racial Disorders," *American Sociological Review* 41 (October 1976): 773; Bryan T. Downes, "The Social Characteristics of Riot Cities: A Comparative Study," *Social Science Quarterly* 49 (December 1968): 509.

53. *Kansas City Star*, 11 April 1968.

54. Hardy, *Mayor's Commission*, 29.

55. Ibid.

56. *Kansas City Star*, 11 April 1968.

57. Ibid.

58. *Kansas City Times*, 11 April 1968.

59. Hardy, *Mayor's Commission*, 30.

60. Ibid.; *Kansas City Times*, 11 April 1968.

61. Seymour Spilerman, "The Causes of Racial Disturbances: A Comparison of Alternative Explanations," *American Sociological Review* 35 (August 1970): 644. Unfortunately, when riot intensity and frequency declined in the late 1960s, scholarly interest in the subject also waned. As Vietnam, the antiwar movement, and campus violence captured the lion's share of America's attention, riot scholarship eventually "slipped into oblivion on the relevance factor." David C. Perry, review of *Violence as Protest: A Study of Riots and Ghettos*, by Robert Fogelson, *Journal of Politics* 34 (August 1972): 987.

62. Jerry Murtagh, "Collective Racial Violence as a Rational Choice" (PhD diss., University of Georgia, 1983), 35; Hardy Papers.

63. Human Relations Task Force on Civil Disorders, *Three Year Report: The Quality of Urban Life* (Kansas City, MO: Advisory Commission on Human Relations and Department of Human Relations, 1971), 3.

64. Alvin Brooks, telephone interview with author, Kansas City, 15 August 1995; Thompson, telephone interview.

65. Fogelson, *Violence as Protest*, 16.

Contributors

David Boutros is the associate director of the Western Historical Manuscript Collection and the University Archives at the University of Missouri-Kansas City. He received MA and MPA degrees from the University of Missouri-Kansas City.

Nancy J. Hulston is the director of the University of Kansas Medical Center Archives and the Clendening History of Medicine Museum, Kansas City, Kansas. She received an MA degree from the University of Missouri-Kansas City.

Warren A. Jennings retired as a professor emeritus of history from Missouri State University, Springfield. He received a PhD degree from the University of Florida. (Deceased)

Edward D. Jervey is professor emeritus of American history at Radford University in Radford, Virginia. He received a PhD degree from Boston University.

Gary R. Kremer is executive director of the State Historical Society of Missouri. He received a PhD degree from American University, Washington, DC.

Lawrence H. Larsen is professor emeritus of history at the University of Missouri-Kansas City. He received a PhD degree from the University of Wisconsin-Madison.

James W. Leyerzapf is a senior archivist at the Dwight D. Eisenhower Library in Abilene, Kansas. He received a PhD degree from the University of Missouri-Columbia.

Henry C. McDougal was a prominent lawyer in Kansas City. (Deceased 1915)

Tom N. McInnis is a professor of political science at the University of Central Arkansas, Conway. He received a PhD from the University of Missouri-Columbia.

Kevin C. McShane taught American history at Center South Junior High School, Kansas City, Missouri, at the time of publication of his article.

James E. Moss served as associate editor of the *Missouri Historical Review* and then as director of the Houston and Harris County Heritage Society, Houston, Texas. He received an MA degree from the University of Missouri-Columbia.

Ann Davis Niepman retired as a teacher of history from Winnetonka High School in the North Kansas City (MO) School District. She received an MA degree from the University of Kansas.

Gail K. Renner retired as professor emeritus of history from Missouri Southern State University, Joplin. He received a PhD degree from the University of Missouri-Columbia. (Deceased 2004)

Joel P. Rhodes is an associate professor of history at Southeast Missouri State University, Cape Girardeau. He received a PhD degree from the University of Missouri-Kansas City.

Thomas D. Wilson is a resident of Watertown, Massachusetts. He received an MA degree from the University of Central Missouri, Warrensburg.

William H. Wilson retired as a professor of history from the University of North Texas, Denton. He received a PhD degree from the University of Missouri-Columbia.

Index

African Americans, 220–299
    in Leeds, 252–276
    riot of 1968, 277–299
Armour, Philip Danforth, 143–144, 148
Aviation, 185–205

Benjamin, Henry, 175–176, 179–180
Bingham, George Caleb, 106, 115–117
Bluford, Lucile, 232, 240-241, 245
Boggs, Lilburn, 54-56, 58–60
Brown, Darius A., 158–159, 161
Bullock, Eugene H., 171, 175, 179–180
Burney, Clarence A., 156–157, 159-161, 167

Central High School, 281–283, 292
Chouteau, Berenice, 27–29, 34, 37, 41
Chouteau, Cyprien, 29, 34, 39–40, 43
Chouteau, Francois Gessau, 27–41, 43
Church of Jesus Christ of Latter-Day
    Saints, 47–70
Civil War, 96-121, 142
Clay County, Missouri, 34–37
Cook, James W., 124–126, 135–137
Cooley, Elizabeth Ann, 71–95
Coronado, Francisco Vázquez de,
12–13, 15
Corrill, John, 51-56, 58
Cowgill, James P., 172, 174

Davis, Ilus W., 281–282, 284–285,
    288–289, 294
Dibble, Philo, 49, 53–54

Election fraud, 209–211, 225-226,
    233–235
Ewing, Thomas, Jr., 96, 98–99, 101–
    107, 109–117

Fort Osage, 22, 32, 34,
Franklin, Chester A., 220–251
Fur trading, 27–46

Gannon, A. J., 170–173, 176, 178–181
Gilmore, Solon T., 158–159
Great Depression, 201, 270–272
Griffen, Wentworth Edward, 158–160,
    162–165

Holland, Louis, 185–195, 197–201
Housing conditions
    Leeds, 255–257

McClure Flats, 175–176

Industrial Workers of the World (IWW), 153–169
Influenza epidemic, 1918, 170-184

Jackson Democratic Club, 206, 207, 215

Kansa Indians, 25, 27, 29
Kansas City Call, 220, 222–225, 227–229, 232, 237–239, 241–245
Kansas City Journal, 122–123, 125, 127, 130–136
Kansas City Star, 123, 127, 133–137
Kansas City Times, 122–130, 132, 134–136, 138
Kelley, Clarence, 281, 282, 291
King, Martin Luther, Jr., assassination aftermath, 277, 279–281, 283–285, 296
Ku Klux Klan, 225, 226, 243–244

Lane, James H., 100–101, 103–105, 114, 117
Lazia, Johnny, 211–214, 217
Leeds neighborhood, 252–276
"Lily whitism," 220, 226–228
Lincoln, Abraham, 96–99, 102–104, 114
Lincoln High School, 253, 263, 269, 281, 282, 292
Lindbergh, Charles A., 193–194
Little, Frank, 155–158
Louisiana Purchase, 16–20

McClure, Elizabeth Ann Cooley. *See* Cooley, Elizabeth Ann
McClure, James W., 71, 73, 77–92
McCoy, John Calvin, 28–39
McElroy, Henry F., 192–194, 199–200, 207
Maddux, Jack, 199–200
Majors, Alexander, 55, 57
Malone, Dolly Mosby, 254–255, 263, 267–268, 271

Meat packing industry, 141–152
Missouri River, 15, 21–25, 27–47, 56, 60–61, 63, 98–99, 104, 109, 122
Mormons. *See* Church of Jesus Christ of Latter-Day Saints
Motley, William P., 172, 176, 179, 181

National Air Transport (NAT), 189, 191–194, 197
National Guard, 282, 289, 292–295
Nelson, William Rockhill, 123, 133–137
New Deal, 241–245

Order No. 11, 96–121
Organized crime, 210–214, 217
Osage Indians, 21–23

Parks, origins of, 122–140
Pendergast, James, 206, 210
Pendergast machine, 192, 200, 206–220, 225, 241
Pendergast, Thomas Joseph, 176, 206–217, 225–226, 228, 231, 233–235, 240–241, 270–271
Plankinton and Armour, 144–149
Pratt, Parley, 50–53, 61–63

Quantrill, William Clarke, 102–105

Ray, Kenneth E., 255–257, 261, 264, 266, 273
Reeves, Albert L., 211, 214–215
Refugees, 60–65, 107–114
Rice, Martin, 107–109
Richards Airfield, 186, 189, 192–193
Roe, Albert, 155, 158–159
Roosevelt, Franklin Delano, 209, 237–238, 241–245, 270
Ryland, John F., 53, 55

St. Louis, Missouri, 17, 181
Schofield, John M., 96–98, 102–107, 114–116

Segregation, 223, 227–228, 230, 234–236, 241, 252, 260, 265, 269, 277–278
Shannon, Joe, 176, 225–226
Stark, Lloyd, 214, 235, 237
Swift, G. F., 147–149

Teaching, 82–92
Thompson, Vernon, 279–282, 286, 288, 296

Transcontinental and Western Air (T&WA), 198, 200–201
Truman, Harry S., 209, 215–216, 220, 225–226, 228–246

Vine Street Corridor, 253–254, 264, 266

Welch, Casmir, 225–226, 229–231
Wilson, Yvonne Starks, 255, 267